Saul Stroogenke

About the Author

MEREDITH JACOBS is the founder of the popular Web site ModernJewishMom.com. In 2004, she created and developed a series of workshops about Shabbat for women's groups, which inspired this book. Jacobs writes a monthly column on family and parenting that appears in Jewish newspapers in Baltimore, Los Angeles, Cleveland, Phoenix, and Detroit. She lives with her husband and their two children in Rockville, Maryland.

For more information, check out www.ModernJewishMom.com.

The Modern Jewish Mom's Guide to Shabbat

HARPER

NEW YORK · LONDON · TORONTO · SYDNEY

The Modern Jewish Mom's Guide to Shabbat

CONNECT and CELEBRATE—
BRING YOUR FAMILY TOGETHER
WITH THE FRIDAY NIGHT MEAL

MEREDITH L. JACOBS
Illustrated by Jackie Ross

HARPER

Grateful acknowledgment is made for the following:

Translation of Eishet Chayil from *Likrat Shabbat: Worship, Study, and Song for Sabbath and Festival Services and for the Home*. Compiled and translated by Rabbi Sidney Greenberg, edited by Rabbi Jonathan D. Levine. Copyright © 1973 The Prayer Book Press of Media Judaica, Inc., Bridgeport, CT. Reprinted with permission.

Excerpt from *Teaching Your Children About God: A Modern Jewish Approach*. Copyright © Rabbi David J. Wolpe, Henry Holt & Company, New York, 1993. Reprinted with permission of Rabbi Wolpe.

The Modern Jewish Mom logo is a registered trademark of Modern Jewish Mom Inc. Used with permission.

FIRST EDITION

Designed by Sarah Maya Gubkin

All illustrations © 2007 Jackie Ross

Library of Congress Cataloging-in-Publication Data is available upon request.

ISBN: 978-0-06-112065-7
ISBN-10: 0-06-112065-0

07 08 09 10 11 ❖/RRD 10 9 8 7 6 5 4 3 2 1

For my parents, who taught me

For my children, who inspire me

For my sister, who laughs with me

For my husband, who believes in me

And for my grandparents . . . who would have been so proud.

Contents

x

The Modern Jewish Mom's Guide to Shabbat

Introduction

SOMEWHERE ALONG THE WAY I became my mother. What's more shocking to me is that somehow I became "the source for all things Jewish" for my friends. Why? How? After all, I'm not very observant. Maybe my friends think of me as an "expert" because of my involvement in my synagogue and local Jewish community. But more likely, it is because of the way I've chosen to keep my home and raise my children.

A lot of what I do is because of what my parents did. We had a mezuzah on our door and kosher meat in our freezer. My parents were very active in our synagogue, sent my sister and me to Hebrew school, and encouraged us to be involved in the synagogue youth group.

All the same, we didn't light Shabbat candles often—rarely, in fact. But when we did, it was magic: My mom would set out the candlesticks in the special-occasions-only dining room. She would cover her head with a paper napkin, light the candles, wave her hands as if to gather in the warmth of the flames, and while covering her eyes she would whisper the ancient blessings. This is one of my most special, earliest memories.

But in my childhood home, the simple blessings over the candles, the wine, and the challah were really the only way Shabbat was distinguished from any other dinner. As I've explained, ours was very much a Jewish home, but I think we didn't go beyond the basics of Shabbat because on some level we didn't need to. We ate together every night. Every dinner conversation included me and my sister. Many nights after dinner we put together puzzles or played games as a family. Many Saturday mornings we went to services together, and we often spent weekends exploring museums or taking day trips.

Life was different then. When I was growing up, my father could come home at six o'clock every night. My sister and I didn't have soccer games on the weekends. We didn't have the amount of homework or number of activities our children do today. We modern moms have very little extra time on our hands.

So when my children came home from nursery school and said, "Mommy, it's Friday. We have to have Shabbat," my reaction was, "Ach, like I have time for this." But I had signed up for the school challah program (meaning I had paid $100 to have my daughter, Sofie, come home with a braided loaf in her backpack every Friday), so I already had the challah; I also had candlesticks (a wedding present) and knew that somewhere in the pantry was a box of candles (that my mom probably bought). What I didn't have was an excuse. Was I really going to tell my children, "Well, Daddy and I think it's important enough to send you to a Jewish nursery school, but we don't really feel like putting into practice what you're learning about?" That would have been ridiculous. As a bonus, my husband, Jonathan—who is usually able to come home only well after the kids and I have eaten—promised to leave the office early enough to join us for dinner. So I made chicken (because isn't that what you're supposed to have?) and we had Shabbat.

The kids said the blessings. We talked about what they had learned at school. It was very cute. Not so cute that I felt compelled to repeat it *every* week—I mean the first couple of times you hear your three-year-old say the blessings it's adorable, but it gets old. Plus, at the end of the busy week, takeout was calling to me; it would be so much easier to just pick up the phone and order pizza—then I wouldn't have to clean pots and pans. So that was Shabbat in my home for many years. Although I was involved in our synagogue, Friday nights came and went like any other night. We would go out to dinner, maybe watch a movie, or order in. No different from Tuesday. Sure, once in a while the kids would come home from nursery school on Friday and ask to have a Shabbat dinner. I'd put out the challah and the Shabbat *chazzerai* they had made in school, but other than these things, it was no different from other nights. And after they graduated from synagogue nursery school and entered the public elementary school, they no longer had "Shabbat Sing" to remind them—and me—that Friday night was more special than others.

Then I heard a story that set my life and my family's life in a new direction. During a synagogue board meeting we were debating changing the time of the Friday night service. An argument was made for starting the service earlier to allow families to go home and have Shabbat dinner. In support of this change, the Sisterhood president spoke about the Shabbat dinners she'd had as a child. Her smile widened, and I was transported to a different time as she told us how on Friday evenings her family would attend services and then go home to eat. Family and friends would eat and sing and talk for hours. Every Friday night! When I saw that joyful look on her face as she reminisced, I was enchanted by her memory and reminded of standing with my little sister as our mother lit the candles, and how special that was to me.

Over the next few weeks, I spoke to older women in the congregation about their families' observances and they shared memories of their Shabbat celebrations over the years—the uninhibited discussions at the table, the concentration on family, the connections made with their children. I suddenly saw Shabbat not as a burden that would take extra time and effort, but as a gift I could give to myself and my family. I wanted a wonderful family dinner every week, one that would give Sofie and Jules memories of spending quality time with Jonathan and me, and here was the vehicle.

I came home and talked to Jonathan about it—after all, he would have to buy into this idea. I wasn't sure how he would react. But he loved the thought of committing to a Shabbat dinner. Growing up, his family had dinner together every Friday night and he wanted to re-create this tradition in our home with our children. He remembered the beautiful dinners served in the dining room, and eating and talking with his family for hours. For him, it wasn't only about being Jewish—it was about being a family. We made a deal: if I promised to make Shabbat dinner, he would get home in time to eat with us.

But what would I do? I knew about the paper napkins and the basic blessings, but what else? I began to learn more. And each week I slowly incorporated those ideas that spoke to me. I learned how to bless our children, and I am so grateful for this precious moment every week when Jonathan and I tell Sofie and Jules how much they mean to us. I learned how to relate the weekly Torah portion to our lives, and use these passages as a way of teaching the kids critical lessons in ethics and responsibility. Shabbat became a guaranteed time Jonathan and I could spend with our children and give them the tools to become the kind of people we pray they will grow to be.

But to be honest, it's not always easy. As modern moms, we juggle crazy schedules. We are all very busy—with working and volunteering and keeping a home and raising a family, and on top of that are our active children who have music lessons, dance classes, and sports, and need us not only to help them stay organized, but also to schlep them to their myriad of activities. So things like synagogue services, observing holidays, and spending time together can get shoved to the background. Who has time to make a brisket, let alone have Shabbat?

This is what I mean when I write about being a Modern Jewish Mom. How can we simply take time out to remember to enjoy our family? How can we incorporate our beautiful traditions into our busy lives? And how do we give our children a foundation that not only grounds them spiritually but gives them an identity that connects them to their family and gives them pride and strength?

We turn to Shabbat.

Shabbat is the time we turn off the outside world and connect with one another. It is a wonderful way to ensure that in this day of ridiculous schedules and pressures, we have at least one meal per week together as a family. Unlike other holidays, Shabbat is not once-a-year special—it's once-a-week routine. It's "wake up, have coffee, get the kids ready for school, get some work done, bake (or buy) challah for Shabbat" routine. It's the time we carve out each week to continue a centuries-old practice and by doing so, connect not only with our children but with generations who came before us.

We can and should raise children who enjoy spending time with family, and Shabbat can help us. This doesn't mean we have to become *frum* (religious). It doesn't mean you do everything. It means taking the time to figure out what feels comfortable and what works for you and your family. Only you can decide that. As the moms, we set the tone for the household, and incorporating new traditions does not have to be time-consuming. It takes just twenty minutes to make challah dough. And really, nothing sets the tone of the house faster than the smell of challah baking in the oven.

Sure, there are Fridays when I don't feel like baking challah or cooking or setting the table all fancy, Fridays when I wish we could just go out for dinner. But I force myself to make Shabbat (and maybe on those busier weeks I'll buy the challah or even order in) because my children have come to expect it from me. By now, Shabbat is part of the routine of their lives that gives them comfort.

Isn't that what we need now? Comfort. And peace.

When I asked my son, Jules, if he liked when we had Shabbat dinner, he said he does like it because it's something that "Mommy and Daddy do with us."

That Mommy and Daddy do with us. I realize that it's our *doing* that makes an impression on our children. It is not "do as I say, not as I do." For children, it is "do as I do"—whether we intend for that to be or not.

Our actions matter. Just as we lead by example, we parent by example. Like it or not, our children are watching us, judging us, subconsciously deciding which actions of ours they will choose to reenact as adults. In other words, the kind of adults they will be is directly related to what *you* do as an adult now.

When my children attended our synagogue nursery school, and it was my turn to come to class on Friday morning and be "Shabbat mom," I put a paper napkin on my head as I always do before I light the candles. "Why are you doing that?" the children asked. And I told them that this was the way my mother lit the candles and the way her mother lit the candles, and so now that I'm a mommy, it is the way I light the candles.

For me, it's not about needing to cover my head—for then I could use a yarmulke or a lace doily or even a cloth napkin. It is fiercely important for me to have that paper napkin on my head because that's what my mother and grandmother did.

I realize now that it was those little things my parents did that gave me a strong identity and sense of where I belong. And it is this knowing where you fit and belong that gives you the strength to move forward. It is the thought behind our actions that matters. It is the strength that comes from family and then through our faith that will carry our children. I want my children to be strong. I want them to know they have a place in the world. I want them to know where they come from and take pride in that.

So I think of Shabbat as a practical parenting tool. Using Friday night dinner to discuss lessons from the Torah or what is going on in the world provides a built-in excuse to teach our children morals and values and to enable us to gently find out more about what's happening in our kids' lives. Using candlesticks and kiddush cups that were once our grandparents' gives us a chance to tell wonderful stories about family who are no longer here. Blessing our children each and every Friday reminds them at least once a week that we love them and they are so very special to us.

More and more, we are looking to put meaning into our families' lives and give our children a sense of place in the world. Although we want our children to be successful and want them to have all they desire, we also want to give them knowledge of something deeper, something larger than themselves and more meaningful than the material things they can acquire. In giving them this bigger picture of the world and teaching them how they fit into that world, we are helping them realize that they are not alone—that they will always be part of something.

My mother once told me the greatest gift you can give to your children is to teach them how to love. Show them the strong relationship you have with your husband. Let them see you argue, and let them see you make up. Let them know you respect and appreciate and bless each other. Show them that a strong, lasting relationship is important enough to work on and put time into. I think about how close I am now with my mother and am mature enough now to recognize that our relationship is what it is because of the effort she has always made. By carving out time on Friday night to celebrate Shabbat with your family, you will find that you are teaching your children not only about your family and Jewish traditions, but also those lessons you can't learn from any textbook. So while I'll give you ideas for making Shabbat less nerve-racking and time-consuming, hopefully I will convince you that whatever it will add to your extremely full schedule, the effort will be more than worth it.

I'm not the only Modern Jewish Mom who rediscovered the joy in connecting on Shabbat. My friend Evie is married to a major movie studio producer. Years ago, she rebelled against her strict Sephardic upbringing and moved away from her family to California. She lived the fabulous Hollywood life. But even with her incredible, exciting life and her wonderful friends, she realized she was missing something. Once her daughter was born, Evie realized she missed her family and the support system they provided, so she and her husband and daughter moved back East. On one of her first days back, her mother called to ask if they had plans for Friday night. "We're going out," Evie said. "But it's *Shabbes*," her mother replied. In California, Shabbat had fallen off Evie's schedule. Her mother's invitation to Shabbat dinner made Evie remember how crucial this tradition was to her feeling of family. This was what she missed when she was in California. Now she has Shabbat every week. She told me, "Our traditions have lasted thousands of years. Just because it is 'in' now to behave a certain way doesn't mean the tradition should change to reflect the now. If we did that—if we kept changing the tradition to meet our modern needs, it never would have lasted. The beauty is in the timelessness. I used to rebel against it, feeling it was old-fashioned and out-of-date. Now I understand the wisdom behind it."

Through my family's Friday nights together I have come to experience personally the wisdom behind Shabbat. I love that Shabbat brings Jonathan home to us early, and I believe Shabbat brings us closer as a family. I wanted to share what I've learned with other families, and that's why I wrote *The Modern Jewish Mom's Guide to Shabbat*. I am not a rabbi. I am not a Torah scholar. I am a young Jewish mom, and if what I do with my family inspires you to use any tradition to bring a sense of wholeness and peace into your home, then I know I've done good.

The Modern Jewish Mom's Guide to Shabbat is not about doing everything at once. I don't believe there's a "right" way to do Shabbat. It's about taking baby steps. Start with what speaks to you, and I promise, it will build from there. Each family is unique and will respond to different traditions. Some families will want to sing, others to debate, and others will simply say the blessings and eat together. Take from this book what you think will be meaningful for your family. No matter what you do, you will feel the essence of Shabbat in spending time with your husband and children.

The Modern Jewish Mom's Guide to Shabbat focuses on the *shabbesdik* (feels Shabbes-y) rather than the halachic (according to the law, or what the Torah and the sages tell us to do). Although we will discuss some laws, or *halachot*, of Shabbat, what I am stressing is the *spirit* of Shabbat and how you can use the traditions of Shabbat to bring you closer to your children and give them memories they will want to share with their children.

I don't remember the specific lectures my parents gave me over the years (I must admit there were many). But I do remember the wonderful evenings I spent with my mother, father, and sister. I remember boisterous holidays with aunts, uncles, and cousins and the wonderful, warm feelings those family-filled evenings brought. I remember my family calling me at college to sing with me the first time I lit Chanukah candles alone. I remember my little sister, Jennifer, and I, standing by our mother as she lit the candles, imitating her with paper napkins on our heads, and whispering gibberish into our hands because we did not yet know the words.

And I remember getting my first pair of candlesticks at my bat mitzvah. They were blue-and-white ceramic. I remember putting them in the china cabinet, knowing one day, when I was a mommy, I would put a paper napkin on my head, light the candles with my children by my side, and know what to whisper into my hands.

1

A Little Kabbalah to Go with Your Challah

I THINK IT'S IMPORTANT TO UNDERSTAND the reasoning behind the rules. I'm more likely to do something if I understand the rationale behind it. It's the child in me asking, "Why?" and craving more of an answer than "Because I said so." For example, when I was in Hebrew school and we were learning the laws for keeping kosher, I asked why we separate milk from meat. My teacher explained that this was because we shouldn't boil a baby animal in its mother's milk. That answer struck a chord—it spoke to me on a humane level and is one of the reasons I keep a kosher home (the other being that it's what my mom does).

So knowing that most of us like more of an explanation than "because that's just how it is," we're going to talk about why we do what we do on Shabbat and get into a little "kabbalah lite." It's not true kabbalah (the mystical branch of Judaism), but some of the explanations for the rituals we perform on Shabbat—lighting the candles, blessing the wine, and eating the challah—are based in kabbalah and the Torah. Other explanations I will share are from the Talmud, written by the great rabbis in the second and third centuries CE. (The Talmud is made up of the Mishnah, the oral law, and the Gemara, the commentary on the Mishnah.)

Let's begin with the basics. Shabbat technically begins eighteen minutes before sunset on Friday night and ends when there are three stars in the sky on Saturday. I love the idea of watching the night sky to signal the beginning and end of the Sabbath. It draws our attention to the heavens.

Shabbat falls on the seventh day of the week. Why the seventh day? According to the very first chapter of Genesis, the first book of the Torah, God took six days to make the world. In chapter 2, we read that on the seventh day God did not work but rested and took pride in what He'd created. Even more than simply resting, God blessed the world on the seventh day: "And God blessed the seventh day and made it holy . . ." (Gen. 2:3).

Now, if God can do anything, did He really work for six days and then say, "Whew, I'm pooped. I'll stop now and pick this up again tomorrow"? He may have chilled out on Shabbat, but there is also a great mystical or kabbalistic reason for Shabbat being the seventh day, which I learned during a Torah study with Rabbi Yaakov Lipsky. The rabbi told us to think about a book (after all, Jews are also known as the People of the Book). How many sides does a book have? Your instant answer might be six: top, bottom, left, right, front, and back. But that's not so; a book also has an *inside*—the seventh side. We cannot understand a book until we look inside—that's the most important part, where it all comes together. The outside of the book gives you the immediate, superficial information—what kind of cover it has, what the title is, and who wrote it—but to gain true knowledge of the book, you have to go inside. In the story of the Creation, on the seventh day, God rested and looked and appreciated. This is what we are supposed to do on Shabbat—look inward.

This concept of looking inward to find meaning, to eliminate the distractions of the outside, is especially important in the crazy world we live in. Modern reality is to focus on the outside, the material, and then . . . to feel empty. We need to come inside to appreciate the outside. Connection is not found by going out and acquiring more, but by going in. Shabbat allows us to stop doing and appreciate what we have, to connect with our family. This is where we truly find fulfillment.

Exodus, the second book of the Torah, continues with the concept of Shabbat. Exodus tells the story of the Israelites leaving Egypt and slavery for freedom. Slaves, by definition, work. Only once they were free were the Israelites able to rest. Shabbat, therefore, is a celebration of freedom. When the Israelites were in the desert, God gave the people the Ten Commandments as well as codes of ethics and rules of worship. The commandment to have

Shabbat is given twice in the Torah. The first time the commandment is given is in Exodus when God commands Moses: "Remember the Sabbath day to keep it holy" (Exod. 20:8). In this verse, the commandment is written using the Hebrew word *zachor*, for "remember." Moses reiterates the commandment in Deuteronomy, the fifth book of the Torah: "Guard the Sabbath day to keep it holy" (Deut. 5:12). Notice that the commandment is slightly different. This time the Hebrew word *shamor*, "guard," is used. So which one are we supposed to do—remember or guard? And what's the difference?

The explanation is found in the song "Lecha Dodi," which we sing during the Friday evening service. Composed in the sixteenth century by the great kabbalist Rabbi Shlomo Alkabetz, the song begins with the line: "*Shamor v'zachor b'dibur echad.*" This means "*Guard* and *remember* uttered as one." The rabbis of the Talmud explain that when God gave these commandments to Moses, Moses heard and understood the words *guard* and *remember* at the same instant. We can take from this that these two concepts are equally important. They are two halves of a whole. Without one, you cannot have the other. The two candles we light to signify the start of Shabbat represent these two versions of the same commandment—to *remember* and to *guard* the Sabbath.

Each word has its own special meaning. When we "remember" (*zachor*) Shabbat, we do things that show that this day is different from the others. We perform acts that we do only on Shabbat—as our *bubbies* would have said, acts that are *shabbesdik* (in the spirit of Shabbat). We light candles, drink wine, eat challah, sing, pray, talk . . . all good things. This active remembering by signifying the day with ritual is probably what many less observant families do, even those of us like myself who describe ourselves as Conservative or even traditional.

We "remember" Shabbat by *actively* lighting the candles, eating the challah, and saying the prayers. But the two versions of the commandment imply a duality of the nature of Shabbat; therefore, we need the corresponding action (or inaction) to make the whole. This is where "guard" (*shamor)* comes in. When we guard Shabbat, we *don't* do certain things. In our fast-paced modern world, this is, of course, much harder. People who strictly observe the laws of Shabbat—people who are *shomer Shabbat*, who literally "guard" Shabbat—don't do work, drive, use electronics, write, talk on the phone (even hands-free), or shop. In other words, should refrain from doing those things we normally have to do during the week in order to separate Shabbat, making it a more special day—a day of rest (as God rested on the seventh day).

Technically Speaking

What are the official restrictions for guarding Shabbat? In the book of Exodus we learn the three categories of forbidden activities: traveling more than two thousand yards from your home (because that's not really relaxing and would be considered work); making a fire; and engaging in work. The rabbis further detailed thirty-nine restricted activities. They are:

I. Growing and Preparing Food

1. Plowing
2. Sowing
3. Reaping
4. Stacking (as in stacking bundles of wheat)
5. Threshing
6. Winnowing
7. Selecting out (as in separating the chaff or pod from the wheat)
8. Sifting
9. Grinding
10. Kneading
11. Baking/cooking

II. Making Clothes

12. Sheep shearing
13. Bleaching/washing
14. Combining raw materials
15. Dyeing
16. Spinning
17. Threading a loom
18. Weaving
19. Removing a finished cloth
20. Separating threads
21. Tying knots
22. Untying knots

I know what you're thinking: "When was the last time I threshed or winnowed or sheared a sheep?" Or maybe you're saying to yourself, "No problem, I promise not to trap an animal on Shabbat." While we're all laughing at the thought of weaving our own cloth or trying to figure out what "separating the chaff" means, understand that the rabbis developed these categories centuries ago based on the work done by society at that time. These categories encompass daily agricultural tasks as well as the Israelites' duties for building and visiting the Temple. Modern rabbis interpret these categories for modern times. For example, driving a car is considered "kindling a fire" because you "light" the ignition. And turning on the lights is "completing an object" because you are "completing the circuit."

The prohibition against kindling a fire is also why the first blessing we make on Shabbat is the blessing over the candles. When the candles are lit, we can do no more "kindling" until three stars appear on Saturday night. Once Shabbat has officially started, if the candles aren't lit, well, too late. You just skip this blessing. (Remember, there are degrees of observance. Here I'm telling you what is technically correct. Later on, we'll discuss other options and what you can do in your home.)

There are also three categories of other activities that are prohibited in order to "guard" or preserve the spirit of Shabbat. These are:

1. **MUKTZEH**—We are forbidden to handle items (those called *muktzeh*) that are used during the week for work, such as a hammer, telephone, pens, and candlesticks. (Technically, once you light your Shabbat candles, you can't touch them, so you should light them where they can remain in place until after Shabbat.)

2. **SH'VUT**—These are acts we are forbidden to perform that are not in line with the spirit of the day. We're also not supposed to ask a non-Jew to perform an act that a Jew is forbidden to perform or give a non-Jew instructions to perform these acts on Shabbat. (Asking before Shabbat is fine; for example, I have some friends who are shomer Shabbat and live in an apartment building in New York City. Before Shabbat they ask their doorman to press the elevator button for them when they come back from synagogue.)

3. **UVDIN D'CHOL**—We are forbidden to do things that are "weekday" in spirit. For example, we should not discuss business on Shabbat. (This one I look forward to having the excuse to invoke. Although I am not shomer Shabbes, I have made it a point to not work on my book or Web site on Shabbat. If I am writing about Shabbat, I feel it would taint the work by doing any of it on that day.)

I work from home, and it's sometimes hard to separate relaxing at home and working at home. There are plenty of nights when I can't sleep at 2:00 a.m., so I go into my office to catch up on a project. On Shabbat I sometimes have to force myself not to work. But by doing so, I turn my attention away from work and toward my family. This, in a nutshell, is why *not doing work* protects or guards Shabbat; by not working on Shabbat we can pay attention to the really important things, like family and friends.

Can we have *zachor* (remember) without *shamor* (guard) and still observe Shabbat? Yes. Honestly, in my home (and probably at most of my friends' homes) we *remember*—we make the Shabbat meal and all that goes with it—but do not *guard*—we do not keep the stricter rules. Do we have Shabbat? Yes. Could it be more meaningful? Always.

Strangely enough, it was Christmas that helped me understand Shabbat. One year, while we were still in that Shabbat-every-once-in-a while phase, Christmas fell on a Sunday. Every store was closed (I know, I know . . . except for movie theaters and Chinese restaurants). There had been a big snowfall that week, so my husband and I didn't feel like driving anywhere. The radio stations were broadcasting church services and Christmas music, and the television stations were playing Christmas shows. So my family spent the day at home together with the radio and TV turned off. We played games, we talked, we had a great time . . . *together*. I remember thinking, "This is great. Christmas kinda forced us to be together in a meaningful way as a family. I wish we had this more often." Then I realized, "We could have this once a week on Shabbat." This is the meaning of *shamor*. By guarding, we eliminate the distractions that prevent us from connecting with one another, with ourselves, with Shabbat, and with our spirituality. *Shamor* in this sense is not negative; all the restrictions make it possible to make the connection. Just as when we stop our children from eating too much candy or playing too close to the fireplace or wandering around the bookstore alone, we're not trying to ruin their fun, we're trying to protect them. In these cases, "restriction" is really protection, and on Shabbat what we are protecting is our relationship with one another. With this understanding, lighting the two candles takes on deeper meaning. With each flame, we are signaling our intent to remember and to guard the Sabbath day—to perform one of the most significant mitzvot (righteous deeds), one that has been part of the Jewish heritage since the time of Moses.

In the desert and in the time of the Temples, the *kohanim* (priests) were responsible for performing all of the rituals, one of which was offering sacrifices. A quick word about these ancient sacrifices. The kohanim were not throwing innocent virgins into volcanoes to appease an angry god, nor were they slaughtering animals to "feed" God. The sacrifices were tithes—offerings of meat, fruit, and vegetables, which served as recognition that the farmer did not raise the food by himself. The offerings recognized and gave thanks for God's role in life. When we say the blessing over the challah, we are doing a modern version of thanking God for giving us bread from the earth. Noam Zion in his book *A Day Apart: Shabbat at Home* explains that the word *challah* is actually derived from the Babylonian word for "pure" and signifies a sacred gift to God. Zion contends that the translation for *challah* should be "bread from which an offering has been removed." In this sense, the challah we eat on Shabbat symbolizes these ancient sacrifices. (Some people even sprinkle salt on the challah while blessing it as the priests salted the sacrifices.)

The challah at our table also represents the portion of food (manna) God provided for each person during the forty years the Jews wandered in the desert. The Bible says that the manna rained down from the heavens each day, and every person would gather his or her due. However, on the sixth day, God provided a double portion. The second portion was to be saved for the seventh day, so that no one would have to work to gather food on Shabbat. This is the reason many families have two *challot* at their Friday night table.

Under King Solomon, the Tabernacle (the sanctuary that the Israelites carried with them through their journey in the desert) was replaced by the *Beit Mikdash* (the Temple), and the priests continued to perform the rituals. However, after the second Temple was destroyed, the rabbis decentralized and democratized Judaism by creating synagogues, instead of rebuilding the Temple again. The old system of bringing sacrifices for the Temple priests to perform was replaced by the new system of prayer in synagogues. Rather than offer sacrifices, we were encouraged to come to synagogues to pray and to do mitzvot in order to bring ourselves closer to God. The individual alone, not via a priestly act, was now responsible for her own observance.

As another part of the decentralization, the rabbis told the Jewish people to bring the rituals of the Temple into their homes. So, instead of making animal sacrifices at the Temple before Shabbat, Jewish people light candles and make blessings and say prayers in their homes. This is based in what we learn from the Torah. In Exodus, we read that God commands Moses to build a *mikdash* (Tabernacle), and promises that His Shechinah (Divine Presence) will dwell there among the people. This way, God showed that He was with the Israelites throughout their journey, and His presence among them gave them comfort and peace. When we make Shabbat, we try to create a peaceful environment. In a sense we are creating a sanctuary—a holy place—of our home. According to the Torah, candlesticks and kiddush cups were used by the kohanim in the original traveling desert Tabernacle (and later in the Temples in Jerusalem). The ritual objects we have on our table, combined with a peaceful family environment helps us transform our home into a space where God's spirit can dwell. This is known as creating a *mikdash me'at* (a small sanctuary), and by doing so we are bringing ourselves closer to God. (I sometimes use this idea to my advantage: on those rare occasions when my children aren't behaving during Shabbat dinner, I'll ask them, "Pretend God was sitting at the table with us. How would you act?") From the destruction of the Beit Mikdash we now have mikdash me'at in our home.

By making a temple of our home we are essentially making our home sacred. This is the key to Shabbat—making the ordinary sacred—so that when Shabbat comes, our homes reflect the purity of the day. Shabbat is considered more "pure" than other days, and for this reason the day is sometimes referred to as a bride (*kallah*) visiting our home. We sing of this bride on Friday night in the song "Lecha Dodi" with the verse "Come, my friend, the Bride to meet. The holy Shabbat let us greet."

The idea of Shabbat being a bride is rooted in Jewish mysticism, and while mainstream Judaism no longer teaches the esoteric beliefs of kabbalah, some of the kabbalists' beautiful imagery remains. The Shabbat Bride is an extension of the Shabbat Queen (Shabbat haMalka), an idea that is quite ancient—there are references to her in the Talmud, which dates to the second and third centuries. Shabbat is the Queen to God's King. The Queen descends from Heaven to dwell with us on Shabbat, and so we prepare our home as we would for a queen's visit. The Shabbat Queen graces us on Shabbat, making the day more special than the rest of the week and establishing the seventh day as one of peace and beauty. (She also solidifies the importance of the female-wife-mother in Judaism.) The personification of Shabbat as a Queen also refers to the idea of the Shechinah. Remember, God promises that His Shechinah will dwell with the Israelites in the Tabernacle. Shechinah is the Hebrew word for the Divine Presence of God. The Hebrew language has both masculine and feminine words and Shechinah is feminine and so Shechinah is considered the "feminine" side of God. Although it is believed that God does not have a gender, God is often referred to as He. If you think in terms of yin and yang, two halves making a whole, the same idea of duality behind the two candles, and shamor and zachor, the idea of a Shechinah completes the idea of (a male) God. Therefore it follows that if our home is a temple, a sacred space, during Shabbat, then it is the place where God will send his Shechinah to spend time with us. When we greet the Shabbat haMalka (the Shabbat Queen), we greet the Shechinah.

Just as the Shechinah is partnered with God to complete the male side of God, the Jewish people are partnered with the Shabbat Bride. The kabbalists examined the story of the creation and formed partners of the days of the week based on what is created in them. For example, on the first day, God created light, and on day four, He created the luminaries (the sun, the moon, and the stars); therefore, we can link days one and four. Days two and five are linked in the creation of heaven and earth and the creation of the creatures of the sea and the birds of the air respectively. Days three and six are connected in the creation of land and all creatures that live on the land. Only the seventh day, Shabbat, was left alone. In the Mishnah, Rabbi Shimon bar Yochai (author of the Zohar, the great book of Kabbalah) concluded that the Jewish people are Shabbat's partner. We make an intimate connection with Shabbat, and Shabbat becomes our "bride." "She" is the day that makes us whole—the day we go inward.

And while we greet our Bride with a beautiful Sabbath table and a sense of holiness, it is, in fact, a romantic meal, complete with candles, wine, and song.

Technically Speaking

The Hasidim add to the romance of Shabbat by reading the beautiful love poem Song of Songs. Found in Ketuvim (The Writings), one of the sections of the Bible that contains verses written by past kings, Song of Songs was written by King Solomon and is considered a love story between God and the Jewish people. Traditionally read on Passover, Song of Songs contains the verse spoken by Jewish brides at their wedding: *"Ani l'dodi v'dodi li"*—I am my beloved's and my beloved is mine.

There you have it—some reasons why. Whether performing simplified rituals originally performed by priests or simply eating in our homes, Shabbat is about connection with the sacred. It's carving out holy space for you and your family. Focus on this as you proceed with your Shabbat preparations. Shabbat connects us with our present, our past, and our future. When you strike the match that will light the Sabbath candles, imagine the flame extending to the candle the woman is lighting in the Jewish home next door . . . in the home around the corner . . . in the next state . . . in other countries . . . throughout time. Look at your children and imagine a time yet to be when they have homes and light their own candles with their children, and envision how their flame connects with their world. This is the beauty and magic of Shabbat. By making Shabbat each week, you can help your children see and feel this connection. This is what I mean when I say that observing Shabbat gives your children a home in the world.

2

It's the Mood, Not the Meal: Your Shabbat Table

SO IT'S FRIDAY MORNING (or maybe even Friday afternoon). You're suddenly inspired to have Shabbat. But you have hardly any time to prepare—what can you do?

Don't worry. Start small. Think baby steps. While I was learning from other moms about what they do to make Shabbat every week, my friend Paula gave me an amazing piece of advice. She said, "It's the mood, not the meal." She meant that the focus should be on Shabbat and the time spent with your family, not dinner. You don't have to be a gourmet chef, or even a good cook, to pull off Shabbat. And, here's something sure to be controversial—you don't even have to make chicken soup or brisket to have Shabbat! You can order in! Thinking this way relieves the pressure to cook a huge meal. What you *should* do is find little ways to make the meal meaningful. The hardest part is making the commitment to have Shabbat dinner—the rest will fall into place.

So start by answering this question: what would make tonight different from all the other nights?

Maybe the rest of the week you eat on paper plates. On Friday night, set the table with china. Or add some flowers to the table. Or eat in the dining room. Or just eat together. Do something different to set the meal apart from the others, to make Shabbat unique.

Imagine you are a decorator or a set designer, and set the stage for Shabbat. Think of how the table usually looks when your family comes in for dinner. Now imagine the table is covered with a white tablecloth and set with beautiful plates, fresh flowers, and glowing candles. Imagine how your family will feel sitting down to a dinner like this. With the mood set for Shabbat, it doesn't even matter what you serve.

You can be creative. I know a family who struggled to balance their sons' soccer schedules with Shabbat. So for the end-of-season party, they hosted a Shabbat barbecue! Everyone gathered around as they lit candles and said the blessings, and then all enjoyed a Shabbes meal of hamburgers and hot dogs!

Such Genius

I know a group of three families who get together every Friday night for Shabbat. They take turns, rotating homes; they light candles, say the blessings, and always have pizza! Starting a Shabbat dinner group guarantees a wonderful Shabbat each week, and you'll be responsible for the preparations only once a month. Plus, your kids will look forward to seeing their Shabbat friends.

Don't get me wrong. I don't want you to abandon the idea of cooking a Shabbat dinner. A casual meal helps us busy moms juggle our schedules and still have Shabbat. Save these for the times when you think that without the pizza option, you're not going to be able to have Shabbat. It's a judgment call. The point is, don't let the food or the *idea* of making the food stop you from having dinner. Plus, these days, there are plenty of restaurants and supermarkets that offer take-home rotisserie chicken—and even deliver!

Here's a quick story: One Friday night, Sofie had her Girl Scout father-daughter dance. This was a big deal, and truthfully, I do make exceptions for having us all together for Shabbat if those of us who can't be home are attending a family event (like a father-daughter dance or a father-son camping trip). We lit the candles together as a family and said all the blessings, and when Sofie and Jonathan left for the dance, Jules and I went out for a mother-son sushi Shabbat. But even though we were at a restaurant, I made sure to keep the spirit of Shabbat through our conversation. We talked about fish—how some people say that fish were the witnesses to the Creation and how some Jews eat the heads of fish on Rosh Hashanah. From that we talked about what it means to be the head of your community and what it means to be a leader. It was a Shabbat with my son that I will not forget.

Not What You Would Call Kosher

OK, the whole pizza for Shabbat thing is fun, but it's not such a great idea to order one with pepperoni (or sausage or ground meat). Look, it's Shabbat. Regardless of what you do during the week, pepperoni pizza on Shabbat just seems, well . . . not kosher. The same goes for wontons.

Ideally, we should serve a traditional, home-cooked meal. I love to try recipes my grand-mother made, even though they usually call for more eggs than one should eat in a month and have scary ingredients like Nyafat. (Her amazing recipes are from the pre-low-cholesterol, low-carb, whole grain, lactose-free, low-sodium, sugar-free days). Whenever I make one of my grandmother's recipes, I think about my family, like the time when I was a little girl and my great-aunt Celie told me that after cracking an egg I should wipe my fingers in the bro-ken shell and smooth the raw egg white on my face as a moisturizer. (I never did it, but she had beautiful skin even into her nineties. So I guess I should start.) Some recipes create more than food—they conjure up memories and serve as history, both cultural history and family history. The women who are part of our history are in our recipes, and they live on through the foods they lovingly prepared. When you have the time to make one of your  family's recipes, you'll bring so much more to the table than just food. You probably don't eat brisket on a regular basis, but if you make it for a special meal like Shabbat, you can tell your children that this is what their grandparents ate, or that this is their great-grandmother's recipe, and by the way . . . let me tell you about her.

If you want to have a traditional meal, turn to the recipes in chapter 8. They're not hard; we're not talking complicated gourmet stuff here. Roast chicken is pretty easy to make, and after years of making truly awful, dried-out brisket, I've finally found a wonder-ful and (dare I say it) foolproof recipe.

If you don't have to worry about the food, the easiest way to set your Shabbat meal apart is to decorate your table a bit fancier than you do for your normal dinners. Elevate your home and the atmosphere around the meal from every other day of the week. To truly make Shabbat we create a sacred time, which is different from secular time. Setting a beautiful table with ritual objects is one way to make Friday night dinner sacred. For example, use a white tablecloth. To me, a white tablecloth feels different from a colored tablecloth. There's just something about a table set with a white tablecloth that says "Jewish holiday." I know a little girl who absolutely refuses to let her mom use their white tablecloth for anything other than Shabbat. "It's the Shabbat tablecloth," she insists. Now, this is all well and good, but her mom only has two tablecloths and sometimes would like to use the white one for a dinner party! So make sure you have enough other tablecloths in case your children designate one as "the Shabbat tablecloth." Look at it this way—it's a great excuse to go shopping.

To be honest, I don't use a tablecloth (I save it for the High Holy Days), and we eat in the kitchen. But I try to make the table special. I put out fresh flowers, use my pretty placemats (OK, they're actually really funky wood chargers that I love), cloth napkins, and my good crystal wine glasses. I like to use whatever I have that brings our family to my table.

When I say "whatever brings my family to the table," I'm not talking about only my husband and children; I'm also talking about my family history. We use a few of my grandma Hilda's kiddush cups (pretty little pink glasses), and I use some of the kiddush cups my husband received when he was born. My children use their own monogrammed kiddush cups. I also use the candlesticks my mother received at her wedding, some pieces of Grandma Fannie's china, and Great-Mama Mil's silver platter. Not only does the table look lovely (this is certainly not everyday tableware), but I use these items the way I use my old family recipes, as an excuse to talk to my children about our family—to share stories of our family's history. It also makes me feel good to look at the table and feel that my ancestors are somehow with us and a part of our Shabbat celebration. (For those of you who don't have kiddush cups or family china, this is your chance to make your own heirlooms. In chapter 9, you will find instructions to make your own special Shabbat items. Who knows, maybe one day your grandchildren will use the "Button Candlesticks" they made with you and tell your great-grandchildren all about what a wonderful influence you were on them!)

After all, family is the key to Shabbat, and here's proof. My husband usually comes home well after Sofie, Jules, and I have eaten dinner, but he makes a point of coming home early on Friday evenings for Shabbat. I didn't realize the impact these little changes to our normal meal made until one Tuesday a few years ago when Jonathan called to say he was leaving work in time to have dinner with us. I was making salmon and decided since he was coming home early, I'd set the table nicely for him to come home to. Jules, who was three at the time, looked at the table and asked, "Is it Shabbat?" To him, a nice dinner with Daddy meant Shabbat.

What else sets the mood for Shabbat? I love the smell of fresh-baked challah cooling on the counter—as my mother always says, "then the house smells like *yontif*." If you have time to bake challah, do so. There's nothing like it. Making challah is actually easy, fun, and if you're stressed, kneading dough is a great way to work out tension! (I've been known to grumble out loud while pounding on challah dough.) Read chapter 7 and you'll be a pro challah baker in no time!

So you've got the challah cooling (or resting on the counter in the plastic bag fresh from the supermarket—I know, I know, baby steps . . . next week you'll bake it!), and you've got the chicken roasting or you're waiting for the delivery guy to arrive with your food. Now you need to set the table. Here's where you bring in the kids. In my house, Sofie and Jules set the Shabbat table. It's Sofie's job to handle the plates and glasses (the breakable stuff), and Jules's duty to get out the silverware. We keep kosher at home, and setting the table for Shabbat gives me a great opportunity to highlight that we have both milchig (milk) and fleishig (meat) dishes and silverware.

Involving the children in the preparations gives them responsibility, shows them I trust them with such a significant part of the Shabbat meal, and also starts the training (for lack of a better word) for when they are adults and will be completely responsible for a meal. They're learning where the fork goes and where the spoon goes so they'll be all set for fancy dinners when they graduate from Harvard. (I may be modern, but I'm still a Jewish mother.) Having them set the table not only helps me out while I'm busy finishing up dinner, it encourages their creativity and gives them a sense of ownership and pride in the Sabbath table. It includes them in the meal even before the meal begins.

Such Genius

The Sephardim have a tradition that the single girls set the Shabbat table. They believe it brings them good luck—as in good luck finding a nice

Jewish husband. (I wonder how old Sofie has to be before I start nudging her about this?) If there are no single girls in the house, the mother helps her young children set the table to teach them how.

I let my kids add their own special touches to the table. They choose from the challah covers, candlesticks, and kiddush cups they've made. They even select the yarmulkes.

Let me say a couple of things about yarmulkes (I call them yarmulkes, not kippot, because I grew up hearing the Yiddish). Our yarmulke collection has grown almost as fast as our Barbie collection, and weekly yarmulke selection has become a thing. We have some unique yarmulkes that make the selection process even more fun for Jules. When Jules was three, a friend of mine who manages a local Jewish gift shop gave Jules an elephant

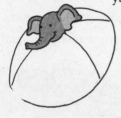

yarmulke because Jules loves (and I mean to the point of obsession) elephants. Now, this wasn't some little yarmulke with an elephant painted on it. It was a yarmulke with a mini Beanie Baby kind of thing coming out of the top. When he wore it, he looked as if he had a stuffed animal on his head. We've since progressed to a suede yarmulke with Harry Potter painted on it. We have loads of yarmulkes from special occasions—they're wonderful to have as they always bring back memories when I glance at the underside and see the stamped date and names from weddings and b'nai mitzvot we've attended. And I love it when Jonathan wears one of the yarmulkes from our wedding. I'm amazed at the plethora of yarmulkes out there—football teams, cartoon characters, flags—and I promise you can find just the right ones for the men in your life.

And if you can't find it, you can make it! I created some projects to make special yarmulkes, so check out the projects in chapter 9. You and your children will have fun making these, and they serve as wonderful memories.

To help your kids help you, be sure to make the Shabbat items easily accessible. When I was a child, the china closet seemed magical—the fine pieces locked inside were treasures to be touched only by the grown-ups. I would stare at the delicate teacups through the glass doors and wonder when I would be old enough to be trusted with them. Today I love unlocking the doors to let my children pull out the Shabbes candlesticks and kiddush cups that I purposefully place on the bottom shelf so they can reach them. Other families store their Shabbat objects in a Shabbat box.

A Shabbat box is a box used to hold the items your family uses to turn your dinner table into your Shabbat dinner table. The box can be as large or as small as you need. (Check out chapter 9 for directions on how to make your own.) My friend Suzi uses her box to store CDs of Shabbat songs, all the Shabbat chazzerai her kids made in nursery school, and special games and puzzles her family plays after dinner. Adding these games and books to the Shabbat box emphasizes another wonderful aspect of the Friday night meal and, I think, one of the most important reasons to do Shabbat. Continue connecting with your family by dedicating the time after dinner to playing games, doing puzzles, reading or telling stories, or whatever your family enjoys doing together (or would like to enjoy but hasn't found the time to do). Paula's family plays word games. Carol's family has political and philosophical debates (her children are older and brilliant). Use Shabbat as the excuse to do whatever your family likes to do (or would like to do).

This is important: the more the children enjoy spending time together as a family, the more likely they will continue to carve out Friday night as the family time when they are teenagers and have many other options.

Such Genius

My friends Robin and Larry have a traveling Shabbat box. It's actually a zip-up food storage bag (easier for packing) filled with Shabbat candles, candlesticks, kiddush cups, yarmulkes, and a challah cover. They bring it with them when they travel over Shabbat to turn their Friday night restaurant table into a Shabbat table. They take pictures of their meal and often look at them when they return home. These are their family's favorite Shabbats. Robin often tells the story of the time they were traveling with two other families in Jamaica. They celebrated a truly spectacular Shabbat at a restaurant by the beach. The sun was setting, the waves were . . . waving. It was beautiful. Robin's husband got up from the table and passed by another table of guests who he noticed had been observing them. They stopped him and told him they were visiting from Israel and that they were touched to have traveled so far from home and still see Shabbat. They said it was the most beautiful Shabbat dinner they had ever witnessed. This "compliment from Israel" filled my friends with much *naches* and inspired them to continue their travel box tradition.

You can take this idea a step further and hang a map on your wall and use pushpins to mark all the places you've celebrated Shabbat. This can be a wonderful geography lesson for your children and an inspiration for your entire family to dream of where else in the world you could have Shabbat.

One of the easiest ways to turn your table into one fit for Shabbat is to set out a vase of flowers. It's also a wonderful excuse to bring flowers into your home. My father-in-law

always brings home a bouquet of flowers for his wife on Friday afternoon (what a lovely way to start Shabbes). Being creative with your arrangements doesn't have to mean expensive. I love using one color and various kinds of flowers. Or buy the supermarket bunch and separate the flowers into several small vases. When I bring home my bunch of flowers, I like to play around with the various blooms to bring a special look to the table. It's quite impressive how you can set the table with the same plates each week, but bring a completely unique look to your table with different flower arrangements.

Here are some seasonal flower arrangements that I do, but they can work throughout the year, too:

For fall, use a square glass vase with high sides. Fill the bottom with fresh cranberries. (I like using fresh ones because they have that plump, lush look and fill the container with their deep red color. Dried cranberries, although yummy in salads, would look like little shriveled pebbles at the bottom.) Cut red roses so that the entire flower (head and stem) is the height of the vase. Insert stems straight down into the berries so that the flowers stand in straight rows flush with the top of the vase. You can experiment with different berries and flowers—perhaps blueberries and huge blue hydrangeas. (When I use hydrangeas, I allow the flower heads to sit above the vase, covering the top like a lid.) By the way, roses and hydrangeas mixed together make gorgeous bouquets.

For spring, take a tall drinking glass, two wide rubber bands, and a bunch of fresh asparagus stalks. Place one rubber band a third of the way down from the top of the glass and the other a third up from the bottom. Carefully insert the asparagus stalks vertically under the bands on the outside of the glass, so that it appears the glass is made of asparagus. The bands will secure the stalks to the glass. Cover the rubber bands with wide ribbon, and tie it into bows. Fill the glass with pretty spring flowers. You can also incorporate delicate stems that drip down between the stalks.

For summer, collect fresh flowers from the yard; ask your children to help you. Tiny stems from flower bushes, like azaleas, work well. Don't worry, you don't have to have magnificent flower gardens in your backyard—even dandelions will work! Put the flowers in tiny vases, kiddush cups, or short drinking glasses around the table. I like placing one at each setting. I find that tiny vases add color without taking up room or impeding vision.

For winter, make a dramatic arrangement of twigs. Walk outside and find long thin branches, or ask your florist for twisted willow. Fill a third of a tall glass vase with plain dried rice, which will anchor the twigs. This arrangement will last forever!

Any time of year, play with mixing fruit and flowers. For example, place six fresh green apples in a shallow glass bowl, one in the middle, five circling it (or however many will fit, depending on the size of the bowl). Since the apples are spheres, they don't fit together flush, so insert flowers in the gaps. Cut your stems short, so that the heads of the flowers rest on the tops of the apples, but don't put in so many that they completely cover the apples. I like using brightly colored flowers against the green apples, like hot pink Gerbera daisies or purple spider mums.

You can also do a variation on this arrangement with a tall glass vase. Fill it with apples or lemons or limes or oranges, and place taller flowers (like gladioli) in the vase, using the fruit to anchor the stems.

Another easy way to show that the evening is more special is to dress up for dinner. Just as we try to look our best when going out to a nice restaurant or a party, we dress for Shabbat. This extra effort shows respect, not only for the others at the meal but for Shabbat itself, and can make it feel more like a celebration. We can also invite guests to our home to share Shabbat with us.

Technically Speaking

Showing hospitality is one of the 613 commandments, or mitzvot (plural for mitzvah, a righteous deed), that are found in the Torah. Throughout the Torah there are numerous examples of hospitality, the first of which is found in Genesis, when Abraham welcomes the three angels into his tent. In Hebrew the phrase is *hachnasat orchim*. So having guests at your Shabbat table is both fun and a good deed!

Having company on Shabbat (while, yes, adding to the work involved) helps teach our young children how to behave while dining with others and can make it a fun evening (that is, if you invite their friends, too).

Also (and I get into this more in the teen chapter) to create a more sacred atmosphere, elevate your speech. Pretend you're in shul—you wouldn't curse or yell or gossip there. (Well, at least you'd *try* not to gossip, but have you seen what you-know-who has been wearing lately?) So try to watch what you say during Shabbat. You're on holy time now. You'll see how what you say—or don't say—changes the mood of the house during Shabbat.

All of these things—the tablecloth, the flowers, and the (old or newly created) family heirlooms—go toward setting the mood. You could plop scrambled eggs down on the plate and the food would somehow seem extraordinary. I promise you, if you do this, your home, your meal, and in turn your family will feel special. Your bubbie would be so proud!

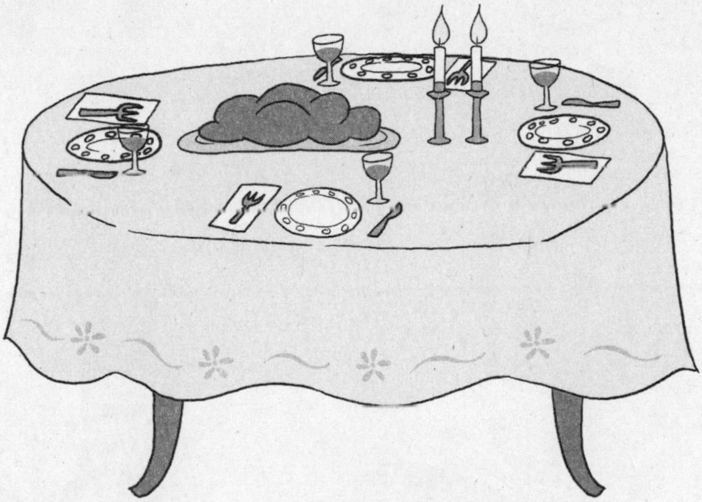

3

Wine, Not Whine: Creating Shalom Bayit Friday Night

DOES THIS SOUND FAMILIAR? You come home on Friday after a whole day of working or running errands, and you're late bringing your three children to three different activities, you have a pile of laundry to do, the dog needs to be walked, and you have ten phone calls and thirty e-mails all waiting for a response. Make a nice Shabbat dinner? Yeah, right, maybe next week.

Or perhaps you decide, no, this is important I'm going to find time to make a nice meal and set a beautiful table. So you're preparing the chicken, you're proud of yourself, things are going well, and then the kids start fighting, the dog starts barking, the phone rings, the doorbell rings (it's a deliveryman who needs a signature), and while the door is open, the dog runs out, the kids start crying, the phone rings again, and it's your husband and he's running late. You glance over to see the braided challah dough sitting on the counter and realize you forgot to put it in the oven, and now it won't be ready until seven o'clock. Then you smell something burning—it's the chicken. A peaceful Shabbat?

Oy, vey iz mir!

Don't let this discourage you. Be strong. Judaism has survived thousands of years, and Jewish mothers have faced much tougher circumstances than whiny kids and busy schedules. Focus on what is important. When it gets really nuts, think about what it really means to make Shabbes, and that you are carving out a time for yourself and your family.

When we imagine the mood of the house during Shabbat, holiness and peace is our goal. Make Friday night (and Saturday) sacred to you, and it will become sacred for you.

As moms, we set the tone of the house. I've noticed that everyone seems to feed off my mood. When I'm stressed, the kids sense it, get uneasy, and then the house is stressed. When I'm "cranky mommy," sure enough "cranky children" and "cranky daddy" soon follow. It's not fair, I know—my husband's moods don't affect the family like this. But to spin it positively, part of me likes knowing that I have a powerful impact on my family. And besides, I know that when I'm in a silly mood, the house is fun. So do what ya gotta do to get your house in a good mood.

This is called *shalom bayit* or "peaceful home." I remember once talking to my über-Orthodox sister-in-law, Elinor, about what her life is like. (She's a *ba'alat t'shuvah*, meaning that she moved to Israel, became very religious, agreed to an arranged marriage with my brother-in-law, and, amazingly, had six children in six years.) Surprisingly enough, she told me she doesn't know how *I* do what I do considering my family's schedule and that her life is much calmer and simpler. I couldn't believe this—is my life, with all its luxuries and conveniences (and the fact that I have two young kids and not six) harder than hers? Elinor told me that rather than running in a million different directions, her single focus is to create shalom bayit and that everything stems from this. Her husband's success and the whole family's success is contingent upon her creating shalom bayit. As a modern American woman, I have a hard time swallowing this "woman makes the home so the man can work" idea, but in Judaism there is actually a great deal of respect for a woman's traditional role and the important contributions she makes to her home and how they affect her family. Taken in the truly respectful manner in which this is intended, it is a beautiful statement, and I think about this sometimes when I debate whether or not I have time to make Shabbat. No matter how modern I consider myself to be, it's up to me to make sure we have shalom bayit. I consider it step one in making Shabbat.

This chapter will help with the mechanics of the Shabbat celebration—when, how, and why you can do what you need to do and keep the "whine" to a minimum and the shalom bayit to a maximum.

COUNTDOWN TO FRIDAY NIGHT MEAL

Moms can multitask. It's our secret superpower. Realize that Shabbat is coming, and try to prepare as much as possible before Friday. Fridays are usually busy days for me, so I try to eliminate last-minute runs to the grocery store, which can add to the stress of the day. I try to buy ingredients for Friday's dinner earlier in the week, but for backup I always keep extra chicken and meat, bags of frozen vegetables, and at least one challah stocked in the freezer at all times. And in the pantry I try to have on hand boxes of my family's favorite rice and a few bottles of wine and grape juice. This way, even on those really crazy weeks, all I need to do is defrost. To be honest, I usually plan meals that need little prep time (check out chapter 8 for my personal faves) and save truly gourmet attempts for days I know I'll have a lot of free time (or when we have company joining us). Even if you are planning to order in, there are things you'll need, such as challah, grape juice, wine, and candles.

Let's start with challah. When you're food shopping during the week remember to buy yeast, flour, eggs, or sugar if you don't already have them. Having these items readily available at home will allow for flexibility in making your challah. This way, if you have some time during the week, make your challah then and freeze it.

Such Genius

Here's the beauty of making your own challah—it's a time-saver (who'd have thought?). Basically, one challah dough recipe makes between two and four loaves, depending on how big you want them. Therefore, if you make the recipe one night while you're watching TV, you'll be set for the month.

Here's another tip: I like to make huge loaves, so I get only two loaves out of my recipe. But we eat only one challah each week. So I put the two loaves out to make the blessing, but after dinner I freeze the second loaf. After two weeks, I always have two challah loaves sitting in the freezer as backup!

I can't tell you how many times I have forgotten to get grape juice. (Those nights, we pour water into the kids' kiddush cups and pretend.) Now every time I pass the juice aisle at the market I grab a bottle. Even if I have some in the refrigerator, the extra bottles will keep in the pantry. I like white grape juice. It tastes the same but doesn't stain the same as the dreaded purple.

If you are like me, you may have thought you had to have that sickly sweet syrupy wine that's more like a combination of grape juice and maple syrup. But here's the good news: you *don't* have to have Manischewitz (unless, like my husband, you like it). Yes, traditionally we drink sweet wine, but it should be good wine—you should enjoy it. And if you keep kosher there are lots of new, quite good kosher wines.

Such Genius

Here's some great news I learned from my rabbi friend Susan: according to the Reform and Conservative movements, all wines that are made in North America are considered kosher because of the process used to make the wines (something about the grapes being squashed by machines). So enjoy that cab you picked up in Napa!

And make sure that you have candles—these are, of course, essential. If you don't, go to the supermarket or local kosher market, and buy a box of Shabbat candles (the white ones).

Technically Speaking

Can any candle be a Shabbes candle? Actually, no. To be kosher, Shabbat candles should not contain any animal fat (in case they drip on the food). But you really don't need to worry about this—most candles today are made of paraffin wax. They should also burn for three hours, the idea being that their light lasts throughout the Sabbath meal.

I like to use disposable aluminum candleholders. These are easy to find and are shelved in the same section as the boxes of Shabbat candles. Placed into the candlesticks, these foil cups serve as liners, so that when the candle melts, you just throw away the foil—no messy wax to clean up. You can also find glass candleholders (known as bobeches) that fit into the candlesticks. They're inexpensive and can be found in any Jewish gift shop. These, of course, are not disposable.

Such Genius

Phil Ratner, a Washington, D.C., artist who specializes in Judaica, told me he puts a bit of water in the bottom of the glass candleholders, so that when the candle burns down, the water both extinguishes the flame and prevents the wax from sticking to the glass.

FRIDAY: EREV SHABBAT

If you are able to make your challah dough (or buy it) Friday morning, great. Then you can braid it and put it in the oven an hour before you plan to serve dinner so it comes out nice and hot. (You can also ask your husband to pick up the challah on extra-busy Fridays.)

If you buy frozen dough (or freeze your homemade braided dough or already baked loaf), then all you need to do is take it out of the freezer the night before or in the morning and let it defrost.

Try to buy your flowers that day (or better yet, ask your husband to pick some up). If you and your husband work, you can even try to pick up flowers during your lunch hour. Flowers are probably not an everyday purchase for you, so they can really feel like a nice treat and this tiny thing makes a huge impact on the table.

When I have time, I love to start my Friday mornings at the market (the fancy organic one). I get inspired by the gorgeous flowers and fresh vegetables. Then I come home, arrange the flowers, and make my challah dough. Afterward, I try to finish whatever work I have to do before the kids come home from school.

Once they're home, Shabbat starts. Promise me you'll get the kids to help you set the table. This helps you out and will occupy them.

Turn on the answering machine and screen your calls. (Believe me, people will start to figure out that you will not take calls on Friday afternoon.) Forget about the laundry or cleaning the house or all the other errands you have to do. They can wait until Sunday. Understand this is also your time. Give yourself permission to turn off everything but your family.

After I get dinner in the oven I try to have a quick run on the treadmill. This is especially important if I feel stressed. If I don't have time, or if the kids are a little meshugge, I'll put on fun music and we'll bebop around the house. If it's nice outside, Sofie, Jules, and I take Mac, our crazy dog, for a walk around the block (which helps ensure *he'll* be good during Shabbes dinner). Exercise really helps calm me down and puts an end to the workday. Then shower and change into your Shabbat clothes.

Such Genius

"I hate Shabbat!" One Friday evening as I was putting the finishing touches on dinner, Jules was screaming.

Great. Here I am, Miss Make Friday Night Shabbat, and my son is yelling that he hates Shabbat. Not good.

The real issue? He didn't hate Shabbat; he was hungry. On Fridays Jonathan makes a point of coming home by seven so he can eat dinner with us, but Sofie and Jules are used to eating at six, so celebrating Shabbat was forcing Jules to wait, and he was hungry. I didn't want to start Shabbat like this, so I instituted a kid-friendly Shabbat happy hour. I put out some juice and heated up some hors d'oeuvres. I found that these take the edge off the hunger and are especially useful if you're going to services before dinner. I don't put out too much so that the food spoils their appetite—just enough to stave off the hunger pangs. We keep kosher, so depending on what I'm serving for dinner, I can heat up those frozen potato puffed-pastry things. Or if I'm serving salmon or tuna steaks, I put out cheese and crackers. Fruits and veggies are always an easy and healthy option. Teenagers will enjoy these too, and this can be another great chance to chat with them while you're finishing up dinner. And if you have grown children or another family over, you can have some wine with the hors d'oeuvres.

WELCOMING SHABBAT

So the table is set, the challah is cooling, but you're still a bit stressed from your crazy day. Here's another tip: Think *Fiddler on the Roof* and summon your inner Golde. If you don't know that I'm talking about Golde, Tevye's wife, put this book down right now and rent *Fiddler on the Roof*. Don't worry about me, I'll wait. Seriously. It's important background information for what I'm going to be talking about . . . so go.

All right, so here's how you can summon your inner Golde: Sing a *niggun*. A niggun is a wordless song. Sing a song you know without the words, like "Lie lie lalalala lie lie" (I wish I could sing this for you so you'd know), or make one up. Think of Tevye singing the "biddy biddy bum" part of "If I Were a Rich Man." It sounds silly and feels goofy, but take a deep breath and try it. Singing a niggun at the start of your dinner is definitely calming.

Here's a true story: One Friday afternoon as I was putting Shabbat dinner on the table, the house was crazy—the kids were yelling at the video game, which was, by the way, blasting, and the *farkakta* dog was jumping on everyone and barking—hardly a peaceful Shabbat mood. I don't know what possessed me, but I started singing a niggun the cantor had taught us. "Lie, lie, lalalala lie lie. . . ." Suddenly, the kids got quiet and started singing along (it's easy for others to join in when they don't need to know the words). I walked over and turned off the TV, led the kids to the table, the dog quieted down, and shalom bayit was back. I know . . . kinda weird. But it worked. Now when my husband or I feel not so much in the Shabbes mood, we sing the niggun.

There's something otherworldly about it. The beauty lies in the simple, old-fashioned tune. It immediately recalls our heritage and makes everything seem simpler. Starting the dinner with a niggun is different from the Shabbats when I just call everyone to the table with the announcement that it's time to light candles. Singing the niggun changes the feeling in the house—it truly feels like the Sabbath bride has entered our home.

It is a common tradition to begin the Sabbath meal by singing the song "Shalom Aleichem," which means "peace to you." Most assume the "you" means the other people at your table, but the "you" in this case are angels. The story is that two angels accompany everyone home from synagogue on Friday night. When they enter your house, if the candles are lit and the table is set, the good angel will say, "May it be God's will that it be this way next Shabbat." And the bad angel is forced to say, "Amen." However, if you come home from shul and the candles are not lit and the table is not set, the bad angel says, "May it be God's will that it be this way next Shabbat," and the good angel must answer, "Amen." Now, my family is not so into singing; however, every once in a while I'll sing "Shalom Aleichem" instead of a niggun to call everyone to the table. I must admit, singing is not one of my strengths, so my family usually rushes to the table knowing that once they all sit, I'll stop.

Another wonderful way to begin Shabbat is with *tzedakah* (charity). Giving tzedakah is an important part of Jewish culture. Teaching our children early on that giving is part of what and who we are helps shape them into caring and generous adults. Sofie and Jules receive their weekly allowance before I light the Shabbat candles. They then contribute part of that allowance to the tzedakah box. Set an example by putting in some coins from your wallet. This also helps set the meal apart from the rest of the week. Beginning with an act of charity adds to the holiness or spirit of Shabbat.

After tzedakah, we officially welcome Shabbat by lighting candles. You may ask all the women or girls present to recite the blessing with you, you may ask the children to recite with you, or you may choose to say it alone as the woman of the house. This is traditionally not something the men do. It is the woman's responsibility to light the Shabbat candles—this is our honor.

Not Quite Kosher

I don't go by the official time to light the candles (I know—how scandalous). I find it more meaningful to light the candles at the table with my family. The "kosher" way is to light the candles no later than eighteen minutes before sundown. This is because you are forbidden to create a fire after Shabbat begins. (This is also why during Chanukah we light the menorah before the Shabbat candles.)

You can find candle lighting times on many Jewish calendars and Web sites. In the winter this may mean that you will be lighting the candles (by yourself) in the afternoon. This is still beautiful and meaningful (even if you are alone) because you are following the law, and when your children come home from school, they will see the candles burning and know it is Shabbat. Some more observant women even refuse to light candles if they missed doing so at the correct time.

We are also forbidden to move the candlesticks once they are lit because they are *muktzeh*, an instrument of work, so we should not even touch them. (Honestly, I move mine because I light them at the kitchen table and have to make room for the chicken.)

As a married woman, I must cover my head to say the blessing, and I do this with a paper napkin, as my grandmother and mother did. For me, the paper napkin helps bring my mom and grandmother and a wonderful childhood memory into my Shabbat. You can use whatever you want—a beautiful lace head covering, a vintage scarf—you don't have to be fancy, but if you're married you should cover your head.

Such Genius

My friend Jen turns off all the lights in the house before she lights candles. This is particularly beautiful and moving, with the only source of light coming from the Shabbes candles. Her five-year-old son, Ethan, always closes his eyes while his mom lights the candles because, he explains, he uses this time to talk with God.

Once you have the candles in the candlesticks, cover your head and light the candles. Hold your hands with your palms facing you, slightly cupped, and circle your hands around the tops of the flames, as if you are drawing the warmth in toward you. Circle three times, and after the third, place your fingertips lightly on your forehead and cover your face.

Technically Speaking

Why do we circle our hands around the flame and cover our eyes? As my rabbi friend Susan explains, this is an act of "legal fiction." Technically, we are supposed to say the blessing before doing the action. But since we are not allowed to light candles after Shabbat has started, we have to first light the candles and then say the blessing. By covering our eyes, we're pretending the candles are not already lit and then when we remove our hands—surprise! They're lit! But I love covering my eyes—there's something quite mystical about it.

My mother would whisper the *brachah* into her cupped hands, covering her face. As a young child, this always struck me as very beautiful, mysterious, and spiritual. In my home, I say the blessings out loud in order to teach my children; however, I plan to switch to whispering once they know the words by heart.

Now recite the blessing over the candles, either whispering into your hands or out loud.

Blessing:

בָּרוּךְ אַתָּה יְיָ אֱלֹהֵנוּ מֶלֶךְ הָעוֹלָם אֲשֶׁר קִדְּשָׁנוּ בְּמִצְוֹתָיו וְצִוָּנוּ לְהַדְלִיק נֵר שֶׁל שַׁבָּת.

Baruch atah Adonai, Eloheinu, melech haolam, asher kid'shanu b'mitzvotav v'tzivanu l'hadlik ner shel Shabbat.

Blessed are You, Lord our God, King of the Universe, Who has sanctified us and commanded us to light the Shabbat candles.

Don't worry if you don't know the blessing—you'll learn. My friend Patricia, a modern grandma, told me a story about when she was a young mom. Her mother had believed that boys, not girls, should be educated in religion, and that performing acts of tzedakah was a more meaningful way of practicing Judaism than "reciting some ancient words." It follows then that Pat did not grow up having a Shabbat dinner. So when the time came to raise her children, she insisted on having a nice family meal on Friday, and although she knew to light candles, she did not know the blessing. When her daughter Aviva was seven, she asked her, "Mom, why aren't you saying the brachah?" "Because I don't know it," Pat replied. "Will you teach it to me?" And that was how Pat, who's now Orthodox, first learned the blessing over the candles.

Once you've lit the candles, bless your children. Not everyone does this, but I guarantee these blessings will be a significant addition to your traditions—unimaginably meaningful to both you and your children.

When I saw *Fiddler on the Roof* again recently, I loved the scene that takes place during Shabbat dinner, when Golde and Teyve practice the tradition of blessing their children and sing:

May you be like Ruth and like Esther.
May you be deserving of praise.
Strengthen them, Oh Lord,
And keep them from the stranger's ways.

What I love most about this scene is when the voices of other parents in the village join Tevye's and Golde's, and we begin to see other families in *their* homes, blessing *their* children. This captures the magic of Shabbat. Even though it is a tradition celebrated by individual families, we are connected as a community, knowing that in every Jewish home families are saying the same words, making the same movements, offering the same blessings as our people have said and done for centuries. It's at once humbling and empowering to be part of continuing such a significant tradition. Think of this when debating whether or not to have Shabbat; think about your responsibility in continuing this tradition.

The traditional way is to begin with the oldest child. The child stands in front of his or her mother and father. The parents place their hands on the child's head and say the following blessing:

For girls:

יְשִׂמֵךְ אֱלֹהִים כְּשָׂרָה רִבְקָה רָחֵל וְלֵאָה.

Y'simech Elohim K'Sarah, Rivkah, Rachel, v'Leah.

May God make you like Sarah, Rebecca, Rachel, and Leah.

For boys:

יְשִׂמְךָ אֱלֹהִים כְּאֶפְרַיִם וְכִמְנַשֶּׁה.

Y'simcha Elohim k'Ephraim v'che-Menashe.

May God make you like Ephraim and like Manasseh.

Technically Speaking

Who are these people we are praying our children should be like? Sarah, Rebecca, Rachel, and Leah are our matriarchs. Many popular books have been written about the lives of these women. Fiction writers have tried to imagine what life was like for them and, in this way, we can garner some understanding about who they were. From what we read in the Torah, we know that they were strong, brave, and righteous and fiercely believed in God. We also know they were praised for their beauty and adored by their husbands—all nice things to wish for our daughters!

We don't pray that the boys should be like the patriarchs Abraham, Isaac, and Jacob. Instead we find inspiration in the story of Joseph. Joseph was the favored son of Jacob who had the beautiful multicolored coat. His jealous brothers sold him into slavery in Egypt, and there he rose to great power. Although he did assimilate somewhat into Egyptian culture, he never abandoned his Jewish faith. We pray that our sons should be like Ephraim and Manasseh, Joseph's sons by his Egyptian wife. Even though their mother was Egyptian (and not Jewish), Ephraim and Manasseh held fast to their Jewish identities. In the Torah, Joseph explains that the names of his sons represent his struggles and eventual success. Ephraim means "God has made me fruitful in the land of my affliction" and Manasseh means "God has made me forget all my toil and all my father's house." Throughout the Torah, the meanings of names are very significant. I take from these meanings that praying for our sons to be like Ephraim and Manasseh means we want our sons to forget or overcome any hardships they've had growing up and be able to go out and find their own paths and be successful.

Then say for all the children (both boys and girls):

יְבָרֶכְךָ יְיָ וְיִשְׁמְרֶךָ.

יָאֵר יְיָ פָּנָיו אֵלֶיךָ וִיחֻנֶּךָּ.

יִשָּׂא יְיָ פָּנָיו אֵלֶיךָ, וְיָשֵׂם לְךָ שָׁלוֹם.

Y'varech'cha Adonai v'yishm'recha.
Ya-er Adonai panav eilecha vichunecha.
Yisa Adonai panav eilecha v'yasem lecha shalom.

May God bless you and keep you.
May God's face shine on you and may He be gracious unto you.
May God lift up His face toward you and grant you peace.

This last part is actually from the Priestly Blessing (*Birkat Kohanim*). You may remember your rabbi saying this to you at your bat mitzvah, or maybe you have heard it at other times (it is a regular part of services). In Numbers, the fourth book of the Torah (Num. 6:23–27), God instructs Aaron (the high priest) to bless the people with these specific words. After the destruction of the Temples, the job of delivering the blessing went to the rabbis (although in some synagogues, this honor is given to those congregants who are kohanim). Even though this prayer began as the sole domain of the Temple priests, anyone can say it. (And, yes, it's true that Leonard Nimoy took the hand gesture used by the priests when making this blessing in the Temple as the Vulcan greeting for Mr. Spock on *Star Trek*.)

45

Technically Speaking

Notice how the lines of the Priestly Blessing form a pyramid, growing progressively longer with the increasing number of syllables in each line. Rabbi Stuart Weinblatt explained to me that this was done on purpose as it's not only a blessing, it's a remarkably beautiful poem.

Repeat with each child in age-descending order.

Here's a variation we tried that I learned from one of the women at my shul. When I first heard the idea I couldn't wait till Shabbat to try it. Rather than only recite the prayers in Hebrew, my husband and I use this time as an opportunity to share a special moment with our children. After we recite the Hebrew blessings, one child goes to Jonathan and the other to me. We then speak quietly just to that child so only the child can hear what we say. For example, I may say, "I feel blessed that you are my son because you are so bright and funny and I really had fun playing Pokémon Coliseum with you. I am blessed to be your mommy."

Or I might say, "I feel blessed that you are my daughter, and I was so proud of how brave you were this week when you broke your finger. You have handled this, as you do everything, with such maturity. I am blessed to be your mommy." Then I hug my child and give her a kiss. Then we switch, so the child who was with me goes to Jonathan and the child he was speaking to comes to me for a blessing. These individual mom-and-dad-made blessings were more significant to our children than the Hebrew words they did not yet understand.

The first time we did this, Jules, then six, was so moved he hugged me and told me he would be with me forever. And Sofie asked if she could bless us—and then gave her special blessing to me and then to Jonathan. And then they got a little meshugge and went and blessed the dog.

When he was in first grade, Jules had an assignment to give an oral presentation about a tradition celebrated at home. He picked Shabbat (of course)! I was curious as to what he thought about our Shabbat observance, so when he came home from school I asked him to repeat his presentation for me. Jules reported that he'd said, "I really like when my parents bless me. It makes me feel special. My dad says, 'I'm blessed to be your daddy, now let's go back to the table to eat.' But my mom always says something nice about me, and it always makes me cry." Then he concluded with, "My favorite part of Shabbat? Chicken!"

Shabbat is that time to connect with your family. The blessings over the children is a built-in time each week to let our children know how special they are to us, so you can tailor your message to something specific for the week. Let your kids know you are paying attention to their lives.

I promise you will not forget the look on your child's face—no matter the age—the first time you do this.

After I started blessing my kids, I read a special book, *My Grandfather's Blessings* by Dr. Rachel Naomi Remen, in which she tells of how when she was a young child her grandfather would bless her every week. Her grandfather passed away when she was seven, but the power of these blessings stayed with her throughout her adult life. Her moving story strengthened my resolve to continue to make blessing my children an integral part of our Shabbat.

It took awhile before we were comfortable blessing our children when another family joined us for dinner (especially if it was a family who didn't celebrate Shabbat or didn't go beyond the basic blessings). Finally, I figured out a way to introduce this tradition to guests. After I light the candles I explain, "At this point in our Shabbat dinner, Jonathan and I like to take a moment to give a special message, kind of like a blessing, to Sofie and Jules. We're going to do that now and if you would like, you can do the same with your children. There are also Hebrew blessings that I can teach you if you'd like." And then we bless the kids quietly as always and our guests usually do the same. Our friends have commented how nice it was and how they will continue this tradition in their own home.

I hope you didn't think you were going to go through all this and *not* have your husband sing your praises! Even with young couples who don't yet have children, the husband is supposed to give a blessing in praise of his wife. I love this. In many homes, the husband, along with the children sing a song called "Eishet Chayil." The beginning of the prayer is translated into a very familiar passage:

What a rare find is a woman of valor—
Her worth is far beyond that of rubies.

The song goes on to praise the wife for doing things like seeking out wool and extending her hands to spin flax . . . and I have to be honest and mention that I can't remember the last time I spun flax. Seriously, though, this is a beautiful song found in chapter 31 of the book of Proverbs and is believed to have been written by King Solomon. Having your husband (and children) sing or recite this represents not only respect for traditions, but respect for the mother (and the million things we do). Some families recite and others sing this to the woman of the household—maybe your family could start its own tradition and make up a tune. Of course, your husband can also praise you in his own words.

This is an excerpt of "Eishet Chayil" that was translated by the late Rabbi Sidney Greenberg. He was my rabbi when I was growing up and is the author of *Likrat Shabbat*, the prayer book many Conservative synagogues use during Friday night services.

Eishet Chayil—A Woman of Valor

A woman of valor who can find?

She is more precious than rubies.

The heart of her husband trusts in her,

And he has no lack of gain.

She does him good and not evil,

All the days of her life,

She extends her hand to the poor,

She reaches out her hands to the needy.

She is robed in strength and dignity;

She confidently faces the future.

She opens her mouth with wisdom,

Lovingkindness is on her tongue.

Her children rise up and call her blessed,

Her husband sings her praises:

"Many daughters have done worthily,

But you excel them all."

Charm is deceitful, and beauty is vain,

But a woman who reveres the Lord, she shall be praised.

Give her of the fruit of her hands,

And let her works praise her in the gates.

If reciting "Eishet Chayil" is a bit much for your husband and kids, try this variation: tell your husband you love him, and let him tell you the same. There is no tradition about praising the husband, but if you want, and he's been good, you can bless him, too. Just as with the kids, it's nice to know you're loved and appreciated.

If you're like most of us, the most significant part of your time together is probably when you are both sleeping. Otherwise, you are living parallel lives—each of you going about your daily life, in the same direction, but more side by side than connecting. Your conversations may chiefly involve relaying what each of you did (individually) that day, your concerns or struggles or achievements and successes. These daily conversations serve to keep you updated as to what your lives are like when you are apart. When you are together, you are most likely with your children or talking about your children. Even when you go out, you may be sharing the evening with friends. Let Shabbat be the time to reconnect as man and woman. A simple "I love you" can be quite powerful.

Now that you're all feeling loved and blessed and appreciated, it's time to get ready to eat. So we start with the kiddush, the blessing over the wine.

There are two versions of the kiddush—a long one and a short one. Technically, the long version is kiddush. If you have a child studying to become a bat or bar mitzvah, this may be a good time for her or him to practice reciting it. Or if your uncle is a cantor (as mine is), you will hear the extended version when you have Shabbat at his table. Most likely, you'll do the shorter prayer, which is really just the blessing of the wine, but many non-Orthodox Jews still call it kiddush.

Kiddush is supposed to be offered by a man and definitely by someone over bar mitzvah age (meaning he should be considered an adult in the Jewish community). I can tell from the way he offers this blessing that Jonathan likes being the one to say it—I guess it's a dad thing, or maybe just as I feel a certain pride that it's my honor as the woman of the house to be the one to light the candles, he takes pride in the fact that kiddush is his honor as the man of the house. It is also a lovely honor to invite a guest to recite the kiddush. My uncle, the *chazzan*, will recite it and then will invite each man at the table to repeat it if he wishes.

בָּרוּךְ אַתָּה יְיָ אֱלֹהֵינוּ מֶלֶךְ הָעוֹלָם בּוֹרֵא פְּרִי הַגָּפֶן.

Baruch ata Adonai, Eloheinu melech haolam, borei pree hagafen.

Blessed are You, Lord our God, King of the Universe, Who commanded us to drink the fruit of the vine.

By the way, "fruit of the vine" equally refers to wine and grape juice.

My friend Lisa told me about a piece of Judaica that she found at a local Jewish gift store which has added a wow factor to her Shabbats: a wine fountain. Imagine a tall kiddush cup with six to twelve spouts. Beneath the spouts are smaller kiddush cups, all resting on a silver tray. It's quite impressive just to look at, but to see it in use is quite fun. You pour wine into the center cup and watch it flow into the smaller cups below. Then everyone takes an individual cup and drinks the wine or grape juice. Amen!

Some of my friends consider these wine fountains a modern version of another custom. Traditionally, the father (or the one who makes the kiddush) drinks first from the cup. He then passes it to the men in the room, who drink from the same cup in age-descending order. Then the cup passes to the women and children. (Yes, exceptions can be made so anyone nursing a cold can drink last.) Other families drink from the same cup in age-descending order regardless of sex. I know one family whose members use their own, smaller kiddush cups, filled by the father after he says the blessing, from his larger kiddush cup. The fountain, therefore, is a way for small cups of wine to be poured from one cup (in essence a hygienic way of allowing everyone to drink from the same cup), uniting everyone at the table.

Here's another lovely kiddush tradition: I know a family whose grandfather keeps pouring wine into the cup until it overflows, so that "life will overflow with goodness and abundance." He then looks into his kiddush cup and smiles when he sees his reflection in the wine. Then all the children are invited to gather around to smile at their reflections. In this way, this family's Shabbat begins with an abundance of smiles.

Once you've all had your kiddush wine, it's time for the blessing over washing your hands, or *netilat yadayim*. I'll tell you why I introduced this blessing to our Shabbat table. It wasn't because I read about it somewhere, not because a rabbi suggested it, nor because I observed it at another family's table. I was wandering around a little Jewish gift shop, looking for a gift because we were invited to another family's for Shabbat, and I saw these very pretty two-handled cups from Israel, made of Lucite with beautiful flowers pressed inside. I asked what the cups were for, and the salesman told me they were for the blessing over washing hands. So, fellow moms, I'll admit it, my increase in observance was inspired by a shopping trip!

Now, I know you've probably washed your hands before coming to the table so you are now going to be washing clean hands, but that is the point. This tradition harkens back to ancient times when the priests would wash their hands before performing their duties within the holy Temple. Remember, by making Shabbat, we have made a mikdash me'at, a small temple, in our home, and we are about to (literally) break bread, which symbolizes the "sacrifice." So the washing of the hands and the blessing over the challah are really two parts of one ritual.

Technically, we are supposed to remove all jewelry before washing. Then go to the sink, and using a special cup (if you don't have one, any cup will do), pour water onto one hand (rotate front and back so the entire hand gets wet), then repeat on the other. Then raise your hands up and say:

בָּרוּךְ אַתָּה יְיָ אֱלֹהֵינוּ מֶלֶךְ הָעוֹלָם, אֲשֶׁר קִדְּשָׁנוּ בְּמִצְוֹתָיו, וְצִוָּנוּ עַל נְטִילַת יָדָיִם.

Baruch ata Adonai, Eloheinu melech haolam, asher kid'shanu b'mitzvotav v'tzivanu al netilat yadayim.

Blessed are You, Lord our God, King of the universe, Who has made us holy through the commandments and commanded us to wash our hands.

We raise our hands because *netilat* means "to raise," and this is not so much about getting our hands clean, as much as raising them to make us worthy to be able to go on to the next stage of the ritual.

Now, here's the bonus—no one should speak from the time he has washed his hands until he eats a bite of challah after the *motzi* is made. Not a peep. Enjoy the quiet. Feel free to take a long . . . slow . . . walk back to the table for *haMotzi* (wink, wink).

Finally, the motzi (blessing over the challah).

The challah (or challot if you're using two) are covered with a challah cover. Traditionally, the father says the blessing, but anyone can say it, and I like to ask one of my kids to say the kiddush and the other to say the motzi. They know the prayers, and this allows them to participate rather than observe. And even though the blessings are supposed to be offered by someone over bar mitzvah age, Jonathan and I repeat the prayers after the kids say them, so I think it's kosher.

The person reciting the brachah can sprinkle salt on the challah (a variation is to dip the challah into salt). In addition to doing this because the priests would salt the sacrifices, I've also heard that the salt represents tears of sadness over the destruction of the Temple. (Some families sprinkle salt on the challah after the blessing, but some prefer to sprinkle before—you can split the difference and sprinkle salt during the blessing!)

51

Then the brachah maker puts his hand on the challah or lifts it and says:

בָּרוּךְ אַתָּה יְיָ אֱלֹהֵינוּ מֶלֶךְ הָעוֹלָם, הַמּוֹצִיא לֶחֶם מִן הָאָרֶץ.

Baruch ata Adonai, Eloheinu melech haolam, hamotzi lechem min ha'aretz.

Blessed are You, Lord our God, King of the Universe, who brings forth bread from the earth.

Then the challah is sliced, and everyone gets a piece to eat. Here we enter into the big challah debate: slice or tear. Do you slice the challah, or do you dig in and tear off chunks? In our house, when it's just the four of us we tear pieces off with our hands (another really good reason to start with netilat yadayim!). When we have guests over, we slice it—this just seems more polite. My friend Suzi does the opposite, for an equally good reason. When it's just her immediate family of four, they slice, because she knows the four of them cannot finish the loaf and she wants to neatly preserve slices for French toast. If another family is joining them, there won't be leftovers, so everyone is free to dig in.

Sephardim have a fun tradition. The person who says the motzi rips off a hunk of bread, dips it in salt, and throws it, aiming for people's plates, and does this until everyone is served. The children like to try to catch the bread as it flies toward them, but it's supposed to just land on the plate. I've heard a couple of different reasons, but the one that makes most sense to me is that it symbolizes the manna that fell from Heaven in the desert.

Now that you've done the basics of the Shabbat celebration, let the feeding frenzy begin!

We should talk about a challenging subject that is increasingly relevant in our modern times. Feeling peaceful on Shabbat is essential, and as I've said before, welcoming guests into your home—hachnasat orchim—and making them feel comfortable will add to your Shabbat celebration. Because there are so many family permutations today, most likely at some point you will have a non-Jew at your Shabbat table, and the mitzvah of hachnasat orchim applies to Jews and non-Jews alike. So what do you do if you have a non-Jewish family over for Shabbat dinner? Or, what if your family or your husband's family is not Jewish? Or, what if you are not Jewish?

Perhaps you were not raised Jewish but are raising your children Jewish or teaching them both Jewish and non-Jewish traditions. For many women I've spoken with, their spiritual life was primarily church-oriented until they converted or got married. The home-oriented practice of Judaism was quite foreign to them and required a few adjustments. They invested time in learning the rituals and how to recite the Hebrew prayers. One woman told me that she keeps everything on hand to make Shabbat but lets her kids lead. This way, she respects that her children are being raised with more than one set of traditions, and even if her husband is not home and the children ask to have Shabbat, she pulls out the candlesticks and kiddush cups. Another mom, who has chosen not to convert, sent her children to a synagogue preschool and learned the blessings along with her children at their weekly Shabbat sing.

Such Genius

You don't need to have children in a synagogue preschool to take advantage of Shabbat Sing. Many synagogues have monthly "Tot Shabbat" services that are open to nonmembers. Just call your local synagogue for a schedule.

Now, what about having your family or your non-Jewish in-laws or friends over for Shabbat dinner? Explain that through these rituals you are thanking God for the blessings you have—your family, home, the food on your table. My friend Suzi's mother-in-law is a deeply religious Catholic woman from El Salvador who attends mass every day. From the beginning, Suzi emphasized that Shabbat is a way to bring the family together. As Suzi tells me, her mother-in-law appreciates the warmth of Shabbat and the fact that it brings something spiritual into the home. On their first Shabbat together, Suzi made a point of having books at the table that discussed the meaning behind the rituals. This encouraged her in-laws to ask questions, and when Suzi didn't know the answers, they found the explanations together.

I've heard from many women that their non-Jewish parents try to learn the rituals in order to connect with their Jewish grandchildren. Suzi tells a cute story of overhearing her son try to teach his grandmother "Shalom Aleichem." His grandmother happily clapped along while singing, "Shalom Halloween."

No matter what happens or who you're with, remember that Shabbat should be a fun celebration of the blessing of family. Take what traditions make sense to you and start there. As the weeks go by, you and your family will want to add more and more elements to your Shabbat. You will learn and grow together. And what started with a conscious effort to create shalom bayit will culminate with a wondrous sense of peace throughout your home and family.

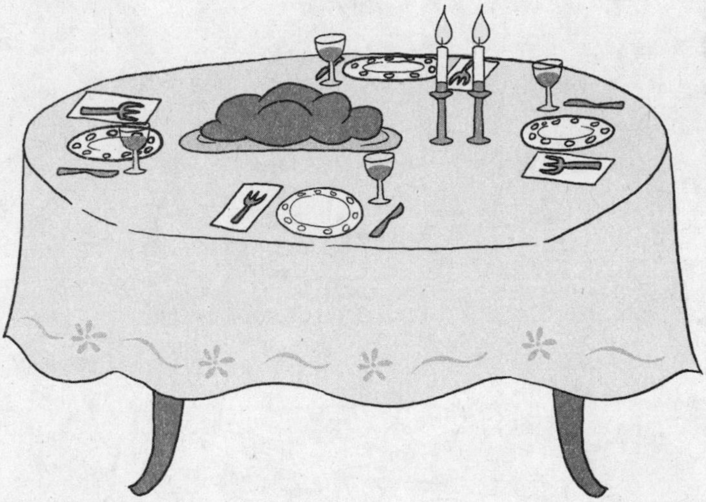

4

Talk the Talk

"YEAH, LOTS OF LUCK WITH THAT ONE," I thought to myself as my rabbi added to the list: "Discuss the weekly Torah portion or some other topic of Jewish interest." I had fallen in love with my family's Shabbat dinners and went to him with the idea to create a series of workshops about Shabbat for our congregation. This was a few years back when I was still a Shabbat novice and needed his help with some of the more advanced topics. I planned to create a nice card with the calendar of dates and titles for all of the workshops on one side, and on the other I was going to write a list of ten ways to separate Friday night from the other nights of the week and "Make Friday Night Shabbat" (which was the name of the workshop series). Together, the rabbi and I wrote up the list, from the easiest and most accessible task to the most challenging:

1. Have dinner together as a family
2. Make it special—eat in the dining room, buy flowers, break out the good dishes
3. Serve a traditional dinner
4. Buy (or make) challah

5. Invite friends over
6. Light candles
7. Recite the blessings over the candles, the wine, and the challah
8. Bless your children—try the Hebrew and then add your own special thoughts
9. Discuss the blessings of the past week, the upcoming Torah portion, or a topic of Jewish interest
10. Attend Friday night services

Nine of the ten were no-brainers that I was already doing with my family—I had even gone to Friday night services a couple of times. But talk about the Torah at dinner? I don't think so.

I was just not comfortable with it. I had no interest in it. The idea of discussing the Torah seemed a bit too religious. But then I attended the challah baking workshop and learned so much more than how to make challah. The teacher, Carol Berman (known in our synagogue as the best challah baker), began the workshop by discussing her own family's Shabbat dinners. She told us that over dinner her husband gave a *d'var torah*, a speech on the week's Torah portion, and used it to incite conversation and debate among their family. She then read the following passage to us:

> *My family always had a Friday night Shabbat dinner before we would be able to go out or play with friends. In addition, my father would always lead a discussion of the weekly Torah portion. This may seem trivial, but in hindsight I learned a valuable lesson about life each week. To this day, I see how happily my parents live their life and understand how valuable their teaching has been.*

This was written by Carol's son, Casey, for his college Jewish mysticism class. And no, his mother did not make him write it. His thoughts about the d'var torah and the discussion at the table truly inspired me. Here was a young man—without prompting by his parents—pointing out the positive effects of having a discussion on the weekly Torah portion at his family's weekly Shabbat dinner. Carol told me that Casey believes his ability to debate and discuss was shaped very early on, during these weekly Shabbat conversations. I thought to myself, "Is this kid for real?" A college student who has put into writing that he liked what his parents were doing, that he admired the way they have chosen to live their life. This was groundbreaking material: Shabbat dinner gives us a chance to do something for which our children will one day thank us! There had to be something to these talks.

Soon after the workshop my family was invited to the rabbi's house for Shabbat. During dinner, his four children, who ranged in age from bar mitzvah to recent college graduate, spoke thoughtfully and eloquently about topics ranging from the Torah to Israel to politics to business. They didn't need to be prompted because this type of talk was an intrinsic part of their Shabbat dinner. I left that night further inspired.

I started asking women in our congregation with grown children if they had these kinds of talks during Shabbat. What I heard were stories of wonderful and wise discussions—and more importantly, I heard again and again reports of teenage children choosing to be home for Shabbat. Some mothers even revealed that their grown children who live nearby want to come home specifically for Shabbat dinner.

As it happens, Carol told me about Casey's paper during the 2004 presidential election. Politics aside, I was deeply distressed that the national debate was shifting from concrete issues that affected the country (economics, foreign relations, etc.) to a discussion of abstractions—values and morals that were not necessarily *our* values and morals. I wanted to make certain that my children had a chance to hear all views and that my husband and I would be the ones who guided them in the shaping of their ideals and opinions. While opportunities come up on a daily basis to discuss various topics with our children, most of our together time focuses on school or work or the stress and frustration of daily life. This is when I realized what a powerful tool I had in my hands—I could use our Shabbat dinner as an excuse (or platform) to engage my children in a different type of discussion from what we were used to. I could begin to discover and understand what my children truly think about their world and share with them what Jonathan and I think. Hopefully, it would become a tradition that would inspire all of us to continue for years and years. Bottom line, if there was a way that one night each week I could guarantee my family would have a meaningful discussion aside from what movie they want to see, I was going to try it.

This is where Shabbat presents another unique opportunity. As I've said before, everything you do to prepare the meal and create shalom bayit should deflate the stress from the week and offer a calm, peaceful atmosphere. Setting aside worries and work and school demands allows everyone to take a deep breath and refocus. Within this environment, the d'var torah can be the starting point for a different kind of family discussion.

When I read stories from the Torah, I often think about Greek mythology. When I was a kid, I loved reading mythology. I recognized that what I was reading as a fairy tale was once a practiced religion. I knew the myths were the way the ancient Greeks explained and understood their world, given the limits of the science of their day—that they believed the sun rises because Apollo drives a fiery chariot across the sky, or that thunder is the sound of a cranky Zeus throwing his infamous lightning bolts. These stories were told to Greek children to teach them about the world they lived in.

I realized that one day, Judaism could be replaced by another religion or philosophy, the same way the beliefs of the ancient Greeks have become myths. The stories of our Torah serve the same purpose. They don't teach science, but they teach what we believe makes us good, makes us holy, makes us Jewish. Whether or not you believe that the Torah was dictated to Moses by God or that the Torah is a written version of oral history passed down for centuries, the Torah teaches us about the Jewish people's relationship with the world and with God. It doesn't matter if what happened in the stories actually occurred, it's the lessons underlying the stories that are important.

The Torah illustrates for us a moral and ethical code. There is a reason so many plays and books throughout time are derivatives of stories found in the Torah: biblical stories are universal. Cain and Abel's story tells us of sibling rivalry. The binding of Isaac demonstrates the power of sacrifice. The struggle between Jacob and Esau is a tale of betrayal and power. Even the personal stories of our leaders and heroes, at their basic level, can be fabulous lessons in leadership. Moses stuttered; he was unsure of his ability to lead the nation of Israel to freedom, and yet he was a brilliant leader. What does that teach us? More importantly, what can that teach our children?

Taken in this manner, the Torah is a practical life text, and we can use the stories within it to teach our children. That is why a d'var torah discussion is an important Shabbes parenting tool. Sitting all together, within the comfortable, joyful, and safe environment of the Shabbat table is when we can teach our children and learn from them and about them.

When I decided to have a d'var torah at the meal, I wanted to start slow. I wanted to help my children understand that the Torah is not just a religious text, but a vehicle to help them understand their life now. So I asked my children why we reread the Torah every year when we don't do this with any other book. I reminded them that when we finished *Harry Potter and the Prisoner of Azkaban* we didn't immediately go back to page one and start the book again, but this is what we do with the Torah. I waited eagerly for any kind of a response.

Sofie and Jules, then seven and five, almost immediately started talking. When there was a lull, Jonathan and I tried to guide the conversation with more questions. By the end of the discussion, the children concluded that the reason we reread the Torah is because we have changed during the year. We have grown and learned new things, so we can understand more and get new ideas from the Torah each year (ach, such brilliance. I was kvelling). I was happy they reached this conclusion because I wanted them to understand that the Torah is a dynamic text, changing and growing as the reader changes and grows. This set the foundation for how we would continue to discuss the Torah stories during future Shabbat dinners.

After a few weeks, I found that our d'var torah topics quickly diverged from the story in the *parashah* to an idea behind the story and how it relates to our children's lives. The story of Abraham welcoming strangers and offering them food and even water to wash their feet (Vayera, Genesis 18) became a discussion of why we are now fearful of strangers and how in today's world we would not welcome a stranger into our home (let alone tell him to wash his feet).

On another night, we started talking about the instructions for building the Tabernacle (Tetzaveh, Exodus 27), and it turned into a discussion on the eternal light above the ark that holds the Torah and why synagogues don't turn off this light, even when no one is there. I asked Sofie and Jules why they thought it's important that even if we aren't in shul, we know the light is burning. My children decided it is important (even Sofie, who is very involved in her school's environmental club and is not keen on wasting electricity) because the light means God is always with us and Judaism will continue.

Yet another night, the parashah (Thazria, Leviticus 12) discusses the laws surrounding leprosy. The commentary explains that leprosy is the biblical punishment for gossip. This became a discussion about *lashon hara* (translated literally as "bad language" or "bad tongue") and we promised (especially Sofie and me) to try to cut down on our gossiping. From this chat, I learned that my daughter, my perfect, good-as-gold daughter, has actually gossiped. I didn't even know that third-graders gossip! (When I was in third grade we dressed up like Pilgrims and celebrated the bicentennial.) Here, at our Shabbat table, Jonathan and I were learning something new about Sofie, and we had the opportunity to talk to her and Jules about gossip without sounding preachy. And I would not have even thought to introduce this topic on my own. It was only because it happened to be in the parashah.

Friday nights have become time for Jonathan and me to learn from and about our children, and we both look forward to it. Even Jonathan, who really let me take the lead on this new aspect of our dinner, will sometimes say, "So what happened in the Torah this week?" This way, if we're spending too much time talking about everyday stuff I'll know he wants to get the *real* conversation started. The d'var torah is a great way to start talking in general. The simple lessons based in Torah offer so much more. Use them to instill some of your own values in your kids.

For example, I'm always looking for ways to talk about leadership with my children, and I use the Torah text to push my agenda (yes, I'm admitting it). When the parashah allows, I ask them about leadership not because I want them to be CEOs but because I want them to have the confidence to think for themselves and not blindly follow the herd. By talking about and analyzing various biblical leaders, I hope to instill in them an inner confidence that says, "you can do it," just as God said to Moses. These are strengths they will need to help deal with peer pressure, or maybe on a tough day give them the courage to raise their hand in class and answer a question.

My mother often reminds me that the best times to really talk with your children are at bedtime and in the car. And it's true—especially bedtime (they'll do anything to stay up). But if you build into your week a time (aside from the fifteen-minute drive to soccer or ballet) that your children know will focus on them and what they're thinking about, they will start to talk on Friday night, too. Be consistent with this type of discussion on Friday night (even if it's like pulling teeth at first), and I promise, you'll create the environment where they feel safe to open up with their thoughts and feelings. If your child has developed a secret on Monday, it can and probably will make its way out on Friday. It's the routine that helps make this work. When our children were babies we learned to keep their schedules routine—when they slept, when they ate, when they were bathed, when they napped—so they knew what to expect and what to count on. The routine made them feel safe, secure, and content. Shabbat is another weekly routine that brings comfort. If you can, start this tradition when they're young, and they will choose to continue being with you for dinner when they're older.

Such Genius

Everything done to prepare for Shabbat not only brings a sense of peace to the home, it brings warmth and good smells and beautiful settings and wonderful tastes—a true feast for the senses. Now add the d'var torah, and you are feeding your child's mind *and* nurturing his or her character.

Yes, in some ways it's easier for those families with young children. Young children love any family activity, and they are also willing to believe. So even if you're not so sure yourself, let them believe. Rabbi David J. Wolpe, in his book *Teaching Your Children About God*, writes:

> *Nothing could be more important than to feel that someone always cares and really understands. For a child to believe in God's concern is not an intellectual proposition or a philosophical decision. It is a way of trusting in the goodness of the world. It is a way of asserting that one is not alone. It is to have what is called in Hebrew bitachon, "trust," a sense of confidence that runs deep inside because it flows from above.*

You may find that your children take the stories at face value. They will not question the existence of God or His ability to perform miracles or speak directly to the patriarchs, but will take these stories as historical fact. It doesn't matter if you believe in God; it doesn't matter if you believe in the Torah. The fact is, your children do—and that belief, that faith, gives them security and comfort.

Developmental psychologists like Bruno Bettelheim and Jean Piaget have written about how children understand their world through fairy tales. Just like with fairy tales, children use biblical stories to gain understanding of good and evil, right and wrong. These stories help children understand and accept difficult and disturbing concepts like the existence of evil, but the idea of good triumphing is important to their developing psyche.

It is OK to reply, "I don't know" when your children ask, "Did this really happen?" First of all, it's an honest answer; second, it opens up the opportunity for you to follow up with, "What do you think?" Get them talking. It's an exercise in active versus passive learning.

How many of us did not like Hebrew school or going to services? How many of us are Jewish, purely because of blood but without meaning or connection? But there is a way to foster a connection—with you and your kids, with you and Judaism, and with your kids and Judaism, and Shabbat. We read earlier how Casey connected in the home. Simple, easygoing family conversations at the Shabbat table shaped Casey and helped forge a deep connection between him and his parents. The discussions that stem from the d'var torah is a great, stress-free, and educational way to do that.

Parents are our first and potentially best teachers. I still listen to my mother's advice.

To this day (and I shouldn't admit this, for future arguments), I don't think the woman has ever been wrong (really). The key is—I respect her. You have to earn your children's respect, and the simplest way to do that is by respecting them. There are so many things we blame our parents for. These days it has become too easy, too accepted, to blame our shortcomings on how our parents raised us. Often, it is not until we become parents that we realize how difficult parenting is and understand what our parents did right. The conversations at your weekly Shabbat table not only foster a connection, but demonstrate the respect between you and your children for what you each have to say and contribute. This has tremendous impact.

You set the example. I read once that if you want your children to love reading, they should see you read as much as possible. Show them how much you love to read, and that positive association will be imprinted upon them. The same goes with learning. My parents retired recently. My sister and I worried about what they would do. Would Dad watch TV and nap all day? Would Mom be calling us every hour? So we were surprised when Dad enrolled in various graduate school classes and Mom started studying to become a bat mitzvah. I'll never forget the phone call from my father telling me he got an A-minus on his history exam. (Of course, I couldn't help reply, "A-minus? I expect A's from you, mister!") And I loved seeing my mom and daughter practice reading Hebrew together. My parents continue to influence and inspire me. Now that they finally have more time, they're using it to learn. Whether they intended to or not, they have sent a strong message to me that you should always find ways to grow through study.

This is what you will be doing when you prepare for your family Friday night discussions. I cannot emphasize how much I have learned from reading the Torah, and I am profoundly grateful for taking this step. I even start the discussions some weeks with "Guess what I learned that I didn't know before?" It is my deepest hope that the work I am putting into preparing for our Shabbat table talks will inspire my children to always be learners.

So, here's how you do it. Read the parashah of the week. In chapter 10 you will find summaries and suggested questions for each Torah portion to start your family's discussions. You can also check the resource directory in the back of the book for other sources of summaries and commentary. And your synagogue bulletin and Web site most likely offer links to parashah sites or even offer a brief d'var. Don't be intimidated. Just as with the rest of your Shabbat preparation, use baby steps to prepare the d'var torah. I'm not a rabbi or a Torah scholar, but each week I learn more, not only about the Torah but about how to lead this type of discussion with my family.

Not What I Would Call Kosher

A word of caution: If you use the Internet to search for weekly Torah portions, you may come upon messianic or Jews for Jesus sites. These sites use Hebrew words and are very deceiving—they look as if they are coming from a Jewish source. These sites will even pop up if you search key words like *parashah* or *parshah*, so read carefully. The resource directory in the back of this book lists safe *Jewish* sites.

Some translations offer explanations on the text, but I try not to read them. For what I'm trying to accomplish, I don't feel the need to know what Rashi or other commentators said or thought about the text. I prefer to find my own meaning within the story and to hear what speaks to me. Then I select what I think makes sense to discuss with my family. However, if you come across phrases that don't make sense in today's vernacular, the commentaries can be very helpful and serve as translations that help you understand and interpret the text. When you have the time, you can learn many interesting things from the commentary.

65

Take It to the Next Level

If you would like to do a true Torah study with your family, research what the rabbis and scholars have said over the years, and then use the information and ideas you have gathered to debate the various meanings. Each source you read will give you a different interpretation of the same text. This type of discussion is better suited to families with older children.

I tend to use the weekly story as a jumping-off point for a more general discussion. Most weeks this is easy, but there are weeks when, for example, the parashah gives tedious lists, like how many sheep were in the tribe of Dan's flocks. Maybe your family would like to discuss sheepherding, I don't know. But if these counting chapters are not so stimulating, you can always go back to another previously discussed parashah or talk about another issue. The point is to get your family talking.

Such Genius

When my friend Shari began including a d'var torah discussion during her Shabbat dinner, the parashah that week was one of the concluding chapters of Deuteronomy. She introduced the discussion with this question: "Guess who led the Jewish people after Moses died?" Her then seven-year-old son, Joshua, was thrilled to learn it was a man named (you guessed it) Joshua! Their conversations have continued and evolved each week, and her other children are waiting to hear if there are any famous Jews with their names.

Oy, Teens

For those with older children, the debate can be deeper and more challenging. As children get older and more cynical, this is the ideal time to test them and to teach them to argue their points intelligently. Be sure to let them know their beliefs are valued and respected—even if they differ from your own. If you are trying to introduce this tradition for the first time with teenagers, try to find a topic that will engage and motivate them. Think of what intrigues them, and find a story with that theme to catch their attention. There are plenty of scandalous passages in the Torah. For example, you may want to check out the parashah Balak in Numbers for a very interesting (and teen-appropriate) story of deception and intrigue.

After you've read the parashah, prepare a brief summary or lesson. Brief is the key word here. If you make it too dense you will lose your kids and it'll feel like school. Don't read them what you've written, just talk in your own words. I write some key points on a piece of paper to remind myself about the story line and what I want to say. Then I ask an open-ended question—yes or no answers defeat the purpose.

Such Genius

If your children are very young, consider reading to them stories from an illustrated children's Bible. They'll love the pictures and the extra story time!

Once you're finished and have asked your question, you and your spouse should shut up. I mean it. If you lecture, they'll tune you out. Treat your kids with respect. Listen to them. I promise you will learn something.

Oy, Teens

My friend Holly's daughter Hillary so enjoyed the d'var torah portion of their Shabbat dinner, she asked her mother if she could be responsible for preparing the summary and discussion questions for her family. Her younger sisters now look forward to the day when they will be allowed to prepare the d'var torah. This is another example of how to involve our teenagers: give them responsibility. Being responsible for part of the meal not only gives them a sense of ownership, it also shows that their parents respect them for their ability to manage the task. Leading the family's discussion also builds leadership and speaking skills.

67

A woman once told me she was too intimidated to try this because her son attended a Jewish day school and he already knew so much more than she. I explained to her that's not what this is about. Honestly, I'm suggesting you discuss the Torah not because I think every child should know the difference between Jacob and Joseph and Esau and Ezekiel. The d'var torah is about talking to your children, not as a rabbi or a Torah scholar but as a parent and fellow student. The Torah is purely the vehicle for initiating discussion—any discussion you want to have with your family.

Introducing this tradition into my Shabbat dinner is one of the single most significant additions I have made in my family's routine. For both Jonathan and me it has been an amazing experience to talk candidly with our children. Each week the stories allow our children to tell us about their beliefs, their ideas, and their dreams. Imagine what else we will happen upon over the years.

5

After Dinner

FOR MOST OF US, Shabbat begins and ends with Friday night dinner. This, in and of itself, can be a meaningful way to not only respect our tradition, but as we've discussed, create a meaningful family experience on a weekly basis. Observing just Friday night is what I call practicing practical Judaism—observing the spirit of the law rather than the true halachah (or law). For example, lighting candles at the table after sundown is not following halachah; however, lighting candles at the table because that's when you have time to do so or (more importantly) because that is how your children can learn the blessings and the tradition is following the spirit or purpose of the law. How you and your family observe and practice is a deeply personal choice and one that will evolve from year to year and possibly week to week.

So let's assume you and your family are really enjoying your Shabbat dinners and would like to add to your experience or want to increase the time you spend with one another. Or perhaps, through your study, you've discovered a personal spiritual interest in Judaism and want to enhance your Shabbat experience in a more observant way. This chapter will explore ways to do so, for various levels of observance.

It is one thing to say "once a week we're making a commitment to having dinner as a family." Anyone can do that. To commit to lighting candles, saying blessings, perhaps even introducing some Torah talk is taking a significant "Jewish" step. If you want to go a bit further, here are some things you can try with your family to add to the Shabbat experience.

Technically we are supposed to conclude the Shabbat meal with *zmirot* (songs), followed by Birkat HaMazon (Grace After Meals). I have attended Shabbat dinners where this occurs, and it can be a lot of fun and makes the meal feel more like a celebration. Did you know the Shabbat dinner is also called the Shabbat seder? Well, just as we complete the Passover seder with songs, zmirot are a great way to end the meal on a joyous note in a joyful mood. Sing before, during, or after dessert, and it will feel like a party!

Now, you may be wondering how you could ever sing zmirot with your kids—how utterly embarrassing! But your little ones will love it and will love to sing along with you. Remember how you loved to sing when you were a child, or think about how uninhibited your young children are when they're singing (or were, if they are no longer young). Start easy—remember those baby steps. Maybe if you don't know the zmirot, sing a song the kids will know—and make sure your hubby chimes in. When we do sing, I love to include the songs the kids learned in nursery school. What ends up happening is that because they are nursery school songs, the adults are comfortable singing because we feel like we're singing to help teach our children.

There is an interesting phenomenon that happens when adults are with their children. It's akin to a mathematical formula: Adults (A) when in the presence of children (C) forget about being embarrassed (UI for uninhibited.) So, therefore:

$$A + C = UI$$

(I know it's math—what do you want from me? I'm Jewish, and my dad is an engineer.) When you apply this formula to a dinner you get adults, who may normally feel self-conscious singing, who become willing to sing when their children are around. Remember how you sang when you were a child? You didn't care how you sounded or even if you knew the words. The louder and longer you sang, the better. As grown-ups we're too worried about how we sound and whether we know the words. But if you apply the formula you'll notice that you (and perhaps the other adults at your table) are more willing to sing and be silly doing so when you are singing for the sake of your children.

Think of all the things you do for your kids that you wouldn't do otherwise. I was always afraid of playground-style rope bridges (actually, bridges of any kind), but when Jules was three he started climbing up a hill covered with tires and crossing a rope bridge at the park (in the section designated for older kids—but did he read the sign? No. But then again, he couldn't read yet.). Once he got started I followed him to make sure he'd be OK. I forgot about being scared and thought only about being close enough to him to grab him if he should fall. When we were both safely on the ground I called my mom to proudly tell her I had finally crossed a rope bridge!

The same happens with singing at dinner. Do it for your kids, forget about being embarrassed, and you'll end up having fun. Before you know it, favorite songs or silly ways of singing will become part of your weekly Shabbat ritual.

Oy, Teens

No one says you have to sing baby songs or even Jewish songs. The great thing about zmirot is that *there are no rules*. Let your teens teach you their current favorite, or you and your husband can do a rendition of a favorite '80s tune. (Doing the pony to "We Got the Beat" can work off a few of those challah calories!) If your children play an instrument or are in a band, this postmeal songfest is a great opportunity for a mini concert. (Just don't light a match if they play "Freebird"!)

Some traditional Shabbat songs include "Shalom Aleichem," "Shabbat Shalom," "Lo Yisa Goy," "Lecha Dodi," "Hinei Mah Tov," "Eileh Chamdah Libi," and "Yismechu Bemalchutecha." There are so many beautiful songs you can sing and you can find the names of a few terrific CDs in the resource directory. There are tons of possibilities and if you don't know the songs I've listed you can ask your kids to sing a song they learned in school. One of my favorite songs from my children's preschool days is "Put the Chicken in the Pot." Not only is this fun for the children, but it teaches them a very important skill: how to make chicken soup! When I sang this with my kids, we acted out the words:

Put the chicken in the pot {pretend to put something in an imaginary p
Stir it up till it's nice and hot {pretend to stir}
Getting ready for Shabbat
Good Shabbat.

Repeat the lyrics, substituting a different ingredient for chicken each time (i.e., carrots, noodles, celery). When you sing about onions, sing as if you are crying. (Because you're working with onions, of course. This is so silly, but your kids will have a ball.) Go around the table and ask each person to suggest a different ingredient. When my kids were little they always wanted to put silly things in to the mix, like an elephant or chocolate ice cream. The nursery school teacher would always insist the ingredients be faithful to chicken soup—the song, after all, was to teach what really went into the soup. (Personally, I think kids know that elephants are not part of the chicken-soup-making process and I am definitely pro-silliness, but I'll leave the ingredient policing to you.)

The next step after zmirot is birkat hamazon, or grace after meals. As with zmirot, reciting the birkat hamazon is another one of those "take it to the next level" kind of things. If anyone at your table went to a Jewish summer camp or was involved in a Jewish youth group, he will remember how much fun singing this can be. It has some boppy melodies, and some people even add some semi-irreverent (but fun) words into the tune, making it a joyfully wacky experience.

To learn the words, you can buy little books called *bentschers* at Jewish book stores (or take the ones your more observant friends put on the table for their children's bar mitzvahs or weddings). These contain all the words to the birkat hamazon and even some songs.

The birkat hamazon is made up of four main blessings: the blessing for food, the blessing for the land, the blessing for Jerusalem, and the blessing of goodness. If the full grace is too much, you might decide to recite just the four blessings in Hebrew or English. You can also express your gratitude in your own words. Or say nothing, but ask your family to at least help you clear the dishes.

בָּרוּךְ אַתָּה יְיָ אֱלֹהֵינוּ מֶלֶךְ הָעוֹלָם הַזָּן אֶת הַכֹּל.

Baruch ata Adonai, Eloheinu melech Haolam, hazan et hakol.

Blessed are You, Lord our God, King of the Universe, Who provides food for all.

בָּרוּךְ אַתָּה יְיָ עַל הָאָרֶץ וְעַל הַמָּזוֹן.

Baruch ata Adonai, al ha'aretz ve'al hamazon.

Blessed are You, Lord our God, for the land and for the sustenance.

בָּרוּךְ אַתָּה יְיָ בּוֹנֶה בְּרַחֲמָיו יְרוּשָׁלָיִם. אָמֵן.

Baruch ata Adonai, boneh v'rachamav Yerushalayim. Amen.

Blessed are You Lord our God, Who rebuilds Jerusalem. Amen.

בָּרוּךְ אַתָּה יְיָ אֱלֹהֵינוּ מֶלֶךְ הָעוֹלָם הַמֶּלֶךְ הַטּוֹב וְהַמֵּטִיב לַכֹּל.

Baruch ata Adonai, Eloheinu melech Haolam, hamelech hatov v'hameitiv lakol.

Blessed are You, Lord our God, King of the Universe, Who is good and does good for all.

So the meal is over, the table is cleared, the dishes are washed (or in the sink waiting for tomorrow morning or the Clean Dishes Fairy, whichever comes first). Is it over? Well, again this is up to you. In my home, Friday night is family night. Continuing the theme of using Shabbat as a vehicle for connecting, Jonathan and I dedicate time after dinner to doing something with Sofie and Jules. This can mean playing a game, going for a walk, doing a puzzle or a project, or watching a movie. I can't encourage you enough to do this. This, I believe, is where special memories will be made, where moments will happen, where tradition will start—one that will make them want to be with you on Friday when they are teenagers and have other options. Let the kids dictate the activity—play Candy Land or watch *The Land Before Time IV*, not because you want to see what happens to that crazy Long Neck and his friends, but because your children want you to be with them. Maybe surprise them with a new game. After wandering in Toys "R" Us, I found that classic '70s games are back. Play these with your kids, and show them how, when you were young, you really kicked butt at Rock 'Em Sock 'Em Robots, Toss Across, or Mousetrap.

After the children are asleep, Jonathan and I spend time together. As a rule, we don't head to the computer to finish up work projects on Friday night. We put work aside and let the answering machine pick up any phone calls—this is the time we've promised each other to connect as a couple. We've all read the magazine articles advising us to make "dates" with our husbands. Think of Shabbat as a guaranteed date night.

So what is the deal with sex on Shabbat? I've heard that it's encouraged—even considered a double mitzvah. But why doesn't it fall under one of the forbidden activities like doing work—or kindling a fire or completing a circuit? (I should stop here.) Seriously though, there is a connection between Shabbat and sex. Mystically, this is the time God's Shechinah (the Divine Presence, personified as the feminine side of God) and God come together. Practically thinking, it makes sense. Shabbat is a time when we not only look our best, but we're relaxed, we've removed distractions and can focus on each other, and, hey, we've even had a little wine. If you think about it, the Shabbat dinner is a romantic meal, complete with candles, wine, and song. Plus, if your husband blesses you with just the right words at dinner . . . you may be in the mood to thank him later (oy, my mother's going to read this).

74

The next day, Saturday, is still Shabbat. Technically, it's a day of rest, one we should spend by going to shul and hanging out with friends. I find going to services kind of like exercising. I'll lie in bed thinking, "I know I should go. I know it's good for me, but I really don't feel like it. I don't feel like getting dressed up. I've got stuff to do today. I'll go next week." To be fair, when I do go, I really enjoy it. It's very peaceful. It's a couple of hours to sit quietly enjoying the familiar sound of the prayers. I feel a wonderful sense of community sitting among my fellow congregants. Whether I know them or not, it's nice to simply smile at one another and say "Good Shabbes." It is nice catching up with people during kiddush (and I love those chocolate brownies they always put out). It's a peaceful way to start the weekend. I always promise myself I'll remember this feeling and go more often. Then I always break my promise.

So, baby steps. There'll be time to go. As my children are getting older and are required to attend synagogue for religious school, I stay for services with them—I don't just drop them off. I really believe if I want my children to believe it's important to be affiliated with a synagogue and attend services, I must show them that Jonathan and I go. If I drop 'em and run, I'm teaching them that when they are able, they, too, should avoid services. But do whatever makes you comfortable or feels right.

My friend Laurie, who taught me how to braid challah, has always brought her children to services. She schlepped them in their carriages. Her oldest, Livvy, is now five and is beautifully behaved at shul. She's comfortable there. She knows the regulars because she, too, is a regular. Laurie brings a Shabbat bag of special toys that Livvy and her younger brother, Artie, play with at services (quiet and nonelectronic, of course). Contrary to what you may have thought, Laurie was not raised with regular shul-going or much religion at all. She taught herself and is now a frequent Torah reader. Because of her example and the pride she has in her Judaism, her husband chose to convert to Judaism and last year read from the Torah.

So it's possible to go to services even if your children are small and even if your spouse is not religious (or not even Jewish). As with anything else, if you want to find the time, you can and you will.

Take It to the Next Level

One woman told me that when she drives to synagogue on Shabbat, she leaves the radio turned off. This is her way of acknowledging Shabbat and making the driving experience more shabbesdik.

Saturday can also be when you spend time as a family. Jonathan usually has to work one day of the weekend, so he chooses to spend Saturday at home with us, partially in honor of Shabbat. Saturday is the day we focus on the children—whether it's hanging out at the house, going to a pumpkin patch, or to a museum. It doesn't matter what we do. We just try to make it fun (so no cleaning out the basement), and we try to do it together.

It's hard. I can get so busy that the only thing that helps me relax is to try to finish whatever work is on my mind. Sometimes it feels like giving up a day of work is more stressful than relaxing. It's a struggle. We're like a toddler who is so overtired, he doesn't even realize how tired he is. He struggles and fights against taking a nap. But he needs rest, and once he quiets down, he sleeps. Taking this rest time and spending the day with my kids does wonders and helps rejuvenate me for the next hellish week.

Our generation of mothers does it all. Very few of our grandmothers went to college—if our great-grandparents could afford college, they sent their sons. Their daughters lived at home until they married, and then they raised their children and ran their homes. More of our mothers went to college and may or may not have worked outside the home. The generations of mothers before us shattered the glass ceiling, and now we, thanks to them, no longer have a ceiling to bump into; however, we may feel obligated to not only climb through the hole they created in the glass, but continue to go as high as possible. But we also are aware of the effects of shattered homes and therefore know how crucial it is to work on our marriages and devote time to our children. We are educated, and therefore, if we choose to stay home, we may feel guilty about not working, so we volunteer what little time we have to our children's schools, our synagogues, or other organizations. And just when our children begin school full-time and our schedules free up a little, some of us start working again and are pulled in another direction. And some of us put time into exercising and trying to stay fit and healthy and dealing with our ideals of beauty, while trying to hide that we're dieting so that our daughters can escape the trauma of trying to achieve an unrealistic body image.

We are driven, maybe even more than any other generation of mothers. It's as if we're on a treadmill, running constantly at full speed.

Our husbands are on the same treadmill. And, unfortunately, even though we try not to, we've put our children on it, too. After all, getting into college is so much more competitive today than it was for us. We simply want our children to be in a position where they will have choices of where they can go to school, of what they will do as a career, so that they can continue to try to do everything they dream of doing.

Running on a treadmill can be very good—it strengthens your heart and increases your endurance—but if you run too far or too fast you can stumble and collapse.

It's as if every member of our family is running on his or her own treadmill—pursuing their own activities and life, parallel to everyone else. We may be running next to one another, we may even be able to shout to one another as we run, but we run alone. Wouldn't it be nice to slow down? Walk together? Maybe even hold hands?

As Jews we're lucky. We have Shabbat, an excuse to slow down. I'm not saying to totally stop—that's your choice, and that's for you to decide on your own. But on Saturday, slow down and walk with your family.

I wish I could learn to relax more. Shabbat is a day off. We are not only supposed to do so, we *deserve* to do so.

Such Genius

I heard a story once about a high-powered Manhattan couple who said that the only reason they can live the life they do is because they celebrate Shabbat. It forces them to stop and rest and rejuvenate.

An Orthodox woman I know told me the marriages and the families in her observant community are very strong—because of Shabbat. She told me to think of the beautiful cocoon that envelopes my family on Friday night, and imagines that feeling and connection lasting twenty-four hours every week. This is what she experiences and this is why she believes Shabbat is the secret to a strong marriage and a united family.

She continued to explain that by spending time in one another's homes for lunch after synagogue on Saturday, her children have gained an incredible sense of community and an understanding of being part of something. By truly growing up enveloped by a community, they learn to feel love and security, not just from family, but from their world. If one child does something good, the entire shul has naches. How's that for incentive?

Take It to the Next Level

Throughout the day, some synagogues offer study sessions in Torah, Talmud, and *Pirke Avot* (Ethics). In between the Minchah (afternoon) and Ma'ariv (evening) services, the third meal of Shabbat, known as *seudah shelishit*, is served. Seudah shelishit is a light meal. Since it is still Shabbat and the ovens cannot yet be turned on, the meal typically consists of cold salads and cake. This can be eaten at the synagogue with other congregants, or at home with family and friends.

Even if you have not spent the day at synagogue and are not Orthodox, you can incorporate the idea of seudah shelishit into your family's Saturday routine by gathering in the late afternoon for a simple snack. This is a wonderful way to check in on one another. Or, take it a step further by inviting friends and neighbors to join you for a casual gathering. Leave the television off and spend time being together.

HAVDALAH

An easy and truly beautiful way to close your Shabbat is with Havdalah. Havdalah literally means "separation." It is a short service that is meant to be done at home, and it takes less than ten minutes.

> ## Oy, Teens
> I've been to a number of bar and bat mitzvahs that start with a havdalah service during the cocktail hour. They'll dim the lights, pass out candles and bags of spices, and everyone comes together for a few moments of prayer.

To do it you'll need a kiddush cup of wine, a spice box, and a havdalah candle. The candle is not an ordinary candle. It is taller than a Shabbat candle and is actually a torch because it has more than one wick; most havdalah candles are four candles braided together. If you do not have a special havdalah candle, you can hold two Shabbat candles together. You can also make a candle at home with your children (I've included instructions in chapter 9).

The rabbis tell us that Shabbat is over once night has fallen—when there are three stars in the night sky and/or approximately one hour after sundown (technically, it's forty-two minutes, but any time after is fine). At this point, gather your family together, and dim the lights in the kitchen (or in whichever room you are holding your havdalah ceremony). Take the kiddush cup and fill it with wine. Have a member of your family hold the cup. Ask another member of your family to hold the spice box. Light the candle.

Take It to the Next Level

If possible, have an unmarried daughter hold the candle as high as possible. Tradition has it that this will insure that her future husband will be tall. (Right, like there are so many tall Jewish guys out there!)

Recite the blessing over the wine:

בָּרוּךְ אַתָּה יְיָ אלֹהֵינוּ מֶלֶךְ הָעוֹלָם בּוֹרֵא פְּרִי הַגָּפֶן.

Baruch ata Adonai, Eloheinu melech haolam, borei pree hagafen.

Blessed are You, Lord our God, King of the Universe, Who creates the fruit of the vine.

Do not drink the wine yet!

Next, hold up the spice box. "Spices" in Hebrew is *besamim*. Recite the following blessing:

בָּרוּךְ אַתָּה יְיָ אֱלֹהֵינוּ מֶלֶךְ הָעוֹלָם בּוֹרֵא מִינֵי בְּשָׂמִים.

Baruch ata Adonai, Eloheinu melech haolam, borei minei besamim.

Blessed are You, Lord our God, King of the Universe, Who creates various spices.

The leader smells the spices and then passes the box around so everyone can smell its contents. I've heard a couple of interesting reasons for why we smell the besamim. One is that we are leaving the beautiful peace of Shabbat and entering into our regular (not-so-peaceful) week. Therefore, we need to enliven ourselves to prepare for work, so the besamim are a kind of ancient aromatherapy. Another reason, based in kabbalah, is that during Shabbat we are given an extra soul (kind of a Divine boost), but when Shabbat ends, this extra spiritual spark leaves us and we feel faint, so we need these spices to revive us.

Next the leader takes the lit candle and recites:

בָּרוּךְ אַתָּה יְיָ אֱלֹהֵינוּ מֶלֶךְ הָעוֹלָם בּוֹרֵא מְאוֹרֵי הָאֵשׁ.

Baruch ata Adonai, Eloheinu melech haolam, borei m'orei ha-eish.

Blessed are You Lord our God, King of the Universe, Who creates the light of fire.

Now everyone raises his or her hands and turns them slowly from front to back in front of the candle, as if to warm their hands in the flame. Ideally, the light should shine through your fingernails, almost as if the fire is emanating from your fingers. There are several reasons for this: the Midrash (the Torah commentary) says that God gave Adam the gift of fire on that first Saturday night, and so the havdalah candle represents this primordial fire. Another is that we need to make use of the light from the candle in order to make the blessing over it. Bringing it close enough to our hands so that we can see the difference between our fingers and our nails gives the light a purpose. And finally, the light, which casts a shadow on our hands, separates darkness from light, which represents the separation of the week from Shabbat.

Finally, the leader takes the cup of wine and recites:

בָּרוּךְ אַתָּה יְיָ אלהֵינוּ מֶלֶךְ הָעוֹלָם, הַמַּבְדִּיל בֵּין קֹדֶשׁ לְחוֹל, בֵּין אוֹר לְחֹשֶׁךְ,
בֵּין יִשְׂרָאֵל לָעַמִּים, בֵּין יוֹם הַשְּׁבִיעִי, לְשֵׁשֶׁת יְמֵי הַמַּעֲשֶׂה.
בָּרוּךְ אַתָּה יְיָ, הַמַּבְדִּיל בֵּין קֹדֶשׁ לְחוֹל.

Baruch ata Adonai, Eloheinu melech haolam, hamavdil bein kodesh l'chol, bein or l'choshech, bein Yisrael la'amim, bein yom hashvi'i l'sheishet y'may hama'aseh.
Baruch ata Adonai, hamavdil bein kodesh l'chol.

Blessed are You, Lord our God, King of the Universe, Who distinguishes between sacred and secular time, between light and darkness, between the people israel and other nations, between the seventh day and the six working days of the week.

Blessed are You, Lord our God, Who distinguishes between sacred and secular time.

Everyone should take a sip of wine from the same cup. After everyone has drunk, douse the candle in the remaining wine. Poetically, just as Shabbat began with a shared cup of wine and the lighting of a flame, so it ends with a sip of wine and extinguishing the fire of the havdalah candle.

After this, some families sing songs, like "Shavua Tov" ("Good Week") or "Eliyahu Hanavi" ("Elijah the Prophet"). These songs are selected because they express hope for a good week or, in general, a messianic age. Of course, as with all the aspects of Shabbat I've mentioned, you can put your own twist on the tradition and substitute your own favorite songs that express wishes for peace, such as John Lennon's "Imagine."

Whether you choose to sing or not, be sure to kiss one another and wish one another *shavua tov*—a good week.

And then Shabbat is over. I hope it was a wonderful experience for you. I wish you a lifetime of peace and happiness. I wish you a lifetime of joy and laughter. I wish you a lifetime of Good Shabbes.

6

Oy, Teens

HEY, BETWEEN YOU AND ME, wanting my children to want to be with my husband and me for dinner is one of the main reasons I started making Shabbat every week. Right now it's easy. Sofie and Jules basically have nowhere else to go, so when I announced we were going to have a real Shabbat dinner every week they were thrilled. However, I can imagine this would have gone very differently if they had been teenagers when I broached the topic. Teenagers are used to having their Friday nights free to do what they want—football games, parties, movies, hanging out with friends, dates (I am *so* not ready for that); so if you suddenly announce, "Hey, guess what? Family dinner night! Yay!" and take away their night of freedom, they might not consider it good news. It would be nice to think we all have children who would be thrilled with the idea of a family dinner where we say blessings and talk about the Torah portion, but the reality is, they're teenagers; family time isn't usually a welcome idea. Don't let this discourage you. It won't be the first time we've had to convince our children to do something they may not have wanted to do but we knew was good for them. You know this is a good thing. You know they'll end up thanking you for it. You're the mom . . . you go, girl!

For many families, the years leading up to a child's bar or bat mitzvah involve a big

Jewish push—required synagogue attendance, family programs or classes, Hebrew school several times a week plus tutoring to prepare for the big day, not to mention attending other bar and bat mitzvahs every other week. For some families, this leads to a new pattern of involvement, and they continue to attend Shabbat services together. For others, the bar mitzvah becomes the conclusion rather than the beginning, and they move on, rarely attending synagogue or making Shabbat. How do you then tell your teens you want to have Shabbat when they have been looking forward to a respite, without starting World War III? Or what if your family has not really observed anything, or your children have not had any formal Jewish education, and suddenly, "Mom's got religion"?

For all the above scenarios—be flexible. First, call a family meeting, but don't make too big an issue out of it. Explain why you're thinking of doing Shabbat. Tell them you love them and want to find a way every week to spend time with them. Talk to them about the kind of conversations you'd like to have at dinner—adult conversations. When you present the idea of Shabbat to your teens, let them know you will work it around their other activities. Remember that the purpose is to connect with your children, not to push them away. This should not be a negative or a gross intrusion on their lives (although they might see it that way at first). It is a fine line—you are suggesting a change in their schedules that won't affect their schedules! If you don't light the candles at exactly the prescribed time, you won't be struck by lightning (really, I'd have lightning hit my house every week if this were true). Start small. As your family comes to enjoy and appreciate this special time together, your desire to make more of Shabbat will grow.

Here are some suggestions on how to work around your kids' crazy schedules. If your child has sports practice after school, wait to light candles and eat dinner until she comes home. If he has a game during dinnertime and into the evening, you have two choices: You can light candles, make a quick kiddush over wine or grape juice, say a quick blessing and eat a bite of challah, and eat after the game or whenever you normally would on game night (this also allows your child to go out with the team after the game). Or, if you know you won't see your child until late at night and you have all eaten, you can do a quick candle lighting, kiddush, and hamotzi when everyone has gotten home. If you can't be together for dinner, make a point of attending your child's game. Make the evening as much about family as you can. Do whatever you can to make Friday feel different.

If your child babysits (or has any other type of after-school job) and has to work that night, light candles with her before she leaves. Your child may reach the point where she chooses to switch schedules or not accept jobs on Friday nights, but don't force it. Maybe she's interested in baking; let her bake the challah after school—that can be her contribution to dinner. Then she can say the blessing over the challah before she leaves. If she's interested in doing so, ask her to bake the challah with you—it will be a great opportunity to bond while kneading and braiding. Take advantage of the time you have while waiting for the dough to rise to talk to her, and let her guide the conversation. Since she won't be joining you for dinner, use that time to bless her—maybe not a formal hands-on-her-head kind of thing, but let her know how blessed you are to be her mom and why she's special to you. It's the blessing that's important—not that you bless her specifically during dinner.

Remember, this is a family commitment. If you are asking your children to put Shabbat dinner ahead of other activities, you have to be prepared to do the same. A funny coincidence happened the first time Sofie had a true conflict with our Shabbat dinner. She was invited to a good friend's birthday party. The party was scheduled for Friday night and was going to be held at the cheerleading team gym where the girls were going to have a hip-hop dance lesson. She wanted to go so badly and I was tempted to let her go, but it's a slippery slope. Jonathan and I discussed it and agreed that Shabbat dinner was a commitment our family had made and we were sticking to it. Sofie was disappointed, but she accepted it.

Well, the next morning I got a call. A good friend had scheduled her birthday party at the Palm that same Friday night. I wanted to go, but how could I refuse Sofie and then go to my friend's party? I explained Friday night was our family time and made plans to take my friend to lunch the following week. I made a point of telling Sofie about my Friday night invitation so she knew that I was not singling her out and that we all make difficult choices sometimes in order to ensure that Shabbat is family time.

Another way to encourage family time is by getting your kids involved in the making of Shabbat. Yes, they can help you set the table or bake the challah or say the blessings. But bring your teenager's mind into it, too. Consider what else your child is interested in. If he is a musician, ask him to lead the family in songs after dinner. Challenge him to compose a Shabbat rap or rock song, or if that won't fly, just ask for a postdinner concert with his choice of music. If your kid is interested in sports, perhaps ask him to do a Google search on Jewish sports stars. The same goes for scientists, musicians, politicians, etc. This sounds a bit like schoolwork, and some kids will balk at the word *research,* but if it's a subject that is close to their hearts they will probably be more interested. If she is artistic, ask her to make the ritual objects you will use at dinner. Don't give her a design (unless she asks for it); let her be creative—maybe go with her or give her a few bucks to get supplies at the craft store. (The projects in this book will provide some ideas. I designed these projects with everything from molding clay to toy blocks, stuff you probably have lying around the house and most likely won't be using anytime soon.) Allow your child the flexibility to show humor in her art—I've seen some very clever books illustrating such objects as a "Neil Tzedakah Box" and challah plates where the challah rests above a painted face, forming a funny beehive hairdo.

My friend Lianne, who has teenage twins, said it's become a tradition that her son acts like an absolute goofball during the blessings so they always start the meal laughing. She explained, "We've never said a kiddush without smacking him in the head!" (In a loving way of course.) If you have a goofball in your family, embrace that talent. Humor is a major part of Jewish culture. Why not challenge your family to bring the best (nonoffensive) Jewish joke to the table on Friday night? I must get one a day via e-mail, so I know they're out there (most notably the one about the "kosher" computer that my dad has sent me three times). Or teach them about some of the older comedians who paved the way for the ones they know. Maybe even rent a Woody Allen movie to watch after dinner or listen to a classic Jackie Mason recording (I have to mention him because he's my dad's personal favorite). All in all, make the meal kid-friendly—tailor it to your kids, no matter their age.

Teens want to be thought of as adults, as peers. Give them respect and they'll give it back. If they know you're truly interested in what they think and what concerns them, you will help build their confidence and learn that their opinions (and even their goofball antics) have value. Solicit their input on what to do. Ask them, "What do you think would make our Shabbat experience better?" *And then do it*. Ask them what they are interested in—politics, pop culture, the environment—and use these interests as a starting point for the dinner conversations.

If you want to take it to the next level, let it be your job to bring the Torah into the conversation. If you do add a d'var torah at some point in the meal, perhaps relate it to something your children were talking about earlier—whether they were questioning the government or talking about something that happened at school. This shows you were attentive when they were speaking and might also make them think of the world in a larger context. In other words, relate it back to Judaism, help them gain a bigger picture of the world and, even more, with a Jewish perspective. This will engage them in their religion and give them an appreciation for their heritage. Help relate the past to the present.

Over time your discussions will become a more comfortable, natural part of your Friday night dinner, and perhaps they will spark an interest in and a connection to the Torah for your teen. Then you could suggest that your child prepare the d'var torah for the week. Sure, she might decline, but she might also want to try it out. One day my daughter Sofie surprised me by preparing the d'var torah discussion for the night. She read the summary I had on my Web site but didn't use my suggested questions—she thought of her own, and honestly, they were better than what I had come up with. Plus, these questions represented what spoke to her from the story, and she was so proud of herself. True, she was a tween at the time, but you might find you inspire one of your teens to lead the conversation. If you don't think they'll want to do the parashah discussion, you can invite them to pick a debate topic that appeals to them, and present it. Use this as an opportunity to teach your kids how to argue constructively and how to make their point and be convincing (this is, after all, a great Jewish strength). This can only help them in the long run (whether or not they become lawyers).

Such Genius

You can use Shabbat as a peaceful time to introduce difficult topics. For example, the parashah Shemini in Leviticus concerns two priests, Nadab and Abihu, who make a "strange fire" in the Tabernacle and are subsequently punished with death. In the Torah, it is explained that this is because they deviated from God's instructions for performing rituals. However, the ancient rabbis have theorized that Nadab and Abihu's true crime was being drunk; their inebriation caused them to make the fire. Priests were forbidden to drink hard alcohol so that their bodies would remain pure for their duties in the Tabernacle. This theory better explains why Aaron (the High Priest and Nadab's and Abihu's father) was forbidden to even mourn his sons.

This parashah is certain to incite conversation among your teens. It raises opportunities to talk about drinking (and drugs) and how excessive use can seriously impair judgment. Additionally, the fact that Aaron was punished by not being allowed to mourn his sons can spark discussion on how use of drugs and alcohol affects other members of the user's family. This could be a powerful and important family discussion, and yet it's raised in an innocuous nonlecture manner that your teens may be more open to.

Let your teenagers know it is okay to question authority. Relate a story from the Torah that you disagree with and say you thought it was unfair. This teaches your children that they don't have to accept everything at face value. Be prepared, however, for them to come back at you with an issue you had argued about previously like, "Well, it wasn't fair when Lauren got to go to the concert and I had to stay home" or whatever grave injustice you committed. Be open to it—have a conversation about it—don't get defensive, let them know honestly why you made the decision you did, and if through their argument you realize you made a mistake, admit it. The point of Shabbat, as I've said before, is to be together and to be open with one another. If there's one night you let your guard down, let it be Friday night.

Let Shabbat have a different feel. Let it be open to a deeper sharing, a new level of conversation. Shabbat is a spiritual reprieve from pressures—and this is something our teenagers need. Teens have an unfair reputation. They are not lazy; they're tired. They have unbelievably challenging schedules and more pressure than we ever faced. So on Shabbat, give them a break. Don't discuss homework or grades. If you are struggling with issues as a family, take a break from them on Shabbat. Let your teens sleep in on Saturday—don't *hak* 'em.

Take It to the Next Level

Another thing that teens need to learn (and we can use Shabbat to emphasize) is respectful speech. Nowadays, everywhere you turn there's a bad or offensive word coming out of someone's mouth. Specifically, it's called lashon hara, and it should be forbidden on Shabbat. On Shabbat, try to elevate your speech and ask everyone to do the same. This means no gossip, no cursing, no yelling, no arguing, no cruelty. On Shabbat we must think about how we speak *to* one another and *about* one another.

One obvious solution to having Shabbat with teens is to invite friends. Whether it's another family or just their friends, having other teens around will help get your kids in a more celebratory mood. Enlist your child's help in planning the menu or even how the dinner should work. You could also create a Shabbat dinner group with several families and take turns hosting. The kids will look forward to when it's their turn, and the moms will look forward to the weeks when it's not!

My friend Jill's father is Orthodox, and while she was growing up, Shabbat dinner was a big deal. She and her sisters were required to have dinner at home (they were allowed to go out after, but dinner usually lasted so long that it was too late to go anywhere). So the girls took to inviting friends over on Friday nights. Jill confided that she always worried what her friends would think: after all, her father did the whole thing. But week after week her friends enjoyed it—they didn't have dinners like this at home, and they loved the feel of the close family dinner. The big deal was when a new boyfriend was invited. Jill's husband still talks about his first Shabbat with her family.

Jill also lovingly recalled the very decadent desserts her mom always served on Shabbat. Special desserts is another great way to make Shabbat something your family looks forward to, especially if sweets are not a normal part of your weekday meals.

Such Genius

Many Jewish youth groups (either through synagogues or independently) encourage the kids to have monthly Shabbat dinners as a group. They rotate houses once a month and have almost a Shabbat party. This allows them to socialize with friends and observe Shabbat at the same time. Whether or not your child is in a youth group, you can volunteer your home for this kind of Friday night get-together.

If there is a college campus nearby, welcome students over for Shabbat. Your rabbi or the school's Hillel house will help you find students who may miss being with family and would really welcome the idea of coming to a home-cooked Shabbes dinner. Plus, your teens can learn about college and may think it's cool to have a college-age friend.

And don't forget extended family. Include anyone who is within driving distance or make a point of having an extra-special Shabbat dinner when relatives are visiting. Lianne told me, "Even my cool macho son wants his grandparents there and is proud when the table looks nice for Shabbat." Encourage your parents to tell stories about their Shabbats growing up or stories about what they did when you were a teen (all those years ago!).

> ## Such Genius
>
> My friend Robin (she of traveling Shabbat box fame) has a wonderful way to bring family who live far away to her Shabbat table every Friday night—they conference call! Most phones today have speakerphone capability (not all have conference call, but some do). So why not do what Robin's family does? Every Friday call your parents and grandparents, put them on speakerphone, and celebrate Shabbat together via the miracle of technology! (How's *that* for a modern idea?) Now, here's the disclaimer: Technically, we're not supposed to make phone calls. But we're not supposed to do a lot of things. The important point is that this action connects your family on a multigenerational level.

90

AFTER DINNER

If your children went to a Jewish summer camp or are active in a youth group, they may know a fun version of birkat hamazon (grace after meals). Encourage them to sing it (with all the irreverent asides that make it fun), and if you or your husband don't know it, let them teach it to you. I still love singing it when I have the chance because it reminds me of when I was a teenager.

If you have children who like to sing or play instruments, after dinner is a great time to do so. The songs don't have to be Jewish songs—any way to include the tradition of singing songs on Shabbat is wonderful.

> ## Such Genius
>
> My friend Dianne, whose family members all have gorgeous voices and whose Shabbat dinners are joyous and filled with song, told me her teenage daughters have plenty of other activities they could do on Friday nights—parties, dates—but they choose to be with their family for dinner. I don't know about you, but I truly hope I will be able to say this in a few years.

Try to designate Friday night as family night, and let your children pick the activity. Maybe watch a movie together or play a game. Some families I know play word games every Friday. My children especially love playing games in which they know they have the advantage, like any GameCube video game (it makes me dizzy just to watch). Right now they're excited about a new Harry Potter trivia game. Sofie, Jules, and I have read all the books and watched all the movies, but Jonathan would be hard-pressed to name even one character besides Harry. The kids can't wait to team up against Jonathan and me, figuring the two of them will easily beat us. For older children (though there are some older Harry Potter fanatics) try a Saturday Night Live trivia game, or bring out the classics. Playing Monopoly, Life, or even working out a really hard puzzle as a family can be a great way to spend the evening.

Does all this sound a little too *Leave It to Beaver*? If you're more Ozzy Osbourne than *Ozzie and Harriet*, use these ideas as inspiration and make them your own. But I've got to tell you, there's something sweet and wonderful about playing board games together.

SATURDAY

I'm not expecting you to go from just starting to have Friday night dinner to becoming shomer Shabbes. The extent to which you take your observance is personal and will evolve. But you can easily do things to make your Saturdays special and family oriented. If you can go to synagogue it's a wonderful and very peaceful way to end the workweek. Perhaps if you see another family at services, you can invite them to have lunch and spend the day with you. Maybe go to the mall, but don't shop (like when we were kids and we'd spend the day at the mall, but since we didn't have any money, we'd really just hang out and try on clothes and talk about boys).

If you normally work on the weekends, try to take Saturday off and make plans with your kids. Things that are work related, things that are harried should be avoided on Saturday. Make the day more enjoyable—and relaxing. Take a walk together or encourage your kids to take a nap, to rest up from school. Sure, some teens may have homework that they *need* to finish, and they'll be shocked if you suggest an alternative activity or that they put it off till later. But use this to teach them time management. If they know a project is coming, help them find time *before* Shabbat to begin work. By making Shabbat a priority, we are making one another a priority. Help them to schedule their tasks so that they can do what they need to do and still have time for family. This is a precious skill they must have when they are grown and are parents. Then they will have to be able to put work aside. Let Shabbat be the vehicle for teaching this crucial parenting skill.

I remember talking about Shabbat with three brothers now in their thirties and forties. The middle brother quietly said, "I remember Mom lighting candles." The youngest said, "I remember that, too." The air was full of emotion as they remembered their mother, who had passed away. Finally, one broke the silence with a laugh, saying, "Remember how Dad used to argue with our uncles every Friday night?" And with that, they all laughed and talked at once, layering their memories of Friday nights with family.

This is what Shabbat is all about. The moments we have with our children are precious, and as parents of teens, we know how quickly the years pass. Shabbat helps us not let those moments fly away, but capture them, preserve them as memories that will stay with our children always.

7

Challah-Bake Girl!

I BEGAN BAKING CHALLAH for the High Holidays when Sofie was three and Jules was one. Sofie's nursery school teacher gave me the very tasty challah recipe the class had made. (You should have smelled the hallways during pickup—it drove many moms back to carbs.) So as part of our preparations for Rosh Hashanah, I made the dough, divided it into two, and then the kids helped by rolling each half into a snake or rope. Then we coiled the snake around and around (like a rag rug) and baked the traditional round challahs for Rosh Hashanah. This was so much fun that it became part of our annual High Holy Day preparations. The challahs always came out so well, and our home smelled incredible. But I made challah once a year. I loved everything about making challah—involving my kids, the way it tasted, the smell—and really looked forward to it every year. But it seemed like too much hassle to do it more often. Until I met Carol Berman.

I met Carol four years after I started baking my Rosh Hashanah challah when I was planning the "Make Friday Night Shabbat" workshop series. Carol is known for her challah, so I asked her to teach the challah baking class. During her class, I asked her how she found time to make challah every week. Her answer shocked me in its simplicity (and I felt like an idiot for not having thought of it on my own): One dough recipe makes four challahs! You need to make it only once a month, and you will have enough fresh, homemade challah for all four Shabbats. Once I heard that, I started seriously considering homemade challah as more than an annual event. Before this I had thought making my own challah would be bizarre—as if I was jumping into the deep end of frum-dom. But I started talking to other women and learned that there are many who make their own challah. It was as if there was a secret club of challah-baking moms, and I wanted to join. To up the ante, I had my friend Laurie, who won the prestigious "Best-Looking Challah" award in our synagogue challah-baking contest, teach me how to perfectly braid the dough. Now my family has homemade challah every Shabbat.

Believe me, if you do one thing new this year, make challah. It's so much better than anything you can buy, it adds that yontif smell to your home (which store-bought simply cannot do), and you can use it for sandwiches or French toast for the weekend.

Such Genius

My friend in California has added to the challah tradition by convincing her *husband* to be in charge of turning the challah into French toast on Saturday mornings.

OK, here's another secret; these homemade challahs are so amazing, I've used them for barter. My friend Joanne, who happens to sell the most gorgeous accessories, has asked me to bake her a fresh challah each week. In exchange she's giving me this very funky ring I've had my eye on for months. Seriously, once you try it, you'll never go back to store-bought. And if your friends have a taste, they'll be putty in your hands. Your kids' friends will be begging for invitations to your Friday night dinner, your college students will come home for Shabbat. . . . Homemade challah will give you unbelievable powers.

Here's a story sure to inspire you: Sofie came home from school one day to report that her friend Jessica, who had celebrated Shabbat with us the week before, was dancing around the classroom singing, "I love Shabbat and I'm not even Jewish!" When Sofie asked her why she loved Shabbat, Jessica said it was "'cause of your mom's challah!" Now Sofie's other friends are clamoring for invites.

So I'm going to teach you how to make challah. In chapter 8, you'll find other challah recipes. How different can challah be, you ask? Well, some are sweeter, some doughier, some cakier. Find the recipe you like the best or make your own variation. I'm going to teach you how to make the challah that I make every week, and for me, any excuse to have dessert is good, so my challah is sweet.

By the way, Carol recommends King Arthur bread flour (for whatever kind of bread you may bake). Honestly, I don't know enough about the different flours to have a favorite, but as I said earlier, she's the expert, so . . .

MEREDITH'S CHALLAH

Yield: 2-3 loaves

¾ cup sugar

2 cups lukewarm water

¾ cup vegetable oil

1 tablespoon salt

3 large eggs

3 envelopes yeast (each envelope is equal to 2¼ teaspoons, so three envelopes is approximately 2 tablespoons plus ¾ teaspoon yeast)

¼ cup lukewarm water

8–10 cups bread flour (This should be bread flour because the density makes it better for baking bread than all-purpose flour. Any kind of bread flour is fine, but if I see King Arthur at the store, I buy it, simply because Carol told me to.)

Preheat oven to 350 degrees.

Combine sugar, 2 cups water, oil, and salt. In a separate bowl, beat the eggs. Then add the eggs to the sugar mixture.

In a separate cup (I use a measuring cup), mix the yeast in ¼ cup water. Make sure the water is warm—not cold or hot. This allows the yeast to work properly—you'll know it's working if you see little bubbles on the surface. (I've used it even if it doesn't bubble—the dough doesn't rise as much, but it still ends up tasting good.) Then add the yeast mixture to the first mixture.

Add 4 or 5 cups of flour and mix well (I use a spoon for this part as it is too wet to mix by hand). Gradually add 4 or 5 more cups of flour. By judging the feel you will know how much more to add—if the mixture is sticky, add more flour; if it's dry and stringy, add a little water. At this point, it may be easier to mix with your hands than with a spoon.

Now you're ready to knead. Take off your rings, because little pieces can get into the crevices of your jewelry, which is a pain to clean. But kneading doesn't get that messy—I've actually made challah in my of-the-moment jeans (you know the ones—they're ungodly expensive, will probably be out of style tomorrow, and I can barely squeeze my "really need to do some cardio" *tuches* into them).

I like to knead in the bowl. Not that I'm such a neat freak, but I make my challah Friday afternoon and the cleaning lady comes that morning, and I just don't want to clean up flour after the house is finally straight. Times like this I wish I lived in a cooking show—where all the ingredients are prechopped and ready for you in cute little bowls, and you put whatever you're cooking in the oven, and after the commercial break it's done . . . and at the end of the half hour you say something clever to wrap up the show and someone else cleans up.

If, unlike me, you prefer to knead on a cutting board or a table, sprinkle some flour on the board (or table), and place the dough on the flour and knead. Kneading on a flat surface allows you to use both hands (if you use a bowl, you have to use one hand to steady the bowl).

Regardless of what you're kneading in, here's how to do it. Make a fist and push (don't punch) down the dough. You can twist your hand as you're pushing so that you can open your hand from a fist to an open palm as you push down and forward on the dough (by forward, I mean away from your body). Then grab a side of the shmushed dough ball, pull it away from the center of the dough, and then fold it back into the center of the dough. Repeat this, starting at the center of the dough and working around the circumference so you push and pull all of it (rotating the dough or bowl as you work). I must admit, working the dough really helps to relieve stress.

Continue to push down with your fist or palm, pull out, and fold back to center until the dough becomes smoother. You can add more flour if the dough is too sticky or wet. Knead for a few minutes (my recipe says 10 minutes, but I don't have the patience to knead for 10 minutes, so I don't, and my challah still tastes great). You'll know when you're finished kneading by looking at the dough. If all the flour is incorporated and the dough is smooth (or somewhat smooth and you've had enough of kneading and your tendonitis is acting up), stop.

Once you're done kneading, pour a little bit of vegetable oil on a paper towel and wipe it around the inside of a clean bowl (not the one you used to mix the ingredients. I've actually tested this out because I love cooking shortcuts, but the dough does rise better in a clean, oiled bowl). I know olive oil is healthier and I do use it for everything else, but you really want challah to taste like challah, not some healthy, whole grain, hippie-dippie, crunchy thing, so use the ingredients I'm telling you to use—vegetable oil, white flour, sugar, eggs. Don't worry about it: My great aunts all lived well into their nineties (actually, they were older, but they lied about their age), and they ate schmaltz on bread. Schmaltz is rendered fat. Yep, pure fat. They'd slather it on white bread and they were, like, 102 when they died. So use the oil and eggs!

Put the dough in the oiled bowl, and flip the dough over so both sides get a little bit of oil on them. Now, here's my secret trick: lay a piece of wax paper over the bowl and then place a dish towel on top of that. Most recipes will not mention the wax paper, but this is the way I've always done it. I don't know what the wax paper does—maybe makes it warmer for the dough to rise—but this makes the dough really puff up *huge*, so do it.

Let the dough rise for an hour. Leave the house, run errands, call your clients back, call your mother back (yeah, right), go to lunch, exercise (yeah, right), watch *Oprah* (that would be nice), whatever. . . . If you take more than an hour, that's fine—nothing will happen to the dough, I promise.

When you come back, the dough should have doubled in size. (Again, don't worry if it hasn't. I've had dough rise only a little bit, and I swear it still tasted good.) Punch down the dough to deflate it, and knead again for a few minutes to work out any excess air bubbles. Cover with the wax paper and towel, and let rise for another half hour.

Take It to the Next Level

After kneading the dough the second time, we are supposed to remove a bit of the dough and make the following blessing over it:

בָּרוּךְ אַתָּה יְיָ אֱלֹהֵינוּ מֶלֶךְ הָעוֹלָם, אֲשֶׁר קִדְּשָׁנוּ בְּמִצְוֹתָיו, וְצִוָּנוּ לְהַפְרִישׁ חַלָּה מִן הָעִסָּה.

Baruch ata Adonai, Eloheinu melech haolam, asher kid'shanu b'mitzvotav v'tzivanu, l'hafrish challah min ha'isa.

Blessed are You, Lord our God, King of the Universe, Who commands us to separate a portion of dough.

Then you put down that small piece and say:

הֲרֵי זוֹ חַלָּה !

Harei zu challah!

This is the challah!

You then bake the small piece but do not eat it. Some people burn it, some feed it to the birds. Challah is a symbolic offering to God, so removing a piece and burning it is a reference to the burnt offerings of the ancient priests.

After a half hour, you're ready to braid. Take the dough out of the bowl and divide it into two. (This is for your two challah loaves. If you want to make three loaves, divide the dough into three. If you just want to make one huge loaf, then leave it whole. I usually make two loaves.) Then divide each of the hunks of dough into four. Work with one set at a time. Roll the four pieces into snakes. I like to make mine 10–12 inches long. It doesn't matter; just make certain all four are the same length.

Lay the four pieces on the table and pinch the ends of one side together. If you like, you can add raisins at this point by pushing them into the snakes of dough. Take the piece on the left and weave it over the roll of dough next to it, then under the next roll, and finally over the last roll, so that it finishes on the far right. Next take the piece that is now on the far left. Again, weave over, under, and over until it finishes on the far right. Continue to weave the left-hand piece until the pieces are too short to weave. Then pinch the ends together and tuck them under the loaf.

Don't worry if the loaf isn't perfect—mine never are; I always have at least one rope of dough end before the other three. When this happens, I need to improvise (hey, maybe it's a good thing I'm not living in a Food Network show). So here's what I do: I judge the length of the ropes (but not too harshly—I don't want to make any of them feel inadequate because of their size). If the ends are all a bit short, I mush them all together and then tuck them under the loaf. If the others are kind of long or if I want a longer loaf, I gently pull the short rope to lengthen it. That rope may get thinner as a result of pulling it, but no one will notice. Just tell yourself, "It's not uneven, it's homemade."

Repeat with the other set of dough. You'll now have two loaves. Place the loaves on a nonstick cookie sheet (or put down a piece of parchment paper before placing the dough on the sheet), cover with a dishcloth, and let rest for 10 minutes.

Why does the dough need to rest? Who knows? Maybe it's been pulled and pushed and pinched a bit too much and just needs a little break, all right? (Actually, the gluten fibers need to relax so the bread isn't tough. Point is, you can't skip this step.)

While the bread rests, prepare the egg wash, which will give the bread its beautiful shine. Here's a secret: don't dilute the egg with water, as some cookbooks will have you do. Just crack an egg in a small bowl, mix it, and brush onto the braided dough. I love this part; it makes me feel like an artist. You can also shake some sesame or poppy seeds onto the loaves at this point.

Such Genius

OK, since you've been such a good reader I'll give you my secret ingredient: honey. One day I was baking challah and I ran out of eggs for the egg wash. Rather than asking my next-door neighbor, I grabbed a squeeze bottle of honey and zigzagged some on the top of the loaf before I baked it. It was amazing! My family will eat challah no other way. So if you like, forget the egg wash and just drizzle the honey. You'll still get a pretty golden color and added sweetness.

Bake for 45 to 55 minutes (the challah will be that beautiful golden brown color when finished). And let the smells begin. I promise you, once you get the hang of it, you can prepare the dough in 15 minutes. And after you try fresh-baked challah, you're never gonna want to go back to store-bought. (Never mind what *you* think—your family isn't going to accept challah from a bag anymore.)

Here's an idea for fancy-schmancy challah that is perfect for very special occasions:

Take your dough and divide it into ten pieces. Roll each piece into a snake, but instead of making them all the same size, roll four shorter (6–8 inches) than the other six (10–12 inches). Braid the four into a short loaf, and then take the six and braid as you would the four (in the same "over, under, over, under" pattern). You will now have a short loaf and a long loaf. Take the short loaf and place it on top of the long loaf. You're basically stacking two challahs on top of each other, but the bigger one will stick out like a base. Carefully smooth them together where they touch (the edges of the base of the smaller loaf to the top of the larger loaf) to make sure they stick. Then do the honey or egg thing and bake (oh yeah, take the piece out and make the brachah, too).

Save this for company (or when your in-laws visit)—this giant, double-tiered challah is so impressive!

Tell the truth: Now that the challah is baking, doesn't it feel like Shabbes already? Ask your kids. Ask your husband. They'll say it does. And that's kinda nice, right?

Oy, Teens

Challah baking is another wonderful way you could involve your children. My friend Gail learned how to make challah this year. She was so anxious about doing it right the first time that she recruited her family to help her. Her teenage daughter loved baking it so much, she's now in charge of making it every week—to her mother's relief and delight!

Such Genius

You're probably wondering what you're going to do with all this extra bread every week. Here are some options: First, you can slice it and use it for sandwiches. I've also turned extra challah into garlic bread: I cut thick slices (this usually will finish off the loaf), schmear some margarine on it

(I use margarine because it's pareve, but if I'm just spicing up some leftover fish, I use butter), and sprinkle some garlic powder on it. (If you have fresh garlic, you can roast the cloves with olive oil and spread them on the bread—yummmm.) Then I put the challah slices on a cookie sheet and broil in the oven until the margarine melts and the bread toasts. (Watch it carefully so it doesn't burn.)

I've already mentioned the French toast idea (again, it's so much better using the thick challah slices), which is great for brunch, but I have been known to make Chocolate French Toast. This recipe makes four large slices.

In a large bowl, beat 3 large eggs. Add ¼ cup skim milk. (You could probably use any kind of milk; I just have skim milk in my fridge.) Then add 1 tablespoon cocoa powder, 1 tablespoon granulated sugar, ½ teaspoon cinnamon, 1 teaspoon vanilla extract, and a pinch of salt.

Slice challah 1 inch thick. Soak slices in mixture for 10 minutes. While bread is soaking, melt 1 tablespoon unsalted butter in a large pan over a low flame. When butter melts, add slices (only enough to fit in pan) and cook. Using a spatula, press down on the slices to flatten them as they cook. Flip over once to brown both sides evenly (about 3 minutes per side). After the first flip, sprinkle some chocolate chips over the top of the toast (they will melt and get gooey).

Remove from pan, and top with sliced strawberries and whipped cream for some extra decadence (like this recipe needs it!).

If you're really having a problem with lots of leftover bread, make smaller loaves. If you're having guests over, you can make two loaves out of the dough; otherwise, make three or four small loaves, and freeze the extra baked loaves for other weeks when you don't have time to make fresh. Just take the challah out of the freezer Friday morning. It will defrost during the day (you can defrost on the counter—it's not like meat). A half hour before you want to serve the bread, place it in the oven at 350 degrees. It takes only 30 minutes to bring back that fabulous fresh-baked smell. You won't regret it!

8

Recipes

I'LL ADMIT IT. I am a lazy cook. I don't like to knead for ten minutes or mix until all the lumps are out. Or even be super accurate with my measuring. But ask anyone who has eaten at my house and they'll tell you I'm a good cook. Every once in a while (usually after I receive a fresh issue of *Bon Appétit*) I'll make something more challenging. But here I've included my good ol' standbys, which are staples at my house because I can count on them to be delicious. I've included traditional recipes from family and friends as well as more "modern" choices, like Fresh Mango Salsa and Balsamic Steak with Crème de Cassis Onions that are a bit more creative. Basically, if a recipe made it into this chapter, it's easy to make and appropriate for Shabbat dinner.

CHALLAH
(Pareve—milk or meat)
Note on challah recipes: I bake all the loaves and freeze the extra.

MEREDITH'S CHALLAH

For my favorite challah recipe, the one I make every Friday, which I so cleverly named "Meredith's Challah," please turn to chapter 7. There you'll find step-by-step instructions for making any challah, braiding techniques, and great ideas for what to do with leftover challah (including Chocolate French toast!)

CAROL'S CHALLAH

(This is the Carol who taught the challah baking class)
This is a good, basic challah—not too sweet, not too doughy.
Note the variation with walnuts and dried cranberries. Amazing!
Yield: 2 large or 4 small challah loaves
(Pareve)

4 packages dry yeast (3 tablespoons)

4 cups warm water

1 cup sugar

2 tablespoons salt

11–12 cups King Arthur bread flour

2 eggs

1 cup canola or corn oil or combination of the two

Mazola corn oil spray for nonsticking to the 4–5 bread pans or 2–3 cookie sheets (do not use foil baking sheets; they won't support the weight of the dough)

Optional: for 1 of the 4 loaves—¾ cup walnut pieces and ¾ cup dried cranberries

Preheat oven to 375 degrees.

In a large glass or stainless steel bowl, dissolve 4 packages of yeast in 4 cups water. Stir until the mixture is well blended. Add sugar and salt, and stir to dissolve.

Add 5 cups flour. Mix well, then add the eggs and oil. Mix well to incorporate.

Slowly stir in 5 more cups flour. Don't dump it in all at once; it's easier to incorporate if you add 1 cup at a time. Once all the flour is added, the dough will become quite thick. When it pulls away from the sides of the bowl (meaning it forms a clean ball and doesn't stick to the sides of the bowl), take the dough out of the bowl and place on a floured board with the remaining cup of flour (or more if it is sticking). Knead for approximately 10 minutes until dough feels blended and smooth.

Wash and oil your large bowl (or oil a fresh bowl if you are using two bowls and therefore don't have to clean the first at this time. However, using two bowls means you ultimately have to clean two bowls, so actually, it's easier to use one and just wash it halfway through the baking process). Place dough in the bowl, and flip the dough over so that all the sides will be lightly oiled. Cover with a towel and let rise in a warm place for 1½ to no more than 2 hours.

Divide dough into 4 even-size pieces for four challahs.

Take 1 piece and divide into 4 pieces and braid. Do this with the other 3 pieces.

Place into 4 sprayed bread pans or cookie sheets with parchment paper on them (no spray taste this way). Allow to rise again 45 minutes to preferably 1 but no more than 1½ hours.

Brush tops with beaten egg. Sprinkle with poppy seeds or sesame seeds if you like.

Bake for approximately 23–25 minutes or until nicely browned.

Lay out dish towel. Remove challah from the pans and cool on towel or rack.

Variation: Before braiding, knead in walnuts and dried cranberries.

ADRIENNE'S CHALLAH

(Adrienne won best-tasting challah at my shul)
This one is sweet, especially if you add the brown sugar.
Yield: 2 large or 4 small challah loaves
(Pareve)

2 packages yeast (1½ tablespoons)

2 cups lukewarm water

1 cup sugar

1 tablespoon brown sugar (optional)

1 tablespoon salt

7 cups flour

3 eggs (2 whole plus 1 egg white for dough, 1 yolk for egg wash)

½ cup canola oil

In a large bowl pour in the 2 packages of dry yeast. Add 2 cups of warm water that is the temperature of your wrist (lukewarm). Stir the water and yeast together, and let stand a couple of minutes.

Add the sugar (and, if you want, the brown sugar). Add the salt and stir. Add 3½ cups of flour and stir till smooth.

Beat together 2 eggs plus 1 egg white (reserve yolk for egg wash) and stir into the mixture. Add the oil.

Now you can begin to add in the rest of the flour. At this point, the dough is difficult to mix, and I use my hands to add in the remaining 3½ cups of flour. Knead the dough until it's well mixed.

Remove the dough and place on a clean surface so you can clean the bowl.

Coat the inside of the bowl with a tablespoon of oil (use a paper towel to spread the oil). Place the dough in the oiled bowl, and flip the dough over so all sides are lightly coated with oil. Cover the bowl with a towel, and let it sit over the stove or in a warm oven that is not on.

After 1 hour, check to see if the dough has risen. Punch down and fold over in a ball. Let the bread rise one more time for about ½ hour, and punch down and get ready to braid the challah dough.

Place the braided challahs on a greased cookie sheet and let rise.

Now take the reserved egg yolk. Beat well in a dish, and brush on the challah dough.

Put challah in the oven at 375 degrees for 25 minutes, or until it is browned and underneath is brown. This could also take 35–40 minutes, depending on your oven.

DORI'S BREAD MACHINE CHALLAH
Yield: 2 challah loaves

1 cup warm water

¼ cup vegetable oil

3 eggs

Honey (just squeeze in a big glug!)

4 cups flour (bread flour is best and great if you can find the flour labeled "special for bread machines")

1 packet yeast (2¼ teaspoons)

Egg wash (1 egg yolk and ½ teaspoon sugar)

Sesame or poppy seeds (optional)

Here's another way to get homemade challah on the table—make the dough using a bread machine! Simply dump all the ingredients into the machine before you leave for work in the morning, set machine for "dough only" option, and when you and your children return home, take the dough out, braid it, apply egg wash and seeds, and bake. Voilà!

CHICKEN SOUP AND MATZOH BALLS

EMILY'S CHICKEN SOUP

(Fleishig—meat)

Yield: Plenty! It depends on the size of your pot.

1 chicken whole (but remove the neck and stuff from inside)

2 turnips, cut into cubes

1 bag (approximately 6–8) parsnips, cleaned, ends cut off, and cut into chunks

6–8 celery stalks, cleaned and cut into chunks

6–8 carrots, cleaned, peeled, and cut into chunks

3 yellow onions, cut. Leave the skin on as it colors the soup.

1 bunch of dill, cleaned

Kosher salt (a pinch or to taste)

White pepper (a pinch or to taste)

Put everything *except the dill and seasonings* into a large stockpot. Add enough cold water to cover the ingredients but not so much that it boils over. Bring to a boil, then simmer. Let simmer until the chicken is falling off the bone (this should take about 2–3 hours). Line

a colander with paper towels or cheesecloth, and put the colander over another stockpot. Slowly pour the soup through the colander, changing the towels as necessary. You should, in the new stockpot, have a nice broth.

Bring the new broth to a boil, then simmer another hour (this intensifies the flavor). Then float dill in it for 15 minutes and remove. Season with kosher salt and white pepper (Emily prefers this as it doesn't show up in the broth and has a nice strength). Serve with shredded boiled chicken and matzoh balls or noodles.

You can freeze this soup to use other times.

Tip: It's not a good idea to put hot things in the refrigerator. The heat causes the temperature to rise and can allow bacteria to grow. Before freezing soup, allow soup to cool on the stove or counter. Then put in the refrigerator to cool. Then freeze. To reheat, simply place pot on the stove over medium heat.

CHICKEN SOUP — MY MOM'S VERSION

(Fleishig—meat)

Yield: As much as your pot can hold

Cut-up chicken (My kosher butcher calls this a "soup chicken family pack,"
but basically it's a whole chicken cut up into parts)

1 or 2 onions, cut in half

2–3 large carrots, washed, peeled, and cut in rounds

Bunch of celery, washed and cut in big chunks (for easy removal)

Bunch of fresh parsley

4 cubes chicken bouillon

Pepper (a pinch)

Optional: thin noodles

"Clean chicken good" (these are Mom's specific orders). Put all ingredients in stockpot and fill with enough cold water to cover ingredients, but not so much that it boils over. Boil chicken until tender (2½ hours at least—the meat should fall off the bones).

With a spoon, take out the onions, celery, parsley, and chicken, but leave the carrots. Reserve chicken. Once the soup has cooled, place in refrigerator. Skim fat the next morning. Put little pieces of the chicken back in. Reheat and serve.

If you want to use noodles instead of matzoh balls, you must cook the noodles first in cold water and drain well. As much as I love cooking shortcuts, if you cook the noodles in the soup, you will get a lot of starch in the soup and that would be yucky.

The reserved chicken is also perfect for chicken salad. Just add grapes, tarragon, and mayonnaise.

AUNT AILEEN'S MATZOH BALLS (KNEIDLACH)—FLOATERS

(Pareve—meat or dairy)
Caution: These are so big and fluffy you'll find yourself saying,
"Would you like some soup to go with your matzoh ball?"
Yield: 8–10 large kneidlach

8 eggs (extra large)

2 tablespoons ginger ale

4 tablespoons imitation schmaltz like Nyafat (sorry, girls!)

1 teaspoon salt and a dash of pepper

2 cups matzoh meal

1 tablespoon salt for water

Using an electric mixer or a blender, beat eggs, ginger ale, shortening, salt, and pepper. Mix well. Remove from blender (if using) and add matzoh meal. Stir thoroughly to incorporate the matzoh meal. Refrigerate overnight.

Bring a large pot of water to a boil and add 1 tablespoon of salt. Form the mixture into balls and drop into the pot. Return to a boil and cook, covered, for 25 minutes.

Tip: Use the biggest pot you can find. The more room the kneidlach have to expand, the bigger they get.

Remove matzoh balls and add to heated soup.

These freeze well. If you're not serving them right away, place cooked kneidlach on a cookie sheet, cover with plastic wrap, and store in freezer (once frozen, you can transfer them to a freezer bag). When you're ready to serve, simply drop the frozen matzoh balls into the hot soup, where they'll defrost in 10 minutes and plump back up!

Laurie's Nana's Matzoh Balls (Kneidlach)—Sinkers

(Fleishig or pareve, depending on fat used)

Yield: 10–12 matzoh balls

6 eggs, separated

1½ teaspoons salt

1 teaspoon pepper

¾ cup seltzer

2 tablespoons chicken fat (or Nyafat or vegetable oil)

1½ cups matzoh meal

1 tablespoon salt for water

Vegetable oil

Combine all ingredients *except matzoh meal* and *egg whites*. Mix well. In a separate small bowl, beat egg whites until stiff, then carefully fold into yolk mixture. Add matzoh meal and mix well. Refrigerate for several hours or overnight.

Fill a large pot three-quarters full of salted water and bring to a boil. Put some vegetable oil in a small dish for your hands (this prevents the mix from sticking to your hands and makes it easier to form balls). Dip your hands in the oil, then spoon out the mixture and roll into balls. Lower the heat and place balls in pot. Return water to a boil. Cover and cook 30–40 minutes.

If you make these matzoh balls ahead of time, freeze them on a cookie sheet. Once frozen, place balls in a freezer bag. To reheat, toss frozen balls into boiling soup. Warm for about 15 minutes, and then taste test one to make sure it's warm throughout.

GEFILTE FISH

(Pareve)

*This is really more of a casserole that you will cut into square pieces
rather than the traditional oval pieces of gefilte fish.*

Yield: 12–20 pieces, depending on size of baking glass

12 pieces of store-bought gefilte fish

1 yellow onion, grated

1 carrot, grated

¼ cup regular mayonnaise

¼ cup matzoh meal

1 teaspoon lemon juice

½ stick margarine (4 tablespoons), melted

3 eggs

Salt and pepper to taste

Paprika (enough to shake over the casserole to give it some color)

Dump fish in colander and wash out gross jelly stuff. (Even if you like the jelly, you still have to wash it off.) Place fish in bowl and mash. Add all other ingredients *except paprika.* If too watery, add a bit more matzoh meal.

Grease an ovenproof glass baking dish or casserole with margarine. Pour mixture into pan, and smooth as you do when you make brownies. Sprinkle paprika on top for color. Cover with foil and bake at 350 degrees for ½ hour.

Remove foil and bake for an additional 20 minutes. Check for doneness by spearing with a knife (as you would check a cake). If the knife comes out only a little wet, it's done. If too wet, place in oven for 5-minute increments and test again.

CHICKEN

(Fleishig)

WHOLE ROAST CHICKEN

Yield: 4–6 servings (more if you can find a bigger chicken)

Whole chicken (3–4 pounds)

3 yellow onions

3 lemons

4 sprigs of fresh rosemary

6 garlic cloves

Garlic powder

Dried parsley

Paprika

Lemon juice

Water

Preheat oven to 350 degrees.

Wash and clean chicken (make certain to look inside and pull out the neck and anything else the butcher put in there in the plastic baggie). Slice onions and line bottom of pan with them (I use a Pyrex pan for this. Use a pan with sides so liquid doesn't spill out). For a more lemony taste, slice 1–2 lemons and layer on top of onions. Throw in rosemary and garlic cloves. Place chicken on top of onions and lemons. Cut remaining lemon in half and squeeze slightly (let some juice remain in lemon) over chicken. Place lemon halves inside chicken. Sprinkle garlic powder, parsley, and paprika over the chicken. Add lemon juice and water to the pan, as much as will cover onion-lemon layer and a little bit of chicken. Place uncovered in oven for 2 hours (or time recommended by butcher, based on size of chicken). If you have a meat thermometer, you can check for doneness if the deepest part of the breast is 180 degrees and the deepest part of the thigh is 190 degrees. Check and baste often—add water if needed.

THE EASIEST ROAST CHICKEN EVER!
Yield: 1–2 pieces per person

Chicken pieces with bone in and skin on (as much as you need for the number
you are serving)
McCormick Montreal Chicken Seasoning with Garlic

Preheat oven to 350 degrees.

Rinse and clean chicken. Place pieces in one layer in Pyrex baking dish (or even easier—aluminum foil roaster that you can throw away!). Sprinkle seasoning on top of the
chicken. Bake until done (1½–2 hours in my oven). To check if chicken is ready, cut into it
and make certain there is no pink and the juices are running clear. It should have a normal,
white chicken color—otherwise it will be chewy (*eww!*).

EMBARRASSINGLY EASY "ITALIAN" CHICKEN
*Everyone goes a little meshugge over this one. Don't give out the recipe—
it's embarrassingly easy—kinda like Shake 'n Bake.*

Chicken pieces with bone in and skin on
Bread crumbs (Check to make sure they're plain, kosher bread crumbs—
some seasoned bread crumbs have cheese in them)
1 big bottle or 2 small bottles noncreamy Italian dressing (feel free to use
fat-free versions)

Preheat oven to 350 degrees. Wash and clean chicken pieces—do not dry. Put some
bread crumbs in plastic bag (the gallon zip-up kind). Place chicken pieces, one at a time,
into the bag with crumbs and shake to coat. Lay chicken pieces in Pyrex pan (no need to
coat the pan). Repeat until every piece is breaded, refilling bag with crumbs as needed.
Pour dressing over chicken, but don't drown it. Place in oven. Bake until juices run clear.
(This is about 1½–2 hours in my oven.)

Note: I really like the way this tastes with a side of spaghetti and tomato sauce.

JANE'S CHICKEN FRANÇAIS

Your kids will think these are "chicken tenders," so you can keep some plain and serve them with ketchup. Also reserve some of the sauce—it's wonderful with plain pasta.

Yield: 6 servings

6 boneless chicken breasts (cut or pounded thin)

4 tablespoons vegetable oil

1 egg

2–3 cups flour

Salt and pepper to taste

1 cup white win

2-ounce jar (dry weight) capers, drained

12-ounce jar artichoke hearts, drained (it's OK if they're marinated)

8 ounces mushrooms, sliced

2 lemons

Pound boneless chicken cutlets thin (you can also slice them in half to make them thinner). Heat 2 tablespoons oil in sauté pan (add more as needed). In a bowl, beat the egg. On a large dinner plate, place a cup of flour, and sprinkle some salt and pepper on top. Then mix carefully so that the salt and pepper are distributed evenly (you will need to add more flour, salt, and pepper as you work through the chicken). Dip the chicken breast in egg, and then dredge the piece in the flour.

Sauté chicken pieces in hot oil until lightly brown on both sides. You will probably be able to cook only a few pieces at a time, depending on the size of your pan. As the chicken pieces are done, remove them from the pan and place in baking dish (I use my trusty 11x14-inch Pyrex).

When all of the chicken is cooked, add wine to pan to deglaze. (This means you scrape the chicken drippings on the pan from when you sautéed the chicken and incorporate them into the sauce you are now making.) Mix the capers, artichoke hearts, mushrooms, juice from lemons, and until warm throughout. Squeeze lemons over sauce. Pour sauce over chicken and serve.

Tip: There is an eggless version of this recipe. Just rinse chicken in water instead of the egg, then dredge in flour as above. This will give it a slightly less "fried" appearance and taste.

CHICKEN MARSALA
Yield: 6 pieces

6 skinless, boneless chicken breasts

4 tablespoons olive oil

2–3 cups flour

Salt and pepper to taste

½ cup Marsala wine

2 cups water

2 chicken bouillon cubes

2-ounce jar (dry weight) capers, drained

1 garlic clove, crushed

¾ pound fresh mushrooms, sliced

Pound boneless chicken breasts thin (you can also slice them in half to make them thinner). Heat 2 tablespoons olive oil in sauté pan (add more as needed). On a large dinner plate, place a cup of flour, and sprinkle some salt and pepper on top. Then mix carefully so that the salt and pepper are distributed evenly (you will need to add more flour, salt, and pepper as you work through the chicken). Dredge chicken pieces in flour. Sauté chicken pieces in pan of hot oil until lightly browned on both sides. You will probably be able to cook only a few pieces at a time, depending on the size of your pan. As the chicken pieces are done, remove them from the pan, and place in baking dish (I use my trusty 11x14-inch Pyrex).

When all of the chicken is cooked, deglaze pan with wine, add water, bouillon, capers, and garlic, and bring to a boil. Add mushrooms and cook for 5 minutes. Pour sauce over chicken. Bake, uncovered, for 30 minutes, then cover dish with foil and bake for an additional 15 minutes.

Tip: This is really nice served over plain pasta (I like angel hair with this recipe).

MEAT

(Fleishig)

CRANBERRY BRISKET

*Yield: 6 servings—enough for a family of four with leftovers
for brisket sandwiches on challah bread!*

3-pound brisket

Salt and pepper

3 tablespoons olive oil

2 yellow onions

4 carrots, cut into chunks (you can also use the baby carrots—
throw in a whole 1-pound bag)

3 smashed garlic cloves

6 whole garlic cloves

2 cups cranberry sauce

Preheat oven to 350 degrees. Season the brisket with salt and pepper. Sauté brisket in a heavy pan with olive oil until it's brown. Remove the brisket to an ovenproof baking dish or aluminum foil roaster (I find metal roasting pans dry out the brisket).

Add onions, carrots, and all the garlic to the pan. Sauté until vegetables are soft (onions should be golden, and you should be able to easily pierce the carrots with a fork). Remove the pan from the heat and add cranberry sauce to the vegetables. (Sometimes I find a cranberry sauce with oranges—this is nice with this recipe!) Pour sauce over brisket. Cook brisket 2 hours, covered. Remove from oven. Allow to rest 10 minutes before serving.

Tip: Allowing chicken or meat to rest before serving is always a good idea. As the food cools it gets juicier.

AUNT BEV'S BRISKET

Yield: 8–10 servings

6-pound first-cut brisket (This is a less fatty cut. Your butcher will understand.)

1 regular-size ketchup bottle (You won't use this much, but this is an old family recipe, so you have to cook like our grandmothers did and just pour until you somehow know you've reached the right amount. Or ask your mom to show you!)

½ cup brown sugar

Put brisket in roasting pan, and cover with ketchup and sugar. Lightly cover pan and bake at 325 degrees until tender (approximately 2½–3 hours).

BALSAMIC STEAK WITH CRÈME DE CASSIS ONIONS

The steak

Steaks (I use kosher rib steaks. I find two people can share one steak. If you have company, you might want to splurge and buy one steak for each person.)

Balsamic vinegar (Buy a bottle. It's hard to say how much you'll need. Basically, you lay the steaks in a baking dish and cover them with balsamic vinegar to marinate them.)

1–2 garlic cloves per steak, crushed

Kosher salt to taste

Coarse pepper to taste

The sauce

2 red onions

3 tablespoons olive oil

1/3 cup crème de cassis

Marinate steaks in balsamic vinegar and crushed garlic for about an hour. Heat a grill pan (or outdoor grill) so it's very hot (you will see steam). This sears the steaks nicely. Before grilling, season the steaks with salt and pepper. Grill to desired doneness. (I usually do 6 minutes per side and then cut into the steak to see how red it is. I like a medium steak, so I remove the steaks when they are pink inside.) Try not to flip the steaks too much, as this dries them out.

Meanwhile, thinly slice onions. Sauté in olive oil. When onion begins to soften, turn flame to low and add splash of crème de cassis. Stir often and allow to caramelize. Serve on top of steak.

FISH

SALMON WITH GRILLED ASPARAGUS

(Pareve—milk or meat)
This is a staple at my house. Sometimes I use the leftovers
for salmon croquettes or salmon salad.
Yield: 4–6 servings

The salmon

> 1½ pounds fresh salmon fillet
> 1 teaspoon ground mustard
> ½ teaspoon ground ginger
> ½ teaspoon garlic powder
> ½ tablespoon dried cilantro or parsley
> (Sometimes I substitute herbes de Provence for the above list)

The asparagus

> Bunch of asparagus
> 4 tablespoons olive oil (enough to drizzle over all the asparagus)

Rinse the salmon fillet with water, and place on broiling pan. Sprinkle herbs on top of the fillet.

Wash asparagus and snap off ends (you can shave the stalks with a vegetable peeler, but this isn't necessary). Place asparagus around the fillet. Drizzle olive oil over the asparagus. Broil about 25 minutes, until inside of salmon is opaque and asparagus begins to blacken. So delicious and healthy!

Tip: I like to combine this with roasted tomatoes and rice or couscous.

SIDE DISHES

GRANDMA HILDA'S CARROT RING

(Pareve—milk or meat)
This was one of my grandma's favorite recipes.
Yield: 8–10 side servings

½ cup Crisco

½ cup brown sugar

3 eggs, separated

1 cup flour

½ teaspoon baking powder

2 cups grated carrots

2 tablespoons lemon juice

1 tablespoon water

Using an electric mixer, cream together Crisco and brown sugar. In a separate clean bowl beat egg whites till they're stiff. Save yolks. In a separate bowl, sift together flour and baking powder. Combine all ingredients *except for egg whites*. Once ingredients are combined, fold in the egg whites. Pour carefully (so as not to soften the egg whites) into a lightly greased casserole dish. Bake at 350 degrees for 1 hour.

Tip: My mom tells me that my grandma used to make this in a Bundt pan. Then she'd invert it onto a plate and fill the hole in the middle of the carrot ring with peas. This was very fancy in the good ol' days!

SAUTÉED SPINACH AND GARLIC

(Pareve)

Yield: 4 side servings

9 ounces fresh spinach leaves

4 garlic cloves, crushed

2–3 tablespoons olive oil

Wash spinach (no need to dry). Place spinach, crushed garlic, and olive oil in large sauté pan. Sauté until wilted.

ROASTED TOMATOES AND GARLIC

(Pareve)

This side dish is wonderful with salmon, steaks, and lamb chops. And it's so easy!

Yield: 4 side servings

1 dry pint cherry or grape tomatoes or 8 ounces baby Roma tomatoes

1 garlic head, cloves separated and peeled

$1/3$ cup olive oil

Wash tomatoes and place in a glass baking dish so tomatoes are all in one layer (just throw them in whole—do not cut). Throw in peeled garlic cloves (as much as you like). Drizzle olive oil over tomatoes and garlic. Place in warm oven at 400 degrees for 1 hour.

ROASTED VEGETABLES

(Pareve)

These are easy, delicious, and healthy!

Vegetables (see list below)

Olive oil (just grab your bottle and pour)

Garlic (a whole, peeled head—use as much as you like)

Balsamic vinegar (optional)

Cut and clean vegetables and place in an ovenproof baking dish so vegetables are all in one layer. Drizzle olive oil and throw in some whole garlic cloves. If you like, you can also drizzle some balsamic vinegar over the veggies, as this will give them a kick. Roast at 450 degrees for the following times:

Asparagus   25–30 minutes

Cauliflower 25–30 minutes

Onions 25–30 minutes

Zucchini 25–30 minutes

Carrots 40–45 minutes

Leeks   40–45 minutes

Butternut squash 40–45 minutes

MASHED BUTTERNUT SQUASH

(Pareve if margarine is used, milchig if butter is used)
Serve this instead of potatoes!
Yield: 6 side servings

1 butternut squash, peeled and cut into large chunks

4 tablespoons margarine (pareve) or butter (milchig)

½ cup brown sugar

Salt to taste

Boil squash in a large pot of water until you can easily pierce with a fork. Drain water. Mash squash as you would potatoes (a potato masher works best, or use a large fork). Add margarine (or butter, if dairy), sugar, and salt to taste. Stir to combine.

Fresh Mango Salsa

(Pareve)

This is a nice partner to fish or chicken. It's really cool and fresh, so I like serving this in the summer with roasted salmon or seared tuna steaks. This would also work well with grilled chicken breasts or with some tortilla chips.

Yield: 4–6 side servings

- 1 large mango
- 1 large tomato
- 1 avocado
- 1 large red onion
- 1 lime

Cut mango, tomato, avocado, and onion into small chunks (about ¼-inch cubes). Toss. Squeeze lime juice over the salsa and mix. See? How easy was that?

Chef Patrick Moulet's Garden Baby Vegetables in Dijon Chardonnay Sauce

(Pareve)

Patrick is a chef with Ridgewells Caterer in Washington, D.C. This sauce is also wonderful with a simple grilled chicken breast.

Yield: 12 servings

The Dijon chardonnay sauce

- 1 tablespoon shallots, diced
- ½ cup white wine (chardonnay)
- 1 pint low-sodium store-bought brown sauce
- 1 tablespoon Dijon mustard
- Salt and pepper to taste

Combine shallots and white wine in a saucepan over low heat. Reduce by half at a simmer. Add brown sauce and bring back to a simmer. Add Dijon mustard to the pan, mixing well with a whisk or fork. Taste and adjust seasoning with salt and pepper to taste.

The garden baby vegetables

24 baby carrots

24 baby zucchini

24 yellow baby sunburst squash

2 tablespoons olive oil

Salt and pepper to taste

Bring a 6-quart pot of salted water to boil. Wash the vegetables and trim the tops off. Fill a bowl with ice and water, and keep on the side.

When water boils, add the carrots. Cook these for a few minutes until tender. Remove from water with a slotted spoon and place in ice bath. Repeat with zucchini and then yellow squash. Remove all vegetables from ice water and drain.

Heat a large sauté pan over medium to high heat. Add all vegetables and ¼ cup of water to the pan. Add 2 tablespoons of olive oil and salt and pepper to taste. Simmer until heated through.

Tip: To serve, I put the veggies on a pretty plate and drizzle the sauce over them.

CHEF PATRICK MOULET'S ROASTED GARLIC YUKON GOLD MASHED POTATO CASSEROLE

(Pareve)

Yield: 12 servings

3 pounds Yukon Gold potatoes, peeled and cubed

1 tablespoon kosher salt

6 garlic cloves, peeled

½ cup olive oil

6 ounces margarine

Salt and pepper to taste

Preheat oven to 350 degrees. Put cubed potatoes in a saucepot. Add water so the potatoes are submerged. Add 1 tablespoon of kosher salt, cover pot, and bring to boil. Reduce to a simmer and cook until the potatoes are easily pierced with a fork.

Put garlic in aluminum foil with ½ tablespoon of olive oil. Roast in oven until brown and soft (about ½ hour–1 hour).

Drain potatoes and put them back into the saucepot. Add the roasted garlic to the saucepot. With a smasher, mash the potatoes and roasted garlic together. Add margarine and remaining olive oil to potato mix. Stir until it's all soft and smooth. If needed, add more olive oil to make potatoes more creamy. Season with salt and pepper to taste.

Spray a casserole dish with vegetable oil. Place potatoes in dish and put in oven. Cook until heated through or golden brown on top (1–1 ½ hours).

This can be prepared the day before. To reheat, cover dish and put in 350-degree oven for about an hour.

KUGELS

In case you didn't know, *kugel* is Yiddish for a pudding, usually made with noodles.

ONION KUGEL
(Pareve if margarine is used, milchig if butter is used)
Yield: 12–15 servings

3–4 onions, minced

Margarine (or butter if milchig)

1 pound egg noodles (I like the No Yolks brand and buy the broad noodles)

4 eggs

Pepper

Bread crumbs (pareve)

Sauté onions in margarine (or butter) until golden. Cook, then drain, the noodles. Grease a baking dish with margarine or butter. Dump onions into noodles, and add eggs and pepper. Pour mixture into pan. Shake some bread crumbs on the top to lightly cover, and dot with margarine or butter (¼ teaspoon every inch or so). Bake at 350 degrees 30–45 minutes, or until golden brown.

Strawberry Kugel

(Pareve)

Yield: 12–15 servings

12–16 ounces medium noodles (I like No Yolks broad noodles)

4 large eggs

1 teaspoon vanilla

8-ounce jar strawberry preserves

Margarine to grease pan

Cinnamon

Cook noodles as directed. In a separate bowl, beat eggs and vanilla together. Add cooked noodles to the egg mixture. Add the jar of strawberry preserves and mix with noodles. Pour into a margarine-greased pan. Sprinkle cinnamon on top, so it lightly covers the casserole (this adds color and flavor). Bake for 1 hour at 350 degrees.

Aunt Karen's Apple and Raisin Kugel

(Pareve)

Yield: 12–15 servings

1 pound noodles

6 eggs

½ stick margarine, plus extra to grease the pan

1 cup applesauce (chunky is good)

½ cup granulated sugar

½ cup brown sugar

2 teaspoons vanilla

1 cup raisins

Cinnamon

Cook noodles as directed. After you drain the noodles, combine with remaining ingredients. Pour into a margarine-greased pan. Sprinkle cinnamon on top. Bake at 350 degrees for 1 hour.

DESERTS

Jewish Apple Cake

(Pareve)

*My mom says this is called "Jewish Apple Cake" because Grandma Hilda made it
every Rosh Hashanah when we are supposed to eat apples.
Yield: 8 big pieces or 10 regular pieces*

The batter

3 cups flour

2½ cups sugar

1 cup vegetable oil

5 unbeaten eggs

½ teaspoon salt (optional)

⅓ cup orange juice

2½ teaspoons vanilla

3 teaspoons baking powder

Combine all the above ingredients in one large bowl and mix with a wooden spoon
until smooth.

The apple mixture

8–10 apples, peeled and cut thin (Mom recommends Granny Smith apples)

2 teaspoons cinnamon

3 teaspoons sugar

Combine all of the above ingredients in a separate bowl.

In a greased and floured tube pan place 1 layer of the apple mixture on the bottom,
then pour enough batter over to cover. Continue to layer the apple mixture, then the batter.
Top with apple mixture. Bake at 350 degrees for 1 hour and 45 minutes.

Grandma Hilda's Mandel Bread

(Pareve)

This is so good on Saturday afternoon with coffee.

Yield: 36 pieces

½ cup Crisco

¼ cup oil

1 cup sugar

3 eggs

3 cups flour

2 teaspoons baking powder

2 teaspoons vanilla

Hot water

½ cup cocoa powder

Preheat oven to 350 degrees.

Cream together Crisco, oil, and sugar. Add eggs, flour, baking powder, and vanilla. Mix well to form dough.

Divide dough into four sections and place on plate or cutting board. In a small bowl, make a paste of hot water and cocoa powder and mix it into one of the sections of dough. You will now have three vanilla dough sections and one cocoa dough section.

Take the cocoa dough section and divide into three. Roll each of these three so they look like hot dogs. Take the three vanilla dough sections and roll each of them into shapes resembling hot dog buns. Slice them open so they really resemble open hot dog buns. (Do not slice all the way through.)

Now, place one cocoa section into one of the vanilla "hot dog bun" rolls and roll, twist, and shmush to combine. You will end up with three mixed dough sections that still resemble rolls.

Place the rolls onto a greased and lightly floured cookie sheet. Bake for 35–40 minutes. Remove from oven and slice each roll into mandel bread–looking slices (the rolls will still be soft). Carefully separate the new slices and return them to the cookie sheet and put back in the oven for another 5–10 minutes.

CHOCOLATE MOUSSE

(This one is amazing, and if you can find pareve chocolate chips, it's pareve!
Otherwise, it's milchig.)
Yield: 8–10 servings

8 ounces semisweet chocolate

¼ cup water

½ cup sugar

5 eggs, separated

1 teaspoon vanilla

Melt chocolate with water and sugar in a double boiler. Stir until velvety and thoroughly blended. Set in a pan of cold water. Add egg yolks and vanilla. The mixture should be semifluid—if it's too firm, add up to 5 tablespoons of *tepid* water.

Beat egg whites until stiff but not dry. Fold into chocolate.

Spoon into individual dessert cups. Chill 4–6 hours. Enjoy!

CARROT CAKE

(Pareve, unless topped with cream cheese icing and then it's milchig)
Yield: 8 big pieces or 10 regular pieces

The cake

2 cups flour

1 teaspoon baking soda

2 teaspoons cinnamon

1 teaspoon salt

1½ cups vegetable oil

3 eggs

2 cups sugar

2 cups grated raw carrots

1 cup well-drained crushed pineapple

1 cup grated coconut

1 teaspoon vanilla

Preheat oven to 350 degrees.

Measure flour into sifter. Add baking soda, cinnamon, and salt, and sift together. In mixing bowl, beat together oil, eggs, and sugar until thoroughly mixed. Gradually blend in flour mixture. Fold in carrots, pineapple, and coconut. Stir in vanilla.

Grease and lightly flour a tube pan. Bake for 1 hour.

The icing

4 ounces cream cheese, softened

½ pound confectioners' sugar (approximately $1^7/_8$ cup)

1 teaspoon vanilla

½ stick butter

Place all ingredients in a bowl and beat until smooth.

FANCY-SCHMANCY (EASY-PEASY) DESSERT

(Pareve or milchig, depending on the chocolate)

Yield: as many cups as you buy

Store-bought chocolate cups (dark chocolate is pareve, milk chocolate is milchig)

Fresh berries

Whipped cream (nondairy is pareve)

Fill chocolate cups with berries and top with whipped cream. If you want to be super-fancy add a sprig of mint or some chocolate shavings on top.

9

Projects

THE GREAT THING ABOUT making your Shabbat items with your children is that it makes Shabbat special for them—it gives them some ownership of the occasion and builds self-esteem to know that you value their creations more than the fancy silver candlesticks your parents' neighbors gave you as a wedding present. This book is about connecting our children with our heritage and traditions in a meaningful way. And one easy way is to find some time to work on a project together.

Now, I'll admit that while I have a lot of fun making stuff, I am no Martha when it comes to crafts. Believe me, if I can do it, you can. All of these projects have been tested by me and my kids. They are designed to be easy, inexpensive, and fast (I seriously have no patience). All materials were found at my local craft store—nothing fancy-schmancy here. You'll notice some materials are used over and over again so they can be used in several projects. My faves are Sculpey (or any bakable clay you can find), flat-backed gems, a glue gun (a must-have), wooden candlesticks, and various colors of acrylic paint. I also like to use stuff from around the house—buttons, old dish towels, extra pillowcases, and even old toys. The best thing is, we have used everything we've made! It's wonderful having beautiful things on your table, but I love to mix my antique silver candlesticks with the plastic kiddush cups with the fake-o gems glued on. This is what makes my Shabbat table my own. Have fun.

SHABBAT BOXES

SHABBAT BOX

This project was designed by internationally renowned
Judaica artist, Phillip Ratner.

Wooden cigar box

Paint

Any embellishments you choose

Decorate the box to make it special to your family. Paint it, glue glass beads or stones to it, decoupage family pictures or pictures from magazines that make you think of Shabbat, embellish it with lace or other fabric. Use your imagination to make it special and unique to your family.

CURIOUSLY STRONG SHABBAT BOX

Got room in your bag for mints?
Then you have room for a traveling Shabbat box.

Altoids box (or similar)

Flat-backed gems

Bakable clay (like Sculpey)

Shabbat candles

1. Glue gems onto tin box. Tip: plan pattern before you glue.
2. You may need to cut candles to fit into box. (This isn't
   exactly kosher, but the fact that you will observe Shabbat while on vacation is more important. If you can use
   a bigger box that fits the candles without cutting them
   down, that's better.) Measure remaining space, and form

a block of clay that will fit into the box along with the candles.

3. Press candles into clay to make holes for candles to stand.

4. You may press extra gems into clay before baking. Bake clay according to directions. (You may need to glue the gems in again, but this is rare.)

5. Pack and enjoy Shabbat wherever you go!

TABLECLOTHS

MESSY SHABBAT TABLECLOTH

Use this for your Shabbat table, and any grape juice or wine spills will just enhance the beauty of the tablecloth.

White bedsheet (large enough to cover your table)
Watercolor paint

1. Take a white bedsheet.
2. Have your children use watercolor paint to make splashes of color on the cloth. Once dry, the paint should become permanent. Check box to make sure; if not the paint will wash out in the laundry.

FLOWERS

PAPER FLOWERS

Here's a classic. It's sure to make your young children happy when they see their "flowers" on the table.

For each flower

8 sheets of colored tissue paper (pick the size based on how big you want the flower to be. You can also add more sheets to make the flower fuller.)

1 green pipe cleaner

1. Place papers one on top of another.
2. Beginning at one end (shorter end if sheet is a rectangle), fold up about ½ inch and crease.
3. Flip over and keeping the initial fold in place, fold again about ½ inch.
4. Flip over and repeat until the entire paper is folded in accordion pleats.
5. Find the middle of the length of the folded paper. Take the pipe cleaner and knot the end around this midpoint. This forms the stem.
6. Carefully, beginning with one side, pull up top layer of sheet toward the middle (or stem). You will now see the "petals" forming.
7. Repeat on other side.
8. Repeat layer by layer until entire flower has been pulled up.

FELT FLOWERS

For each flower

    1 piece felt (any color but green, to distinguish it from leaves)

    1 piece green felt

    1 green pipe cleaner

1. Cut nongreen felt in the shape of a flower (a simple five-petal design).
2. Make a small hole in the center of the flower.
3. Cut two leaves from the green felt.
4. Make small holes near the base of the leaves.
5. Thread the flower and the leaves on the pipe cleaner.
6. "Knot" the end of the pipe cleaner that is closest to the flower (this will prevent the flower from slipping off).
7. Bend the pipe cleaner so that the flower is facing you when you put it in a vase (this also stops it from slipping down the stem).

YARMULKES

Stamp Art Yarmulkes

Individualize the stamps to make a unique yarmulke for each member of the family,
or buy letter stamps to make monograms.

Plain white yarmulkes (I used both satin and suede)*

Ink pad

Stamps

    *These you won't find in your local craft store.

    You can buy inexpensive yarmulkes at any Jewish gift store.

1. Buy plain yarmulkes.
2. Select ink pad and stamp.
3. Stamp away!

Optional: Decorate with puffy paint. Caution: This is messy. Make sure you and your child wear old clothes, or cover your clothes well while using puffy paint. Make certain paint has completely dried before handling. I learned this after I decided it would be fun to have a bunch of girls make slippers using socks and puffy paint during one of Sofie's sleepover parties. Let's just say that evidence of this project still remains on my basement carpet and my friends' car seats!

137

My Name Yarmulkes

Markers

Plain white satin yarmulkes

Embroidery hoop

Embroidery thread

Needle

1. Have your child write his or her name with a marker on a plain yarmulke or draw a design.
2. Do a simple cross-stitch (sew *x*'s) over the marker to preserve the writing.

TZEDAKAH BOX

Tzedakah Block Box

Wooden toy blocks of any kind. It's fun to mix and match from those you have around your house. I ended up using forty-five for my box, but I used two triangle blocks together to form a rectangle and mix larger building blocks with smaller alphabet blocks.

Glue gun. If you don't have one, go right now and buy one. It's so easy and fun to use and available at any craft store for under $10. You can also use wood glue for this project.

1. Place blocks on a flat surface, and shape into a square base of any size (mine is approximately 5x5 inches).

2. Once you are happy with the arrangement, use the glue gun to glue the sides of the blocks together.

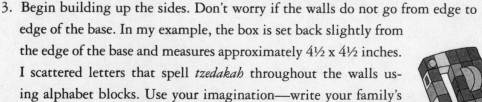

3. Begin building up the sides. Don't worry if the walls do not go from edge to edge of the base. In my example, the box is set back slightly from the edge of the base and measures approximately 4½ x 4½ inches. I scattered letters that spell *tzedakah* throughout the walls using alphabet blocks. Use your imagination—write your family's name, your children's names, the name of the charity you are collecting for, or simply place letters at random for color.

4. Once you are happy with the arrangement, use the glue gun to glue the edges together.

5. Set the box aside and shape the lid. The lid should be the same dimensions as the base (again, in my example it is 5 x 5 inches). Shape the lid so there is an opening in the middle to allow you to drop coins in without removing the lid.

6. Once you are happy with the arrangement, use the glue gun to glue the edges together.

7. Take an arched block and glue it to the lid to serve as a handle. You can also construct a handle out of Tinkertoys.

8. Place lid on box.

9. Decide with your children what charity you would like to contribute to.
Variations: Use Lincoln Logs or any other wooden building toy. If your children are into cars, why not glue a car to the lid for a handle? Or glue flat wooden animals to the sides. Or decorate with beads or small plastic doll shoes. Whatever sparks your children's imaginations.

CANDLESTICKS

SHABBAT CANDLESTICKS

This project was created by internationally renowned Judaica artist, Phillip Ratner.
They were designed to fit into your Shabbat box.

Blocks of Sculpey (or other bakable clay)
Glass candleholders (You can find these at your local Judaica gift shop.)
Paintbrush
Gold acrylic paint

1. Work with clay until pliable. Mold into desired shape (you can roll it into "snakes" for braiding or twisting). Test for balance.

2. Insert candleholder. Twist candleholder into clay to create a larger hole for reinserting the glass candleholder once clay is baked.

3. Remove glass and bake clay according to directions.

4. When cool, apply accents with gold paint.

5. When paint is dry, insert candleholders and candles.

ELEGANT BEADED CANDLESTICKS

These were inspired by an expensive pair I saw in a gift shop window.

Chocolate brown paint (Feel free to choose another color; this is what I used.)

Unfinished wood candlesticks*

Tiny glass beads (bronze, gold, and black)

Golden thread

Paintbrush

Wood glue

1. Paint candlesticks and allow to dry.
2. Thread beads on thread (do not cut thread from spool). Use as many as you like depending on how heavily beaded you want your finished project to be. Allow beads to hang down at the bottom of the thread (the end with the spool). You will be working with just the thread at first. Imagine sitting at a chair holding the end of the thread in your hand and the thread continues down to the spool which is on the floor. As you string the beads onto the thread, they will slide down the thread and stop at the spool. Leave them there until you are ready to bring up two or three at a time to decorate the candlestick.
3. Using the paintbrush, brush glue onto main body of candlestick. (I left the base of the candlestick plain.) Do not put glue over entire candle stick at once. Work small sections at a time.
4. Press end of thread into glue to start wrapping. Brush more glue over top of the thread end to secure it to the candlestick.
5. Continue pressing the thread into the glued part of the candlestick and begin wrapping up the candlestick—add more glue as you wrap.
6. Every so often, bring up two beads from the thread and press into the glue.
7. Continue wrapping and bringing up beads randomly.
8. Finish at top of the main body of the candlestick. (I left the top plain to match the base.)
9. Brush more glue over top of thread end to secure.

*I think it is safer to use an aluminum foil or glass insert for the candles, especially when using wood candlesticks!

BUTTON CANDLESTICKS

Paintbrush

Paint—any color!

Unfinished wood candlesticks*

Glue dots (These are kid-friendly, easy to use, and not messy.)

Buttons with flat back (It's your choice what kind to use, but I found that smaller works better.)

1. Paint candlesticks and allow to dry.
2. Glue buttons to candlesticks. Glue dots are so easy. They come on a strip in various sizes. Simply press the button onto the glue dot, and when you lift the button up, the glue stays on the button. Then, when you press the button onto the candlestick, it stays—no mess!
3. Continue until candlestick is fully covered with buttons or until your children have decided they're done.

*I think it is safer to use an aluminum foil or glass insert for the candles, especially when using wood candlesticks!

ALMOND BLOSSOM CANDLESTICKS

In Exodus (the parashah is Terumah if you want to look it up) we learn the cups of the candlesticks in the Tabernacle were shaped like almond blossoms. Discovering this inspired these candlesticks! Use bakable clay to make your own almond blossom candlesticks, just like in the days of Moses. These are Sofie's favorite candleholders.

For two candleholders

Bakable clay (like Sculpey) in pink, peach, green, and white (Of course, if your kids are obsessed with any other colors at the moment, you can use those!)

Plastic knife

Shabbat candle

1. Beginning with pink block of clay 2-inch x 1-inch x ½-inch (standard size for bakable clay blocks), roll a ball approximately 2 inches in diameter.
2. Cut ball in half using a plastic knife.
3. Cup one of the halves in the palm of your left hand with flat side up. Use your right hand to push and twist a Shabbat candle into the clay. Mold the clay up around the candle so that you form a cup approximately 1½ inches tall with a 1-inch diameter. (Reverse directions if you are left-handed.)
4. Remove candle and repeat with other half. Set cups aside.
5. Using peach clay, make 10 balls approximately ½ inch in diameter.
6. Cup a ball in the palm of your left hand and use your right thumb to press down into the ball—keep your left hand cupped so the finished disk is slightly curved and approximately 1 inch in diameter. Repeat with all 10 balls.
7. Imagine a small circle. Take 5 peach disks (rounded side down) and press the bottom ends of the disks together to form the petals of the flower. The disks will overlap slightly. Flatten the clay slightly so that the petals stay together. Repeat with other 5 disks.
8. Take pink cups and place in center of the petals. Mush slightly so that the cup adheres to the flower. You may need to curve the outer edges of the petals slightly so that they look like real petals.
9. Take the green clay and form 10 balls ¼" in diameter.
10. Using your thumb, press and stretch green balls into teardrop shapes approximately 1 x ½ inch. These are the leaves.
11. Press leaves to the bottom of the flowers in between each of the peach petals, making sure the leaves show (they should extend slightly beyond the peach petals). Use 5 per flower.
12. Take white clay and pull 10 small pieces and roll into little logs approximately ¼ x ⅛ inch (they should look like Tic Tac mints).
13. Press one tiny white piece on the base of each flower petal extending from the pink cup out to the edge of the petal (they will come only about halfway up the petal—this is just to add some detail).

14. Bake clay according to directions on the box. (I put mine in a toaster oven at 275 degrees for 20 minutes.)
15. Remove and cool.

Caution: You cannot put a lit candle directly in these candleholders. The clay will burn. Put foil candleholders in the flowers first to protect the clay from the flame.

LEGO CANDLESTICKS

Rectangular Legos (or other similar building toy)
Aluminum foil candleholders

1. Lay two rectangular Legos parallel to each other.
2. Press two other Legos across the first two to create a square, making sure to keep an opening in the middle.
3. Continue building by repeating steps 1 and 2 until candlestick is desired height.
4. Repeat to create second candlestick (of course, your kids are building these so they don't have to be identical).
5. Place aluminum foil candleholder in each candlestick to hold candles.

CHALLAH COVERS

GROOVY TIE-DYE CHALLAH COVER

This is a mom's version of tie-dye—using food coloring!

White pillowcase
10 small rubber bands
4 small plastic bowls for food coloring
Water
Dishcloth or other rag to protect your kitchen counter
Optional: fabric pen, glue, glitter, trimming

Tip: Wipe up any spilled food coloring from your countertop ASAP to prevent discoloration. You can clean the counter with water and bleach or something like Soft Scrub if simply wiping doesn't work.

1. Grab a section of the pillowcase and twist. Secure twists with rubber bands. Tip: You can also cut the pillowcase in two, if you have more than one child working on this. When you're done, you can alternate using them from week to week. If you do cut the pillowcase, ask your mom to hem it!

2. Repeat step 1 in various sections of case until cloth is fully bunched and twisted and tied.

3. Fill each bowl with warm water, and drip food coloring in each bowl to create a bowl of red, a bowl of green, a bowl of yellow, and a bowl of blue. (For purple, mix red and blue together; for orange, mix yellow and red.)

4. Dip each section into a different color of food color dye.

5. When each section is colored, place dyed cloth on dish towel to dry. Don't use newspaper or paper towel, because the dye may soak through the paper to the counter.

6. Allow to dry overnight.

7. The next morning (or when it's dry), remove rubber bands and untwist. It will be very wrinkly, so you may want to put it in the dryer to smooth out.

8. If you like, you can write "Challah" or "Shabbat" or "Shabbat Shalom" on the case, using fabric pen. Or you can get fancy using glue and glitter: simply write the words in glue, sprinkle glitter on top, and shake off any excess glitter—glitter will stick only to the glue, so only lettering will be glittered. Or you can use puffy paint—sometimes glitter still appears on my table!

9. Another idea to finish the project, instead of (or in addition to) the words, is to add trim—like lace or a pretty grosgrain ribbon along the edge—or even sew fun buttons or beads in any design your child wants. (I have one with a Star of David.) Go nuts with it!

Caution: Don't wash your finished project. Unlike traditional tie-dye, food coloring will wash out. At least it's easy enough to make again!

CHALLAH COVER

This project was designed by internationally renowned
Judaica artist, Phillip Ratner.

White handkerchief

4 permanent or fabric markers

Divide handkerchief into four boxes—boxes do not have to be same shape or size—use your imagination. In one box, write the word *Shabbat* in Hebrew or English. In the second box, draw a challah. In the third box, draw a kiddush cup. In the fourth and final box, draw Shabbat candles. Use only four colors (plus the white of the handkerchief).

KIDDUSH CUPS

DISPOSABLE KIDDUSH CUPS

Here's an easy and fun project to do with the children while they're waiting
for Shabbat dinner to be served.

Plastic (disposable) cups

Foam shapes with adhesive backs (You can find these at many craft stores.)

Give each child a plastic cup. Spread out a variety of foam shape stickers (I found sports shapes, flowers, and farm animals). Allow the children to decorate their cups.

Finished cups become their kiddush cup to use during Shabbat dinner. Easy cleanup because you just throw them away!

145

KIDDUSH CUP

This project was designed by internationally renowned Judaica artist, Phillip Ratner.

Blocks of Sculpey (or other bakable clay)

Glass candleholder (You can find these at your local Judaica gift shop.)

Paintbrush

Gold acrylic paint

1. Work with clay until pliable. Mold into desired shape (can roll into "snakes" for braiding or twisting). Test for balance.
2. Insert candleholder. Twist candleholder into clay to create a larger hole for reinserting the glass candleholder once clay is baked.
3. Remove glass and bake clay according to directions.
4. When cool, apply accents with gold paint.
5. When paint is dry, insert glass candleholder and use as a cup.

JEWELED KIDDUSH CUPS

So easy, yet so fancy-schmancy!

School glue

Flat-backed gems

Plastic wineglasses

Glue gems onto glasses.

Tip: Hold gems in place for a minute to help them adhere to where you want them. If the glue is too wet, the gems will slide down the glass.

NETILAT YADAYIM TOWEL

(Hand-washing towel)

Dish towel   Children's hands

Fabric paint   Paintbrush

1. Lay out a clean dish towel.
2. Pour paint into a pan or bowl.
3. Have a child press palms of hands into paint and then onto the towel.
4. Paint the words *wash hands* on the towel (or the Hebrew prayer if you are ambitious!).

HAVDALAH

HAVDALAH CANDLE

3 or 4 sheets of beeswax. Select different colors of wax for a very pretty effect when the candles are braided together.
3 or 4 wicks
Tip: These materials are not as easy to find in the craft stores as they used to be, but if you search "beeswax sheets" you'll find lots of Internet sites that sell them inexpensively. You may have to order sets of twenty-four sheets, so why not invite another family over for Shabbat dinner on Friday night, and have the kids make their candles as you finish preparing dinner. They'll be all set to celebrate havdalah on Saturday night!

1. Follow the directions that come with the sheets. In some cases, they advise you to warm up the sheets in a toaster oven to soften; other products you can just roll without heating.
2. Cut a piece of wick 1½ inches longer than the height of your candle. (I just use the shorter edge of the beeswax for my height—this eliminates cutting.)
3. Decide which side of the sheet of wax is the length of the finished candle (for example, the sheet is a 9 x 11 inch rectangle and you would like the candle to be 9 inches). Lay the wick parallel to this side, setting it in about ⅛ of an inch from the edge to allow you to roll. Make certain the excess wick extends beyond the top of the wax so that you will be able to light the candle. Fold the edge over

the wick and continue to roll the wax to form a long candle. Don't roll the entire sheet as this makes the candle thick and more difficult to braid. Stop rolling after approximately 5 inches of the wax sheet has been rolled up. It's easiest to use a box cutter to cut the wax, but a kitchen or steak knife will work also.

4. Repeat with the other 2 or 3 wicks and sheets of wax.
5. When the candles are finished begin to braid.

For 3 candles: Braid as you would a hair plait. Lay all 3 candles side by side. Pinch together the bottoms of the candles (the end without the wick). Beginning with the left candle, lift slightly and place in between the other 2 candles so that it now becomes the middle candle. Next, take the right candle, lift slightly, and place in between the other candles so that it is now the middle. Alternate from left to right until the three are completely joined. It may help to flatten the candle as it comes together.

For 4 candles: Braid as you would a challah loaf. Lay all 4 candles side by side. Pinch together the bottoms of the candles (the end without the wick). Beginning with the left candle, weave over and under the other 3 candles until it becomes the rightmost candle. Repeat with the candle that is now on the left side until the 4 are completely joined. Again, it may help to flatten the candle as it comes together.

SPICE BOXES

Spice Bag

Small mesh bag (like the ones used for jewelry)
Spices (cinnamon stick, cloves, bay leaves, rosemary, etc.)

Fill your bag with various spices (how easy is this one!).

Milk Carton Spice Box

This will look like a little house for your besamim.

½ pint paper milk carton (the kind the kids buy at school)

Straight pin

Spices (cinnamon stick, cloves, bay leaves, rosemary, etc.)

Tape

1 Styrofoam cup

Glue (glue gun is too hot for this project; use good ol' white school glue!)

Dry pasta (like elbow pasta)

Gold paint (or any color)

1. Wash and dry out the empty milk carton.
2. Use the pin to carefully poke holes around the top or sides of carton (so you will be able to smell the spices).
3. Fill the carton with spices.
4. Tape the carton shut.
5. Invert the Styrofoam cup (so open end is now the base) and glue the carton to the cup.
6. Glue pasta onto milk carton.
7. Paint the box and the cup.

Tip: Add some sparkle by gluing flat-backed gems to the Styrofoam cup.

10

Summaries of Weekly Torah Portions and Family Discussion Questions

THE CONVERSATION MY FAMILY NOW HAS around our Friday night table is one of the most wonderful ingredients that make this dinner special. I turn to the weekly Torah portion for inspiration for these discussions. I had to take a deep breath when I first initiated these talks, but what Jonathan and I have learned about our children—how they think and what they believe—and watching them mature as participants in thoughtful discussions is worth whatever trepidation I initially felt about bringing the Torah to our Shabbat table. I hope that chapter 4 encouraged you to try this with your family, and to make it as easy and comfortable as possible, I'm giving you quick summaries and family-appropriate discussion questions.

To create these summaries, I read the Soncino Pentateuch, which I used to learn the Torah and haftorah portions for my bat mitzvah. I happen to like the old-time phrasing. For me, phrases like "goest thou" and "lookest thou" lend a Biblical feel to the reading. However, you may want to consider a more recent version for a more modern translation (like *Etz Hayim* or the Plaut commentary). Some of the interpretations are my own, some are from the commentaries found in the Soncino text, and some are from the Midrash. The Midrash is a collection of interpretations of the Torah by the great rabbis of the sixth century CE and incorporates both halachah (law) and Aggadah (folklore or stories that illustrate the law).

In writing these summaries, I tried to be as straightforward as possible (I couldn't resist adding a few comments here and there), but my goal was to provide a somewhat clean canvas for your own interpretation. I encourage you to get a copy of the Torah (Five Books of Moses) to read the entire portion, or parashah, and decide what catches your attention and gives meaning to you and your family. I've tried to provide several questions for various ages. As you read them, select the ones you believe are most suitable for your children.

The parashahs are listed here in order from the first, Bereshit, to the last, Vezot Ha berachah. Each parashah is named for the first significant word in the chapter. To learn which parashah is being read each week, check with your synagogue, Jewish calendar, or other reputable source (a list is provided in the back of this book).

GENESIS
Bereshit

Bereshit means "In the beginning" and "bereshit" is the first word in the Torah. Bereshit is the story of creation. On the first day, God divides the light from the darkness and creates day and night. On the second day, He creates heaven and earth. On the third day, He creates land and sea and all vegetation. On the fourth day, God creates the heavenly lights (stars, planets, etc.), also known as luminaries. On the fifth day, God creates the creatures of the sea and the birds in the air. On the sixth day, God creates the animals of the land and man (male and female). God gives humankind dominion over the earth and all its creatures. God commands us to "Be fruitful and multiply." And on the seventh day God rests. It is significant to note that after each day of creating, God looks upon what He has created and declares it "good."

Man, who is named Adam, names all the creatures. God creates woman so that man will not be alone—she is named Eve. God gives Adam and Eve the Garden of Eden, and tells them that they must eat from every tree, but not from the tree of knowledge, for if they eat from that tree, they will die. A serpent persuades Eve to eat from the Tree, convincing her that if she eats, she will not die, but be like God and know the difference between good and evil. Eve tastes the fruit and then tempts Adam to eat. God, of course, knows what they have done and punishes them, saying that Eve will hereafter have pain in childbirth and Adam will have to work for his food. They are cast out from the Garden of Eden.

Adam and Eve leave the garden and have two sons, Cain and Abel. Abel becomes a shepherd and Cain a farmer ("a tiller of the ground"). One day, the two brothers make separate offerings to God. Abel gives God the best of his flock, but Cain makes a half-hearted offering. God favors Abel because he gave to God from his heart, causing Cain to become jealous and kill Abel. When God confronts Cain and asks, "Where is Abel, thy brother?" Cain answers, "Am I my brother's keeper?" God punishes Cain by cursing him to forever wander the earth, and since Cain has spilt his brother's blood on the ground, nothing will grow from the ground for him.

Cain begs for forgiveness and fears that since he will be a wanderer, he will be an easy target for anyone who happens upon him. God declares that anyone who kills Cain will be punished sevenfold and puts a special mark on Cain to indicate this protection. (The Soncino commentary notes that the phrase "the brand of Cain" has come to be equated with a murderer. The rabbis explain that this is incorrect. The mark is a sign that Cain was a repentant sinner.) Cain leaves Eden and ultimately settles east of Eden, in the land of Nod.

QUESTIONS FOR DISCUSSION

Why does God "rest"? Does God get tired?

Why does God declare His creations to be "good"? What does "good" mean?

The rabbis tell us that since the fish were the first creatures to be created and that they never close their eyes, they were the witnesses to the Creation. What do you think of that idea? Does it change your opinion of fish?

Each day there is a balance to what is created: light and dark, heaven and earth, fish and birds, etc. Could one have been created without the other? What does this say about men and women?

Would you eat from the tree of knowledge?

What if the knowledge from the tree was knowledge of evil and that by eating we could now see (or know) evil and it is that knowledge that destroyed the Garden of Eden? In other words, we can never see the world as a paradise once we know evil exists.

What does it mean to be your brother's (or sister's) keeper?

Are Cain and Abel another "pair" of the Creation? What do each of them represent about humanity?

Noach

In the second parashah, the Torah jumps many years to tell the story of Noah and his sons. Noah is a good and righteous man living in an unrighteous generation. God speaks to Noah and tells him that He is going to cause a great flood to cover the earth and destroy all living things. But since God sees goodness and righteousness in Noah, He has decided that Noah and his family will be saved. God instructs Noah to build an ark (building materials and dimensions are specified) and gives him seven days to gather all the animals on earth. Noah is to gather two of each creature so that they may replenish the earth after the flood. After the ark is built and Noah; his sons, Shem, Ham, and Japheth, and their families; and all creatures of the earth are safely in the ark, the rain begins. And just as God told Noah, it rains for forty days and forty nights. All other living things on earth perish. The waters last for 150 days.

Finally, God sends a wind to ebb the flood, and the ark comes to rest on Mount Ararat. Noah sends a dove to find dry land. When the dove comes back, Noah knows there is no land for it to rest. Noah waits seven days and sends the dove out again. Once again the dove comes back, this time with a freshly plucked olive leaf. Noah waits another seven days. This time the dove does not come back, meaning it has found land. Noah and his family leave the ark along with all the creatures of the earth. God tells Noah and his family to "be fruitful and multiply." Then He promises Noah that He will never again flood the earth and destroy all living things. He makes the rainbow as a sign of His covenant. From then on, whenever it rains, a rainbow may be seen in the clouds as a reminder of God's promise.

It may also be interesting to note that chapter 9, line 18 of the parashah describes

Noah's son Ham as the father of Canaan. We will learn from later stories that the Canaanites are a wicked people.

QUESTIONS FOR DISCUSSION

Why doesn't Noah try to argue with God and convince Him not to destroy the earth? Aren't we commanded to speak up to try to save our fellow man?

After God destroys humankind because it has become wicked, why does He allow Ham to be saved when it is mentioned at the end of the chapter that Ham goes on to father wicked people? Did God know that Ham's children will be wicked?

Why did God choose water as the way to destroy all life? How would the story be different if God had chosen a fire or famine or poison or illness?

Lech Lecha

A lot happens in this chapter.

The chapter begins with Abram receiving the call from God. (Now, you may be thinking, "Oh, I know this story. When Abram was a little boy, he smashed all the idols in his father's shop." Well, that story is not found in the Torah. It's found in both the Koran and the Midrash.) At this moment, Abram turns from his polytheistic religion and gathers his wife, Sarai; his nephew, Lot; all their belongings; their servants; and various people ("souls," as they are referred to, who believe as Abram believes and have decided to follow him and accept one God). Abram and his household journey to Canaan, as God instructed him.

When they reach Canaan, Abram builds an altar to God (somewhere between Beth-el and Ai). Abram is concerned that the land is already inhabited and even more importantly, that there is a famine. So they travel down to Egypt. Abram tells Sarai that because she is very beautiful, he is afraid that the Egyptians will kill him in order to get to her. He asks her to pretend that he is her brother so that the Egyptians will be kind to him. Sure enough, word gets back to Pharaoh that there is a new woman in town and that she is very beautiful. Pharaoh takes Sarai as his wife and heaps all kinds of riches (cattle, silver, and gold) upon Abram as payment for her. God does not like that Pharaoh has taken Abram's wife (even if, in all fairness to Pharaoh, he didn't know) and causes terrible things to happen to Pharaoh's household (the Soncino commentary notes that the kind of sickness that plagued Pharaoh's household "was such as to constitute a safeguard to Sarai's honour." Somehow Pharaoh realizes that Sarai is Abram's wife, and he calls Abram before him and asks why Abram pretended to be Sarai's brother. Abram explains he was afraid, and with that Pharaoh tells him to gather his belongings (including Sarai) and leave Egypt.

So they leave (thanks to Pharaoh's payments for Sarai, Abram is now a very rich man). They travel back to Canaan, to the place where Abram built the altar to God; however, Abram's herdsmen and Lot's herdsmen are not getting along so well. Abram says to Lot that to avoid any more trouble, it would be best for them to split up. He tells Lot to look around and decide where he'd like to go. Lot notices that the plain of the Jordan River is very well watered and so has an abundance of nice grass for the cattle. Off he goes toward the plain to the towns of Sodom and Gomorrah.

After Lot leaves, God says to Abram: "Life up now thine eyes, and look from the place where thou art, northward and southward and eastward and westward; for all the land which thou seest, to thee will I give it, and to thy seed for ever. And I will make thy seed as the dust of the earth; so that if a man can number the dust of the earth, then shall thy seed also be numbered" (Gen. 13:14–16). And with that, Abram builds an altar to God.

Then there is a battle among various kings. The Soncino commentary notes that this recounts the battle by which the great king Hammurabi unites Babylonia. The people of Sodom were involved in these battles. Unfortunately, Lot and his family were living in Sodom and were taken prisoner, and all of their belongings were stolen. When Abram hears this news, he takes his men and they rescue Lot. Abram brings Lot, his family, and all their belongings before the king of Sodom, and the king praises Abram and offers to reward him. Abram refuses any reward, saying basically that it is God Who should be praised. After saying this, God tells Abram that He is Abram's shield and will protect him and reward him. Abram says he is concerned because he is childless and does not want his property going to his servant Eliezer of Damascus. God tells Abram to count the stars, and however many stars he counts, that will be the number of heirs he will have. He tells Abram to sacrifice some animals to Him, and then Abram falls asleep. In his sleep God speaks to him and tells him that he will father a great nation, who will be "a stranger in a land that is not theirs" and will be slaves to another nation whom God will judge in the end. God will then lead Abram's nation to safety and prosperity (Gen. 15:13–14).

But Sarai was unable to have a child. She tells Abram to have a child with her handmaiden, Hagar. Sure enough, Hagar becomes pregnant and once pregnant is very insolent with Sarai. Sarai complains to Abram about Hagar's behavior; he tells her that Hagar is her maid and she can do with her what she wishes. So Sarai deals "harshly" with Hagar, and Hagar runs away. An angel of the Lord finds Hagar and tells her that she will give birth to a son named Ishmael (meaning "God heareth"). The Soncino commentary explains that Ishmael shall be a wild man who wanders the desert, always ready for battle. The actual description is that he will be "a wild ass of a man: his hand shall be against every man, and every man's hand against him" (Gen. 16:12).

God then makes His covenant with Abram, saying if Abram follows Him "wholeheartedly" He will make of him a great nation. God changes Abram's name to Abraham and Sarai's to Sarah. (The Hebrew letter ה which makes an *H* sound, represents God's name, and so putting the ה in the names symbolizes that God is always with Abraham and Sarah.)

God tells Abraham to circumcise all the men and hereafter all male children when they are eight days old. God then tells Abraham that Sarah will have a son. Abraham laughs and is, of course, surprised by this news because he is a hundred years old and Sarah is ninety. God says she shall have a son and his name will be Isaac. Abraham is worried about Ishmael, and God promises to also make a great nation from Ishmael, but it is with Isaac that God's covenant will be established.

QUESTIONS FOR DISCUSSION

Talk about Abraham and Sarah's initial encounter with the Egyptians and Pharaoh. Do you think Pharaoh's "taking" Sarah foretells the future enslavement of the Jews?

What do you think about Abram growing wealthy and benefiting from Sarai living as the wife of Pharaoh? Do you have a problem with this?

Talk about names—*Ishmael* meaning "God heard," *Isaac* meaning "laugh," *Sarah* meaning "princess," *Abraham* meaning "father of a multitude" (*Ab* meaning "father" and *raham* meaning "multitude").

What do names mean in our religion? Who are you named after? Discuss with your children why you named them what you did. What do your names mean—both literally and for whom they honor?

Talk about the description of Ishmael—how does this predict the struggle between the Jews and the Arabs? How does our modern-day struggle find roots in the bitterness between Sarah and Hagar?

Vayera

Vayera begins with three strangers visiting the tents of Abraham while he is convalescing from his circumcision (this gives rise to the tradition of *bikur cholim* "visiting the sick"). Abraham offers the strangers water so they may wash their feet and offers them food without knowing that the strangers are actually angels sent by God. The first angel tells Abraham that Sarah will have a son. At this news, the ninety-year-old Sarah laughs (this is important because her son will be named Isaac, which means "laughter").

God speaks through one of the angels to tell Abraham that He is going to destroy Sodom and Gomorrah because the people there are immoral and depraved. Abraham pleads with God and begs that the innocent not be killed because of the wicked. He asks that God not destroy the cities if there are fifty righteous men within the city. God agrees. Then Abraham asks for only forty-five people; again, God agrees. This goes on until Abraham bargains God down to only ten righteous men. (As if God didn't know how many were righteous to begin with!)

The two angels visit Abraham's nephew, Lot (who lives in Sodom), and tells him to gather his family and get out of the city before it is destroyed. Lot tells his sons-in-law what he has been told, and they think he's crazy. One angel tells Lot to take his wife and two daughters and head to the mountain. Lot complains that the mountain is too far away, could he please go to the little city nearby (Lot is often portrayed as weak and kvetchy). The angel agrees, and the city is thereafter known as Zo'ar, which means "little.") They are cautioned not to look back as fire and brimstone rain down upon Sodom and Gomorrah. You probably know this part: Lot's wife looks back (which may also mean she hesitated to leave, perhaps indicating her connection with the evil society or lack of faith) and is turned into a pillar of salt. (Did she actually turn into salt? The Soncino commentary explains that similar to what happened to the victims of Pompeii, she was probably encrusted with a nitrous and saline substance.)

This leaves Lot and his two daughters in a cave in the mountain. (He ended up in the mountain because he was afraid to stay too close to the cities.) This next part is not appropriate for families with young children: Lot's daughters fear that there are no men left and want to ensure the continuation of their father's line, so each one in turn gets her father drunk and becomes pregnant by him. (The Torah is very careful to note that Lot does not realize what is happening at either time.) The older daughter gives birth to Moab (who becomes the father of the Moabites), and the younger daughter gives birth to Ben-ammi (who becomes the father of the Ammonites). Interestingly, both the Moabites and Ammonites are later portrayed in the Torah as being immoral and lascivious peoples.

Back to Abraham. He and Sarah continue their journey to Canaan and once again Abraham pretends Sarah is his sister for fear the king will kill him to get to Sarah. After Sarah is taken into the king's harem, God speaks to King Abimelech in a dream and tells him that Sarah is Abraham's wife. The king, upon waking, returns Sarah to Abraham along with some sheep, oxen, servants, and silver. (Abraham's practice of "selling" Sarah to various kings is not one of his better traits!)

After they leave Abimelech, Sarah becomes pregnant by Abraham and as God promised, gives birth to a son, named Isaac. Soon after, Sarah sees Hagar and Ishmael and tells Abraham she wants them sent away for fear Ishmael will take Isaac's birthright. Abraham is not happy about this, but God tells him it's OK, that He will make a great nation of Ishmael, but that it will be from Isaac that Abraham's descendants will follow God.

Hagar and Ishmael leave, and Hagar runs out of water. She leaves Ishmael under a bush because she cannot bear to see him die. An angel of God appears to her and tells her Ishmael will father a great nation. With that, she looks up and sees a well of water. She and Ishmael thrive, and he marries an Egyptian woman. (Today, Arab people trace their lineage to Ishmael, and it is in this sense that Jews and Arabs both descend from Abraham.)

The chapter concludes with the *akedah*, or the binding of Isaac. God speaks to Abraham and commands him to take "thine son, thine only son, whom thou lovest, even Isaac" (it is written this way to emphasize the sacrifice Abraham is being asked to make) (Gen. 22:2) and sacrifice him.

159

You may be wondering why it is written "even Isaac." Remember, Abraham has two sons, Ishmael and Isaac. There is a wonderful commentary by

> Rashi that suggests there was a dialogue between God and Abraham that went something like this:
>
> God said, "Take thy son," and Abraham said, "Which one?"
>
> God said, "Thy only son" (meaning the only son of his mother), and Abraham said, "This one is the only son of his mother, and this one is the only son of his mother" (for both Ishmael and Isaac were only children).
>
> "Whom thou lovest." Abraham's response: "I love them both."
>
> Finally God names him: "Isaac."

Abraham takes Isaac and some wood for the offering and goes to the place God told him to go. Isaac asks his father, "Where is a lamb for the burnt offering?" (Gen. 22:7). Abraham answers simply "God will provide Himself the lamb for a burnt offering, my son" (Gen. 22:8). Now, this can be read as "God will provide a lamb (in answer to your question), *my son*." Or, it can be read as "God will provide the lamb (which is you) *my son*." How you read this line will alter your interpretation of whether or not Isaac is aware that he is the sacrifice and therefore willingly goes to his death or if he trusts that God will provide an animal. Either way, it is evidence of Isaac's absolute faith.

At the last minute, God calls to Abraham. Abraham looks up and sees a ram caught in a bush and knows that Isaac is saved, and the ram is sacrificed.

QUESTIONS FOR DISCUSSION

Assuming God knows how many righteous men are in Sodom and Gomorrah, what is the point of allowing the argument or bargaining with Abraham?

Why does the angel tell Lot not to look back at Sodom and Gomorrah? Why do you think Lot's wife looked back? What does this say about her?

In the Torah, we read both the positive and negative traits of our patriarchs. Why is it important to read about Abraham again pretending Sarah is his sister because he fears for his life?

Why do you think God made Abraham and Sarah wait so long to have children?

Discuss the akedah. Why is this moment so crucial? What was this a test of? Faith? Obedience? Do you think Isaac knew he was going to be sacrificed? What would you do if you were Isaac? If you were Abraham?

Chayei Sarah

Sarah dies when she is 127 years old. The Midrash comments that she was as beautiful at a hundred as she was at twenty (and we know of her beauty from previous chapters in which various kings took her into their harems during her journey with Abraham). Upon Sarah's death, Abraham says to the Hittites (the inhabitants of the land) that he is a stranger among them and asks to buy land to bury Sarah. Ephron agrees to sell him land and the cave of Machpelah, where Abraham proceeds to bury Sarah. (By the way, this land is later known as Canaan.)

At this point, Abraham is very old. He asks his servant Eliezer to swear to find Isaac a wife among Abraham's people. Eliezer journeys to the land of Haran and asks God to help him find a wife for Isaac. He sits by the well and waits for the women to gather. He tells God that he will ask the women for water and asks that the woman whom God chooses for Isaac to draw water not only for Eliezer but also for his camels. Rebecca comes by and offers to give him and his camels water. Eliezer asks who her family is, and she replies that she is the daughter of Bethuel (who is actually Abraham's nephew). Eliezer goes with her back to the home of Bethuel and Nahor (Abraham's brother) and asks for Rebecca to marry Isaac. They consent and Rebecca agrees to go back with Eliezer. When Rebecca goes back, she veils her face in modesty (this is where the tradition of the bridal veil comes from). Isaac greets them, likes what he sees, and they marry and love each other.

The parashah ends with Abraham's death. Together, Ishmael and Isaac bury him in Machpelah with Sarah. After Abraham's death, God blesses Isaac. (We are not told what is said in this blessing, just that he is blessed by God.)

Questions for Discussion

Why is the parashah called Chayei Sarah, which means "the lives of Sarah" or "Sarah's lives" when she dies at its start?

Why was it necessary for Abraham to buy land?

Why the emphasis on Sarah's beauty?

Why was it so important to Abraham that Isaac not marry a Canaanite, but someone from Abraham's family?

Rebecca veils her face in modesty. How do you feel about what you wear? How do you decide what is or is not appropriate to wear?

Toldot

It comes to pass that Rebecca becomes pregnant with twins. While in her womb, they struggle and fight. She prays to God and asks why this is so. God tells her that she has two great nations inside her womb, that they struggle as they will always struggle, and the older shall serve the younger. Finally, she gives birth to the twin sons. Esau, who is hairy and ruddy, is born first. Jacob, who is fairer, is born holding onto the heel of his brother. (In fact, the name *Jacob* means "holder of the heel" or "supplanter.") Esau becomes a hunter and is favored by his father, Isaac, who loves to eat the meat Esau hunts. Jacob, who is gentle of spirit and often stays in the camp, is the favorite of his mother, Rebecca.

One day, Esau comes back from the day exhausted and thirsty. He asks Jacob for some "pottage" (which I take to mean some sort of food or drink). Jacob says he will give him some if Esau gives him his birthright. Esau agrees to this exchange. (This demonstrates how little Esau valued his birthright, which he so easily gave away for some "pottage.")

The time comes for Isaac to die, and he tells Esau to go to the field and get some venison so that he can eat his favorite food one more time, and then he will give his blessing to Esau. This blessing is a big deal. Rebecca overhears the plan and tells Jacob to go fetch some goats, and she will cook them to make them taste like venison. Then Jacob should go to Isaac (who is almost blind) and pretend to be Esau and thus get his brother's blessing. Jacob worries that Isaac will know it's him because Esau is very hairy and Jacob is not. Rebecca ties some fur around Jacob's hands and neck.

Jacob goes into Isaac's tent, and after Isaac eats he asks how Jacob found the meat so quickly. Jacob replies that God was with him and sent him speed. This arouses Isaac's suspicions because Esau wasn't prone to talk about God. He asks which son is with him. He feels the fur tied to Jacob's hands and says the voice sounds like Jacob, but the hands feel like Esau. Jacob lies and says he is Esau. Isaac proceeds to give his blessing to Jacob, promising that his brother will serve him: "And let thy mother's sons bow down to thee" (Gen. 27:29).

Esau returns from the fields with the venison and brings it to his father, who tells him that he must have been betrayed by Jacob. Esau is very upset and begs Isaac to bless him, too. Isaac says he has already blessed Jacob with riches and prosperity and has promised that Esau will serve Jacob. The only blessing he has left is that Esau will live by his sword and that although he will serve Jacob, there will come a time when he will break free.

Rebecca fears for Jacob's life and tells him to run away and go live with her brother, Laban. She tells Isaac that Jacob has gone to look for a wife among her family (as Abraham and Sarah did for Isaac). Esau, who knows his parents are not happy that his current wives are not from Abraham's family, takes one of Ishmael's daughters as a wife so that he, too, will marry a girl from Abraham's family.

QUESTIONS FOR DISCUSSION

Even though Esau is portrayed as not caring for God or his birthright, or even marrying within his people, the bottom line is that Jacob stole the blessing that was rightfully Esau's. Why is it set up this way? Why didn't God make Jacob the older twin? Why do you think this struggle and deceit was necessary?

How is the description of Jacob like the stereotypical image of Jews today? Why is the "bad" one the big, hairy, hunter and the "good" one the little, studious one?

Talk about intermarriage. From the first possible "Jewish" boy to marry (Isaac), it is stressed that the girl comes from Abraham's people (Hebrews). What are your views about interfaith marriage?

Do you think it is significant that Esau married into Ishmael's family? Discuss the similarities between Isaac and Ishmael and Jacob and Esau. What about the fact that Ishmael is, like Isaac, a son of Abraham and that by marrying Ishmael's daughter, Esau is marrying into Abraham's family? Do you think this proves he *did* care about the birthright?

Vayetzei

Jacob travels to Haran, to the home of Laban, Rebecca's brother. On the way he falls asleep and dreams of angels ascending and descending a ladder to Heaven. (It is noted in the commentary that the mention of the angels ascending first indicates that the angels of God have been traveling with Jacob and were ascending to Heaven from where they were escorting Jacob. This shows that God was with Jacob.) Jacob wakes and continues on his journey. He reaches a well where he meets Rachel and immediately falls in love with her. He learns that she is Laban's daughter, which makes him happy because Laban is Rebecca's brother and his mother would be happy to know Jacob married someone from her family. He goes with Rachel to her father's home, and Laban invites Jacob to stay and live with him.

After some time, Laban offers to pay Jacob for his work (we suppose this is work in the fields and with the herds). Jacob says he will work for seven years for Rachel and at the end of seven years, Rachel will become his wife. Laban agrees. Jacob works and it is written that so great is Jacob's love for Rachel that the seven years feel like only several days. The time comes for them to marry, but Laban tricks Jacob and sends his older unmarried daughter, Leah, in Rachel's place. Jacob agrees to work *another* seven years for Rachel's hand, though Laban allows Jacob to marry her eight days after marrying Leah.

Of course, Jacob favors Rachel. Leah is hurt by this, and God rewards her by having her conceive many sons. Rachel, meanwhile, is barren. She gives Jacob her handmaiden so he can have more children. Not to be outdone, Leah gives Jacob *her* handmaiden, with whom he can have children. Between Leah and the handmaidens, Jacob has ten sons and a daughter, Dinah. Finally, Rachel has a son, Joseph. From these eleven sons will come eleven of the twelve tribes of Israel.

With all of these wives and children, Jacob says to Laban it's time for him to leave. Laban agrees to let Jacob take all the spotted and striped cattle and goats, and the black sheep from the flock. But once again Laban is sneaky. Before Jacob can select his animals, Laban picks out all such animals from the herd and has his sons take them far away. Jacob takes rods from the poplar, almond, and plane trees and peels them so they appear to be streaked with white. He sets the rods in the ground near where the flocks came to drink. When the remaining animals (those that were not spotted, striped, or black) come to drink and see the rods, they immediately conceive and later give birth to streaked, speckled, and spotted babies. This continues for several generations of animals until Jacob has a very large herd. He tells Leah and Rachel that he wants to take his family and his herd and leave Laban. They agree to go with him. While packing to leave, Rachel steals her father's idols.

Laban catches up with them and is angry—angry because Jacob has a herd greater than his own, because he didn't have a chance to say good-bye to his daughters and grand-children, and because someone has stolen his gods. He accuses Jacob of doing so. Laban searches Jacob's belongings for the idols, but Laban cannot find them because Rachel is sitting on them. Finally, Jacob and Laban build a pillar of rocks and agree that neither will cross to the other's side, and with this they part company.

QUESTIONS FOR DISCUSSION

Talk about Jacob's dream ladder. What does it mean to you?

There is a tradition of angels in Judaism. If you think in terms of *tikkun olam* (repairing the world) or social action, do you know any "angels"?

Eliezer (in the previous parashah) found Rebecca at a well and Jacob finds Rachel at another. What is the significance of the well in this story?

Why was it necessary for Laban to trick Jacob into marrying Leah? How would Jewish history have been altered if Jacob had married only Rachel?

How would things have been different if Rachel had had ten sons and Leah only one?

Why did Rachel steal Laban's idols?

Jacob works for seven years—when else have we read about the number seven being significant?

Vayishlach

As Jacob nears his homeland, he is afraid to see Esau, fearing that Esau is still angry at him for stealing his birthright. At night, he wanders around and comes upon a man, with whom he wrestles. While wrestling, Jacob holds onto the man. As morning approaches, the man grabs the hollow of Jacob's thigh and tells Jacob to let go. Jacob refuses to let go until the man blesses him. It is at this point that we learn that Jacob is not wrestling with a man, but with an angel of God, because the angel says that Jacob's name will no longer be Jacob but Israel, for he "wrestled with God." (*El* as in the suffix of the name Israel is another way to connote "God.") After that, Jacob/Israel limped, and to this day, Jews do not eat the tendon of the thigh vein because of this struggle.

Jacob (as of this point, the Torah calls him Israel, but we will continue to refer to him as Jacob as we more commonly refer to this patriarch) gathers his family and approaches Esau. Esau runs to Jacob and hugs and kisses him, and all is well.

During Jacob's stay in Esau's lands, a Hittite man named Shechem rapes Jacob's daughter, Dinah. Shechem wants to marry Dinah. Jacob's sons Simeon and Levi tell Shechem's father, Hamor, that they will allow the marriage only if every man in Hamor's family is circumcised. Hamor's family is very excited by this because they see that Jacob is wealthy, and so they eagerly circumcise themselves. While they are recuperating, Jacob's sons go to their village and kill every newly circumcised man. Jacob is upset by this and also fears that the inhabitants of the land will be after them now. The sons defend their actions, arguing the murders were done out of vengeance for their sister's rape. (This is the last we hear of Dinah, although Anita Diamant has imagined her story in her popular book *The Red Tent*.)

God tells Jacob to leave and go to Beth El. Jacob does so, and along the way, Rachel has another son, Benjamin (which means "the son of my old age"). She dies giving birth to Jacob's twelfth son (whose descendants will become the twelfth tribe of Israel) and is buried along the road to Ephrath (Bethlehem).

Soon after, Isaac dies, and together, both Jacob and Esau bury him.

QUESTIONS FOR DISCUSSION

Talk about the famous story of Jacob wrestling with an angel of God. What is the significance of this? Why did God have an angel wrestle with Jacob? Have you ever wrestled with God?

Again, God changes a name. When else has God changed a name of a patriarch or matriarch? What does this mean when it happens?

Were you surprised that Esau forgave Jacob? How would you have acted if you were Esau? Have you ever fought with your brothers or sisters?

Why is it important that both Esau and Jacob together buried Isaac?

For teens and older: What is the significance of the rape story and all that comes out of it?

Just for fun: Superman's real name is Kal-El. Do you think the creator of Superman (who was Jewish) was using biblical references in his comic book? Can you think of any other connections between popular culture and the Bible?

Vayeshev

Jacob loved Joseph most of all his sons, and makes for Joseph a special coat out of many colorful fabrics. At that period of time, colorful coats were a sign of monarchy. One may interpret that by giving Joseph this coat, Jacob was marking him the future head of the family—of all the tribes—and Joseph's brothers were jealous. To make matters worse, Joseph told his family about a dream he had in which his sheaf of wheat stood tall and his brothers' sheaves bowed down before it. He didn't win any fans by then telling them about yet another dream in which the sun and moon and eleven stars bowed down to him. (You don't have to be a great diviner of dreams to interpret *that* one.) The brothers were not thrilled by this.

So one day, when the brothers were herding sheep, they discussed killing Joseph. Reuben intervened and convinced the others not to kill Joseph but to throw him in a pit (he planned secretly to return later and free Joseph). The brothers agreed and took Joseph and threw him into a pit. While they are eating, they see a caravan of Ishmaelites, and Judah suggests selling Joseph into slavery. While the brothers are off eating, a group of Midianite traders passes by the pit and hears Joseph. It is they who take Joseph and sell him into slavery to the Ishmaelites (and not actually his brothers; although, it was his brothers who put him into the pit in the first place). Reuben returns to the pit (not knowing that Joseph has been sold into slavery) and assumes that Joseph has been killed or dragged off. He worries that as the eldest brother Jacob will hold him responsible for what the others have done to Joseph. So the brothers take Joseph's coat and dip it in goat blood and show Jacob the bloodied coat, telling him that Joseph must have been killed by an animal. Jacob mourns for his son.

Time passes and Joseph is brought to Egypt and sold to Potiphar, Pharaoh's captain of the guards. God favors Joseph, and Joseph becomes very successful in Egypt. Potiphar gives him a lot of responsibility in his house, and under Joseph's supervision, Potiphar's house prospers. Potiphar's wife is attracted to Joseph and tries to seduce him, but Joseph refuses her advances. During one such seduction attempt, Potiphar's wife grabs hold of Joseph's garment (oy, again with the coat) and pulls it off Joseph. After he runs off, the wife shows the men of her house Joseph's clothing and claims that it was Joseph who was making advances on *her*. Potiphar has no choice but to throw Joseph in jail.

While in prison, Joseph meets Pharaoh's former butler and baker (both imprisoned for committing different offenses). The butler tells Joseph that he had a dream and asks Joseph to interpret it. The butler dreamed about a vine with three branches that suddenly burst forth with grapes. While the grapes were growing, the butler had Pharaoh's cup in his hand. The butler took the grapes and pressed them into the cup and then gave the cup to Pharaoh. Joseph tells the butler that this dream foretells good fortune—that in three days, the butler will be returned to work and he will once again press the cup into Pharaoh's hand. The butler thanks him, but Joseph says there is no need, just to please remember him and tell Pharaoh about him.

The baker is excited to hear Joseph interpreting the butler's dream and wants Joseph to interpret his dream as well. In the baker's dream, he had three baskets of bread on his head. The breads were meant for Pharaoh, and birds ate the bread from the basket. Joseph tells him sadly that in three days Pharaoh will bring the baker out of prison, only to hang him.

Sure enough, in three days, the butler is returned to service to Pharaoh and the baker is hanged.

QUESTIONS FOR DISCUSSION

Was Jacob wrong in favoring Joseph?

Have you ever been jealous of your brother or sister?

Did you ever feel like your parents' favorite? Or that your brother or sister was the favorite?

If you had a dream like Joseph had about his family bowing to him, would you tell your family?

Once again we see how the older brothers are portrayed as "bad" to the younger "good" (Cain/Abel, Ishmael/Isaac, Esau/Jacob, brothers/Joseph). Do you think there is significance in the younger being favored by God? Why or why not?

We will read in Exodus how the Midianites took Moses in after he fled from Egypt. Is it significant that it is the Midianites who now bring Joseph (and therefore the Hebrews) to Egypt?

Miketz

It comes to pass that Pharaoh has a dream. He dreams that seven fat cows come out of the river and feed upon the grass. But then seven lean and sickly cows come out of the river and eat the seven fat cows. He wakes up, disturbed by his dream, and after a while falls back asleep. This time he dreams of a stalk of corn with seven big healthy ears. Suddenly, another stalk appears with seven thin and weak ears, which then devour the healthy corn. When he wakes up, Pharaoh is upset and calls his magicians to interpret his dreams. When they are unable to do so, the butler tells Pharaoh about Joseph, who had correctly interpreted his and the baker's dreams.

Pharaoh sends for Joseph and asks him to interpret the dreams. Joseph says that it is God who will interpret the dream. Pharaoh tells Joseph the dreams. Joseph explains that the two dreams are actually one and the same. The dreams are God's way of warning Pharaoh that He will cause seven years of plenty for Egypt, which will be followed by seven years of famine that will be so bad, everyone will forget the seven good years. Joseph suggests that Pharaoh use the seven good years to store up provisions for the seven lean years. Pharaoh is impressed with Joseph and puts him in charge of this task and, in fact, appoints him so high up in government that only Pharaoh is above Joseph. Pharaoh gives Joseph a woman named Asenat as his wife, and with her he has two sons, Manasseh ("God hath made me forget all my toil and all my father's house") and Ephraim ("God Hath made me fruitful in the land of my affliction").

The years pass and finally there is a great famine in the land. Jacob tells his sons that the Pharaoh has food and sends them to go buy some. He sends ten of his sons and keeps Benjamin with him, for fear that something might happen to him (because Benjamin is the surviving son by his beloved Rachel, Jacob wants to keep him close). The brothers appear before Joseph. He recognizes them, but they do not know him. (To be fair, they probably don't expect to see their brother, who was sold into slavery, now a major ruler in Egypt.) Joseph remembers his dreams, which predicted his brothers bowing down to him. He is purposefully mean to them and accuses them of being spies. They insist they are good men, twelve brothers, one of whom is home with their father and one who is gone. Joseph says if they return to their home and bring their youngest brother back with them, he will believe them and keeps Simeon as a prisoner until they return. The brothers believe this is happening to them because of what they did to Joseph. Joseph tells his stewards to fill the brothers' bags with grain, give them provisions for the journey, and to place the money they had given as payment into their sacks.

When the brothers return home and find their money in their sacks they are afraid that Joseph will think they stole the money and will punish them. They tell Jacob what happened, and even though Simeon is in prison in Egypt, Jacob refuses to let Benjamin go. Time passes and they desperately need food. Jacob tells them to return to Egypt and allows Benjamin to go with them. Judah pledges to protect Benjamin.

The brothers go to Joseph again. They tell his steward about the money, and the steward (probably at Joseph's instruction) tells the brothers that their God must have given them money because Joseph did receive their payment for the grain. Joseph releases Simeon and invites the brothers to dine with him while the stewards fill their sacks with grain. Joseph secretly has the stewards place his silver cup into Benjamin's sack.

While the brothers are journeying home, Joseph orders his men to overcome them and accuse them of stealing. They search the bags and find Joseph's silver cup in Benjamin's sack. The brothers return to Joseph's house, beg Joseph for forgiveness, and plead their innocence. Joseph tells them he will keep Benjamin as his slave and sends the rest home to face their father.

QUESTIONS FOR DISCUSSION

Why is Joseph doing all this to his brothers? Why doesn't he come right out and tell them that he is their brother?

Why aren't the brothers jealous of Benjamin, whom Jacob clearly favors?

The fact that the brothers believe the harsh way they are being treated by Joseph, whom they don't realize is their brother, is some cosmic retaliation for what they did to Joseph, means they feel guilty. Have you ever felt guilty? Did you ever think something bad happened to you because of something else you did?

Vayigash

Upon hearing that Joseph will keep Benjamin in Egypt, Judah begs Joseph to take him instead and allow Benjamin to return home. He explains that their father will surely die of grief if Benjamin is lost to him. It is significant that Judah is the one who tries to save Benjamin. This is the concept of t'shuvah (repentance). Judah, when faced with the same situation (a favored brother), acted differently than he did the first time. He tried to rid himself of Joseph but fights to save Benjamin. For this act of repentance, he and his descendants are blessed. It is said that the Messiah will be born from the tribe of Judah.

After hearing Judah's offer to sacrifice himself for Benjamin and Isaac, Joseph weeps and reveals himself to his brothers. He tells them he is not mad at them for what they had done, and that it must have been God's will, for he was able to come to Egypt and save many lives from the famine. He tells his brothers to go get Jacob and their households and come live with him in Egypt.

The brothers do what Joseph asks. During their journey down to Egypt, God appears to Jacob in a dream and says, "Jacob, Jacob," and Jacob replies, "Here I am" (Gen. 46:2). God tells Jacob to go to Egypt and there He will make him a great nation. When they reach Egypt, Pharaoh allows them to live in the land of Goshen, which has the best pasture.

The famine is terrible. Under Joseph's rule, Pharaoh obtains all the money, herds, and lands of the people of Egypt in exchange for grain. Finally, there is nothing more for the people to give Joseph as payment, so he gives them seeds and tells them to tend the fields. He declares that one fifth of whatever they raise shall be given to Pharaoh as a tax and the rest they can keep for their families. Joseph is praised for his wisdom and judgment in creating this rule.

QUESTIONS FOR DISCUSSION

Would you exchange your life for your sibling's?

Do you think Joseph acted fairly with the people? Was it right to take their belongings in exchange for food? How did what Joseph ultimately do help both Pharaoh *and* the people?

Do you think Joseph is a good leader? Why or why not?

Vayechi

Jacob lives to be 147 years old. Before he dies he blesses each of his sons. This is significant because these blessings determine the future of each of his sons and the tribes of Israel that descend from them. Jacob also includes Joseph's sons, Ephraim and Manasseh, in his blessings. By blessing them as he would his own sons, he makes them part of the Hebrew nation (even though their mother was an Egyptian). Even today, when we bless our sons, we pray that they be like Ephraim and Manasseh.

When Jacob dies, his sons take him to the cave of Machpelah and bury him alongside Abraham and Sarah. After Jacob's death, Joseph's brothers beg him to forgive them. He replies that even though they meant him harm, God meant good and their actions ultimately allowed him to save many lives. He forgives them.

Joseph lives to be 110. He is buried in Egypt.

QUESTIONS FOR DISCUSSION

If God intended for the Jews to end up in Egypt, then He intended for them to become slaves and then to lead them out of Egypt to the land of Israel. Why not just lead the Hebrews to Israel? Why was it crucial for them to be slaves?

What was the significance of Jacob's final blessings? What does it mean to bless your children? If you were giving a final blessing, what would you say? What would you want to hear?

What was your favorite story in Genesis? Discuss your favorite characters. What do our patriarchs have in common? What were their strengths and weaknesses? Were they great leaders? Why or why not?

EXODUS
Shmot ("Names")

After Joseph dies "there arose a new king of Egypt who knew not Joseph" (Exod. 1:8). This king fears the Hebrews, who are numerous and strong, will one day rise up and overthrow him. He calls for the Hebrews to be forced to work for the Egyptians as a form of taxation (in reality this was slavery). Pharaoh hopes that this will break the Hebrews' spirits. However, the Hebrews continue to thrive and multiply. So Pharaoh instructs the midwives to kill any male children born to Hebrew women. But the midwives fear God and do not obey Pharaoh. Instead, they tell Pharaoh that the Hebrew women were strong and did not need the services of the midwives when they give birth. God rewards these women for fearing Him and protecting the Hebrews. Finally, Pharaoh declares that every son born to a Hebrew shall be cast into the river.

During this terrible time, a boy is born to a couple from the tribe of Levi. (Their names are not given at this time. The Soncino commentary explains this is because it is important to move the narrative along. We will later learn that the father is named Amram, the mother is Yocheved, and the sister is Miriam.) The wife hides the baby for three months. When she can hide him no longer, she makes a small ark and places the baby in it. (Interesting note: there are only two times in the Torah that the Hebrew word for "ark" is used—here and in the story of Noah.) The woman puts the tiny ark into the river and tells her daughter (the baby's sister) to watch him so she may know what becomes of her son. Pharaoh's daughter happens to be bathing in the river and finds the little ark. When she opens the ark and sees the baby, she takes pity on it. She realizes he is a Hebrew child, and knowing that an Egyptian woman will not agree to nurse a Hebrew child, she tells her handmaiden to find a Hebrew woman to nurse the baby. When the child is old enough to be weaned, the woman brings the child back to Pharaoh's daughter, who raises him as her son and names him Moses, which means "to draw out" because she drew him out of the water.

Moses grows into a man. One day, while he is walking among the Hebrews, he sees an Egyptian taskmaster beating a Hebrew slave. Seeing no one else around, Moses strikes and kills the Egyptian. The next day, Moses is walking again and sees two Hebrews fighting. Moses says to the one in the wrong, "Why do you strike your fellow?" and the man replies, "Who made you a ruler and a judge over us? Are you going to kill me, as you did kill the Egyptian?" (Exod. 2:14). Moses fears that word has spread about what he had done. Pharaoh hears and wants to kill Moses, so Moses flees to the desert and sits by a well in the land of Midian. At the well he sees the seven daughters of the priest of Midian. When they try to get to the well to draw water for their flock, other shepherds keep them away. Moses helps the girls, so they invite him back to their father's house. The daughters tell their father, "An Egyptian delivered us out of the hand of the shepherds, and moreover he drew water for us, and watered the flock" (Exod. 2:19). It is important to note that Moses does not correct them and allows himself to be introduced as an Egyptian, not as a Hebrew. Moses lives with the Midianites and eventually marries the eldest daughter, Zipporah, and together they have a son, Gershom, whose name means "a stranger," for Moses says, "I have been a stranger in a strange land" (Exod. 2:22).

Meanwhile, back in Egypt, the children of Israel are crying out to God, and God hears them and remembers His covenant with Abraham, Isaac, and Jacob. (We learn from the Soncino commentary it's not that God had truly forgotten, it's just that the time was right for the next step toward fulfilling His promise.)

One day, while Moses is watching his father-in-law Jethro's sheep, he notices a bush that is burning but not consumed, and he turns to look at it. When God sees that Moses has noticed, He calls to Moses. Moses replies, "Here I am." (The Midrash explains that God speaks to Moses in the voice of Moses' father.) God tells Moses to take off his shoes for he is standing on holy ground. He introduces Himself as "the God of thy father, the God of Abraham, the God of Isaac, and the God of Jacob" (Exod. 3:6). He tells Moses that he is to go back to Egypt and lead the Israelites to the land of milk and honey. (This is the first time the Jewish people are called the Israelites.)

Moses is concerned that he is not the right one for the job. He worries that the Israelites will not believe him and wonders what he should tell them when they ask who sent him. He does not think he is eloquent enough to speak convincingly to Pharaoh or to the people. God tells Moses that He will be with him, and that Moses should tell the Israelites that "I am that I am" sent him. He causes Moses' rod to turn into a snake and back into a rod. He causes Moses' hand to become leprous and then to heal. God explains that He gives all men the ability to speak and that He will tell Moses what to say, but also that Moses' brother, Aaron, who is a good speaker, will help him.

God tells Moses to first ask Pharaoh to let the people journey into the desert to offer sacrifices to God. When Pharaoh refuses, Moses is to then insist on the freeing of the people. When Pharaoh refuses, Moses is to say that the Israelites are God's firstborn, and if he does not free them, God will slay Pharaoh's firstborn.

Moses gathers his family and journeys into the wilderness (actually, the land between Horeb and Egypt) and meets up with Aaron. Together, Moses and Aaron meet with the elders of the Israelites. The elders believe Moses and Aaron, and when they hear that God has remembered them, they bow their heads in prayer.

At last Moses and Aaron go before Pharaoh and tell him that the God of Israel has demanded that he "let My people go." Pharaoh says, "Who is the Lord, that I should heed unto His voice to let Israel go? I know not the Lord, and moreover I will not let Israel go" (Exod. 5:2).

Pharaoh makes life more difficult for the Israelites. He refuses to give them straw but insists that they still make bricks. As they can not produce the bricks, they are beaten. The children of Israel complain to Moses that he has made things worse for them. Moses "returns" to God and questions why God is making things so difficult. (The Soncino commentary explains that use of the word *return* is important, for it describes the ongoing communication between God and Moses.) God reassures Moses, saying, "Now shalt thou see what I will do to Pharaoh; for by a strong hand shall he let them go, and by a strong hand shall he drive them out of his land" (Exod. 6:1).

QUESTIONS FOR DISCUSSION

Why do you think the Egyptian midwives helped the Hebrews?

Once again we read that names have special meanings. Discuss how *Moses* means "to draw out," connecting it not only to being drawn out of the water, but also drawing the people out of Egypt; how *Gershom* means "stranger"; and of course God's renaming the Hebrews to Israelites ("Children of Israel" with *Israel* meaning "Wrestles with God"). What about God calling Himself "I am that I am"?

Discuss the image of the burning bush. What is its significance?

Why do you think Moses had to be a shepherd before he heard the voice of God? Why couldn't he hear God when he was living as a prince in Egypt?

We really don't hear any more about Moses' family after this chapter. Why do you think they fade out of the story line?

What do you think of Moses' doubting his leadership ability? Have you ever felt this way? What traits do you think a leader needs?

Moses agrees to lead after he hears that God and Aaron will help him. Can a leader be successful by working alone? How important is it to have a strong team? What does it mean to be part of a team? How about your parents—do they have teams at work?

Va'eira

The Israelites are not happy with Moses. They think he has brought more trouble upon them, and Moses brings these and his own complaints to God. God tells Moses to organize the Israelites into their houses or tribes. This, essentially, organizes them for war, and it is in this manner that they will leave Egypt.

Moses and Aaron again go to Pharaoh. Aaron turns his rod into a snake. Pharaoh's magicians are able to do the same with their rods; however, Aaron's rod eats their rods. Pharaoh continues to refuse to let the Israelites go. God then sends the plagues upon Egypt—the Nile turns to blood and then frogs infest the land. When the gnats come, Pharaoh's magicians admit this must be the work of God. Still, Pharaoh refuses. So God sends more plagues—flies, cattle disease, boils, and hail. Still, Pharaoh's heart remains hard.

Why are the Israelites complaining? Are they right to complain? Should they trust Moses when he says God has a plan? Does this indicate a lack of faith in God?

Is Moses being an effective leader? Should he keep going back to God with the Israelites' complaints?

Doesn't God know the Israelites are unhappy? Why is he making this a longer process than just sending them on their way without difficulty?

Bo

Moses and Aaron again go to Pharaoh and announce that a plague of locusts will come if Pharaoh does not let the Israelites go. Pharaoh's servants plead with Pharaoh to let the Hebrews go, for they are afraid. Pharaoh asks who exactly will go. When Moses replies all the men, women, children, and herds, Pharaoh replies that he knows they are looking to leave Egypt and not just journey into the desert for a couple of days to make sacrifices to their God. So Pharaoh says Moses can leave with just the men, for they are all that is needed to worship God.

God tells Moses to hold his arm over Egypt. With this, swarms of locusts arrive and destroy all of Egypt's vegetation. Pharaoh calls for Moses and Aaron and begs forgiveness. God sends a strong wind to rid Egypt of the locusts. As soon as the locusts are gone, God hardens Pharaoh's heart once more.

God tells Moses to stretch his "hand toward heaven, that there may be darkness over the land of Egypt, even darkness which may be felt" (Exod. 10:21). After three days of heavy darkness, Pharaoh tells Moses he can now leave with the children, too, but the flocks must remain in Egypt. Moses explains that they need the cattle for the burnt offerings. Pharaoh is enraged and tells Moses to get away from him, threatening that if he sees Moses again, Moses will die. Moses replies that he will surely never see Pharaoh's face again.

God tells Moses that there will be one more plague—a plague so terrible, there will be no need for any more. He tells Moses to tell the congregation of Israel (it should be noted that this is the first time the people are called a "congregation," denoting that they are a religion) to gather their belongings and prepare a special meal and eat it fully dressed with shoes on, so they will be ready to leave. They are to prepare enough lamb so that each member of their family will eat to his need (no more and no less). They are to roast the lamb and eat it with bitter herbs and unleavened bread. God explains that this will mark the beginning of the months and that it will be a special day of remembrance, as a festival to the Lord. Future generations are to rid their homes of anything leavened and to eat only unleavened food for seven days. (This describes the holiday of Passover—our first holiday is one that occurs in the home.)

Each household is then to take the blood of the lamb and smear it on their doorposts and lintel. That night, God will kill every firstborn male child and beast in Egypt. Any doorpost with blood will be passed over. (This is also the origin of placing a mezuzah on doorposts to signify a Jewish household. *Mezuzah* literally means "doorpost.")

So it came to pass that such a cry went out over Egypt, for there was no Egyptian home where death had not struck. Pharaoh begs Moses and Aaron to leave with their people and their herds and hopes for a blessing for himself. The length of time the Israelites were in Egypt was 430 years.

The Hebrews flee quickly with their families and their cattle. And God is with them and watches over them and protects them.

And God tells Moses that every firstborn of Israel must be dedicated to Him (this continues today in the ceremony of *pidyon haben*, "redemption of the firstborn son"). God also instructs Moses that the Israelites are to observe Passover every year and to remember that God brought us out of Egypt "with a strong and mighty hand." We are also instructed that the words of God are to be "a sign upon thy hand, and for frontlets between thine eyes" (Exod. 13:16). (This commandment is manifested in the tefillin men wear on their foreheads and wrap around their arms.) God tells Moses how to answer when a child asks questions about why we observe Passover or wear tefillin, thus making teaching children a priority in Judaism.

QUESTIONS FOR DISCUSSION

How does the final plague relate to Pharaoh's decree of killing all male Hebrew children?

Why are firstborn children considered so important? (Think about the time all this occurred and the popular rules for inheritance.)

Talk about Passover in your family—how do you celebrate? What do you do during the holiday that reminds you of what happened in this parashah?

Beshallach

God leads the Hebrews out of Egypt. A pillar of cloud guides them in the day and a pillar of fire by night (the cloud shields them from the hot sun, and the fire lights their way), showing that God never left His people. When they get to the Red (or Reed) Sea, God tells them to stop and camp so that Pharaoh will think he has them trapped. (In Hebrew this sea is Yam Suf—"Reed Sea"—and is still called this today.) God explains to Moses that He plans to overthrow the wicked Pharaoh and thus show the Egyptians that He is the Lord.

When the Israelites see the Egyptians approaching they become afraid because there is nowhere to escape but into the sea! They complain to Moses that they would rather be in Egypt than die in the wilderness! They even remind him that they asked him to leave them alone—that they would rather be slaves than wander in the wilderness. (This is just the beginning of the complaints. Poor Moses—whenever the slightest difficulty arises, the people complain.)

God tells Moses to raise his rod and extend his hand over the sea. With this, the sea parts, so that the children of Israel can walk through safely. But the Egyptians are in hot pursuit behind them, so Moses again raises his hand (per God's instructions) and the sea closes over the Egyptians, drowning them. Upon seeing this, the children of Israel "feared the Lord; and they believed in the Lord, and in His servant Moses" (Exod. 14:31).

With this, the children of Israel sing a song of joy. Part of the song becomes the prayer "Mi Kamocha," with the lines that translate to "Who is like Thee, O Lord, among the mighty? Who is like unto Thee, glorious in holiness, fearful in praises, doing wonders?" (Exod. 15:11).

Now the Israelites are alone in the desert. They begin to worry about how they will eat. Again they regret having left Egypt and begin to think of the meager food they received as slaves as luxury. Murmurings against Moses spread among the people. Moses cries to God that he fears the people will stone him. God tells him that He will provide the people with manna, which will rain down from the skies. (Manna is described as tasting like flat bread sweetened with honey.) Enough will be provided for each person to eat his or her fill. Moses explains that manna will rain for six days. On the sixth day, enough will rain down so that each person can gather two portions. They are instructed to save the second portion for the seventh day. The seventh day will be a day of rest, and there will be no gathering on the Sabbath.

Again the children of Israel complain. This time they are thirsty. God tells Moses to gather the elders of the congregation and strike a rock with his rod. With the elders as witnesses, God causes sweet water to pour out of the rock for the people to drink.

Soon after this, Amalek appears and the Israelites have to fight. Amalek is considered to be the grandson of Esau. (It is noted in the Soncino commentary that every time the Israelites complain, they soon after happen upon Amalek and a fight ensues.) God helps the children of Israel win the war—every time Moses holds up his staff they prevail. After the Israelites ultimately win the war, the Torah says, "The Lord will be at war with Amalek throughout the ages."

QUESTIONS FOR DISCUSSION

Why do you think God waited for the Egyptians to catch up with the Israelites before He parted the Red Sea?

What do you think it would have been like to walk through the sea? How would you have felt if you were an Israelite and you walked through the sea and then watched the Egyptians drown?

Why do the Israelites keep complaining? God continues to shower them with miracles, why do they still doubt and complain?

Why do you think the Israelites have to fight Amalek after they complain?

What do you think of Moses' leadership style so far? At one point, God tells him it is not time for complaining but time for action, and they need to move. When is it time to pray, and when is it time to act? What does this teach the Israelites about their relationship with God?

Yitro ("Jethro")

Jethro, Moses' father-in-law, journeys with his daughter Zipporah, Moses' wife, and her two sons by Moses, Gershom (whose name means "stranger" because Moses described himself as a "stranger in a strange land") and Eliezer (whose name means "God helps" because Moses said "the God of my father was my help and delivered me from the sword of Pharaoh") (Exod. 18:4). When they reach the Israelites, Moses greets them joyfully with kisses. Moses recounts to Jethro all that has happened to them. Jethro declares that God is surely more powerful than all the other gods. He then offers a sacrifice to God with Moses, Aaron, and the elders of the congregation.

The next day Jethro observes Moses counseling and sitting in judgment over the people. All day and all night, Moses helps settle disputes. Jethro worries that Moses has so much to do for the people and wonders why he works alone—Moses will wear himself out. Moses explains that he settles disputes and makes known the laws and teachings of God. Jethro counsels Moses to appoint judges from among the righteous men to help settle the smaller disputes so that Moses' time can be reserved for more important matters. Moses heeds Jethro's advice and sets up a system of judges.

Moses tells the people to prepare for God. They are to stay pure for three days and wash both bodies and garments and avoid certain areas around Mount Sinai. On the third day after these instructions are given, God comes down upon Mount Sinai as fire and smoke. The people congregate at the foot of the trembling mountain, and horns are heard. Moses goes up, and God warns him not to let anyone else up for fear they should see God and perish. Moses responds that the people are following instructions and observing the boundaries set around the mountain.

God then gives Moses the Ten Commandments. They are:

1. I am the Lord, thy God; thou shalt have no other gods before Me.
2. Thou shalt not make unto thee a graven image (idols).
3. Thou shalt not take the name of the Lord, thy God, in vain.
4. Remember the sabbath day and keep it holy.
5. Honor thy father and thy mother.
6. Thou shalt not murder.
7. Thou shalt not commit adultery.
8. Thou shalt not steal.
9. Thou shalt not bear false witness against thy neighbor.
10. Thou shalt not covet thy neighbor's house, wife, or possessions.

QUESTIONS FOR DISCUSSION

Was Jethro right in his counsel to Moses? Discuss delegating responsibility as an important part of leadership. If you were Moses, what traits would you look for in deciding who would be a judge?

What is the significance that the name of this important parashah is Yitro—named for Jethro, a non-Hebrew—and that God gives the Israelites the Ten Commandments in this chapter?

Discuss the Ten Commandments. Why are they ordered the way they are?

There are many laws and rules that we will learn about as we read the Torah. Why are these ten highlighted? How do they serve as general rules for governing behavior?

If you could add an eleventh commandment, what would it be?

Mishpatim

In Mishpatim, we read in more detail the rules of the new society being formed in the desert. We learn about how to treat servants and slaves and those indebted to us, and how to punish those who commit various crimes. Interestingly, if we accept a coat as collateral for a debt from a very poor man, we are to return it to him at night, to save him from freezing to death (remember, it gets very cold at night in the desert). We also learn the concept of "an eye for an eye and a tooth for a tooth," which in practical terms means monetary compensation for damages and personal injury.

Moses tells the people of Israel what God has said, and they declare that all God has commanded, they will obey. God has also promised to deliver the Israelites into the Promised Land and smite those who currently live in the land so that the Israelites can inhabit the land without the risk of the other people swaying them from the ways of God.

Moses builds an altar under the mount with twelve pillars, one for each tribe. The young men offer sacrifices; half of the blood Moses pours on the altar and half he sprinkles on the people, saying, "Behold the blood of the covenant, which the Lord hath made with you in agreement with all these words" (Exod. 24:8).

Moses and Aaron and the elders of the community return to Mount Sinai. God tells Moses to approach and tell the others to wait. Here Moses receives the tablets upon which God has written the laws, which Moses must teach the people. A cloud covers the mountain and Moses walks through the cloud and stays on the mountain for forty days and forty nights.

QUESTIONS FOR DISCUSSION

What does "an eye for an eye and a tooth for a tooth" mean to you? Do you have an example of when someone has hurt you and you felt you needed to be somehow compensated for the injury? Have you ever hurt someone and needed to make up for it?

Compare the forty days and forty nights of Noah's flood with the forty days and forty nights it takes for Moses to receive the word of God. Do you think is it significant that it is the same duration of time? Why or why not?

Do you believe this story? Can you imagine what it was like for the people to hear the word of God?

Terumah

In Terumah we receive detailed descriptions of the interior of the Tabernacle (*mishkan* in Hebrew) with instructions for everything from the size of the altar table (*shulchan*) to intricate gold candelabra (menorah).

QUESTIONS FOR DISCUSSION

We are instructed to build the Tabernacle so that God will dwell in it. What does it mean for God to "dwell" someplace?

On Shabbat, we make our home into a sanctuary so that God's presence can dwell with us. What did you and your family do to make your home special for Shabbat? What other things can you do to make your home a holy space?

Tetzaveh

God says: "And thou shalt command the children of Israel, that they bring unto thee pure olive oil beaten for the light, to cause a lamp to burn continually" (Exod. 27:20). With these words, the Israelites receive instructions for the Eternal Light in the Tabernacle, which still hangs in synagogues today.

Tetzaveh also gives the description of the robes worn by the high priests (*kohanim g'dolim*) when performing their rituals in the Holy of Holies (*kodesh kodashim*). These beautifully colored robes are decorated with bells at the hem so that the congregation will know when the priest enters the Holy of Holies. The priest also wears a headpiece and a breastplate decorated with the names of the twelve tribes.

Finally, Tetzaveh gives instructions for how the priests (kohanim) are to perform sacrifices and care for the altar.

Questions for Discussion

What is the meaning of the Eternal Light? Think about your synagogue: why don't they turn off the light when no one is in the building? Why is it important that it stays lit?

Think about the description of the priest's robes. How do they compare with the way we dress the Torah today?

The priests are required to dress in these special robes when performing very sacred rituals. How does this compare to our dressing special for Shabbat and going to synagogue? Do you agree with dressing up, or should we wear whatever we'd like? How do you feel when you get dressed up? Does this make an event more special?

Consider the word *holy* as meaning "not ordinary." Does dressing up make something holy?

In the days of Moses, only the high priest could perform the rituals in the Holy of Holies. Do you think this was better—for the priests to represent the people—or, do you prefer how we do it today, with each of us having a unique relationship with God?

Ki Tissa

God instructs Moses to take a census of the men (this accounting prepares them for war) and to give everyone a "ransom for his soul," a monetary value assigned to each person. The law of the day stated that if one man kills another, the murderer should be put to death. However, if your ox (for example) kills someone, you will not be put to death, but you will be required to compensate the family of the murdered man what that man was worth (an eye for an eye, a tooth for a tooth). When the census is taken, each man (for only men were counted) must pay the ransom in advance because as soldiers going to war, they are very likely to take another's life. Rich and poor pay the same ransom because, as the Soncino commentary says, all souls are of equal value to God. The money collected was used to maintain the Tabernacle.

The priests are instructed to wash their hands and feet before approaching the altar. So important is this direction that it is written that they wash so "that they die not" (Exod. 30:21).

We are again commanded to keep the Sabbath "for it is a sign between Me and you throughout your generations, that ye may know that I am the Lord Who sanctify you. Ye shall keep the Sabbath therefore, for it is holy unto you; every one that profaneth it shall surely be put to death; for whosoever doeth any work therein, that soul shall be cut off from among his people" (Exod. 31:13–14).

And with this, God gives Moses "two tables of testimony, tables of stone, written with the finger of God" (Exod. 31:18).

While Moses is up on the mountain, the people begin to fear Moses has died and go to Aaron and demand he make an idol for them to worship. Aaron agrees and tells them to collect all their gold jewelry and give it to him. He then melts the gold and fashions a calf.

Meanwhile, on the mountain, God tells Moses that the people have turned against Him and He is going to kill them all. Moses begs Him not to do so. But when Moses returns to the people and sees them reveling around the idol, he grows very angry—so angry, in fact, that he throws down the stone tablets and shatters them. Moses is angry that the people have broken God's first two commandments and cries out, "Who is with me?" The Levites go to him. Moses directs the Levites to take up their swords and kill everyone who has participated in this horrible sin. Moses then returns to the mountain to try to appease God.

Moses begs God not to destroy the people—in fact, he says, "If not, blot me, I pray Thee, out of Thy book which Thou hast written" (Exod. 32:32), meaning if God kills the people, He should kill Moses as well. God tells Moses to go back and continue to lead the people, but it will be an angel, not God who will lead him. (This is because God is still very angry about the whole golden calf thing, and really, who can blame Him. After all, He brought the people out of slavery, He parted the Red Sea, and the minute Moses is late coming back from his meeting with God, they go back to the idols—*oy gevalt!*)

God tells Moses to tell the people that He is angry, and if He descends upon them, He will destroy them. The people are afraid. Moses sets up his tent, which he calls the tent of meeting (*ohel mo'ed*). When he goes into the tent and a cloud descends in front of it, the people know that Moses is talking to God "face to face, as a man speaketh unto his friend" (Exod. 33:11). Only Moses' young attendant, Joshua, son of Nun, may stay in the tent with Moses. When the cloud is in front of the tent, the people pray.

While in the Tent, Moses asks God to teach him so that he will find favor in God's eyes and that Moses, in turn, can teach the Israelites so that God will know they are His chosen people. God agrees and tells Moses that this pleases Him and that "My presence shall go with thee, and I will give thee rest" (Exod. 33:14). This "rest" means that He will lead them to the Promised Land.

Moses asks God to let him see His "glory." God explains that "Thou canst not see My face, for man shall not see Me and live" (Exod. 33:20). God tells Moses that He will pass by and protect Moses with His hand, and then after He passes, Moses can see His back.

Then God tells Moses to cut two stones, the same kind as the shattered ones and to write down what God tells him. God reiterates the covenant—what He will do (basically, protect them and enable them to take over the Promised Land) and in exchange, the Israelites will follow the commandments—observe the festivals, not intermarry (so as to protect the faith), and not have other gods. Moses writes as he is commanded and then comes down from the mount to instruct the children of Israel. As he speaks, beams of light radiate from his face—it is a Divine radiance, and when the people see Moses' face, they believe.

QUESTIONS FOR DISCUSSION

It is explained that the taking of the census was, in part, preparation for war. We often imagine this time in the desert as simply "wandering," but actually, the Israelites fought many battles with various nations they encountered on the way to the Promised Land. Discuss what must have actually occurred in order for the Israelites to get to the Promised Land.

Discuss the golden calf. Can you imagine why the people wanted this, even though God had performed many miracles? Why did Aaron (the high priest and Moses' brother, with whom Moses had gone to Pharaoh) agree to help them? Why did Moses react so severely? Why is it the Levites who come forward?

Discuss what Moses says to God to calm Him. How does this show Moses' leadership—that even though he was very angry, he still defended his people? What do you think of Moses for telling God that if He killed the others, He should kill Moses, too, even though Moses was not involved? What should a leader do in this situation? If you are leading a group that does something wrong, are you responsible even if you are not present when the wrongdoing occurs?

Why can Moses see the back of God but not God's face? What does this mean to you? What do you think God looks like? Is it good or bad that we don't know?

Vayak'hel

Vayak'hel begins with Moses asking the children of Israel to donate jewelry and fine cloth to make the Tabernacle and the clothing for the priests. The parashah goes on to state that not only did the people donate willingly and with open hearts, but they gave even more than was needed. Vayak'hel goes on to describe the details of the Tabernacle, from the size of the altar to the cups and candlesticks shaped like almond blossoms.

QUESTIONS FOR DISCUSSION

In the previous parashah, when the children of Israel ask Aaron to build an idol, he responds by asking them to contribute their jewelry to melt down. The Soncino commentary uses Rashi's commentary to explain that he does this in order to delay having to create the idol (he assumes the people will not want to part with their gold). Contrast that with the description of the people being asked to donate jewelry for the Tabernacle and the willingness and joy with which they donate.

Why is it necessary to go into detail about the Tabernacle?

What do you think it signified to the people to construct this temple to God?

Think of our current synagogues—how important is it to support your synagogue? What ways can you help sustain your shul?

P'kudei

P'kudei, the final chapter in Exodus, marks the completion of the work on the Tabernacle. After four months, the Tabernacle is complete. It is brought into the tent of meeting. Moses lovingly sets up the altar—setting out candlesticks, burning the incense, lighting the lamps, and setting out the bowl for the priests to wash. At last, "the glory of the Lord fills the Tabernacle" (Exod. 40:35). The promise is fulfilled—the children of Israel have built a house for God, God's Presence has descended upon them and dwells among them, and leads them on their journey to the Promised Land.

QUESTIONS FOR DISCUSSION

Why does Exodus end with the completion of the Tabernacle? Why doesn't it end with the Egyptians drowning in the Red Sea? Why is this a more appropriate ending? What does it symbolize?

The creation of the Tabernacle fulfills a promise. Have you ever made a promise? What did it feel like to keep it? What does it feel like to break a promise?

What things exist today in our synagogues and homes that were also ritual objects in the Tabernacle? Now that you know the history of these objects, do you feel differently about the ones you use now?

LEVITICUS
Vayikra

Vayikra is the first chapter in Leviticus. Leviticus means "the law of the priests" and we can see a connection in the word *Leviticus* and the Levites. (The kohanim, or "priests," descended from Aaron, brother of Moses, from the Levites.)

Vayikra begins with details about burnt offerings to God. Any goats, sheep, or cattle brought to Aaron and his sons to offer must be male and without blemish. These represent the finest of the herd, and only the very finest is worthy of becoming a burnt offering. The same goes for an offering of fowl—it must be either a turtledove or a young pigeon. If someone wants to offer meal as a burnt offering, it must be made of the finest flour and oil. No honey or leavening can be used in the meal. The priests were told to salt all offerings before they were burned. After meal is burned, the priests may eat the remains. Instructions are given as to how the priests should slay the animals and what to do with the blood and the body (trust me, being a priest was a gruesome job).

If the sacrifice is a peace offering, the animal can be either male or female, but it still must be without blemish.

Sin offerings are more complicated. If a priest commits a sin, he must offer an unblemished young bull. If the entire congregation commits a sin, the community offers a young bull. If the chief of a tribe sins, he must offer a male goat. And finally, if a common person sins, he must offer a female goat or a female lamb.

QUESTIONS FOR DISCUSSION

On Shabbat, there is a tradition of sprinkling salt on the challah before eating it. Challah represents a sacrifice. Talk about how the law of salting the burnt offerings compares to the modern-day tradition. What else do we do now that is derived from the time of Moses?

No honey was allowed in the burnt offering. Why do you think this was? Today, the Sephardim will not eat challah baked with honey (or any sweetener) on Shabbat. Do you think there is a connection?

Why did the animals have to be "without blemish"?

Why do you think different groups of people were instructed to offer different animals for sin offerings?

Tzav

Tzav continues to instruct the priests about offerings. We learn about guilt offerings, peace offerings, and thanks offerings. The commentary explains that peace offerings fall into three categories: thankfulness for deliverance from sickness or danger; fulfillment of a vow made in time of distress; and offerings made when one's heart simply moves one to make an offering. Thanks offerings are regarded by the rabbis to be the highest offering. (The Soncino commentary theorizes that in the Messianic era there will be no need for sin or guilt or peace offerings, but there will always be a need for thank offerings that express our gratitude.)

Tzav also relays instructions regarding what part of the offering the priests are to eat.

Tzav concludes with Moses sanctifying the sanctuary and the priests (Aaron and his sons). This involves an elaborate ceremony of dressing the priests in their robes and vestments, and anointing them and the tent of meeting with oil, and, of course, sacrificing some animals. At the end of the ceremony, Moses instructs Aaron and the other priests to enter the tent of meeting and not come out for seven days, after which their consecration will be complete.

QUESTIONS FOR DISCUSSION

We don't do sacrifices anymore. What have we replaced them with?

Do we have different prayers for atonement, for peace, and for thanksgiving? Discuss when you've said which prayers and how you've felt.

What do you think it was like to offer a sacrifice (either an animal or meal) in order to communicate with God? Why do you think this system worked in the days of Moses? Do you find prayer helpful or meaningful?

What do you feel like when you pray? Would you rather pray in Hebrew and read the prayers in the prayer book, or would you prefer to offer your own words? Is prayer still important? Why or why not?

Shemini

On the eighth day after the consecration of the sanctuary and the priests, the priests emerge from the tent of meeting, and Aaron and Moses bless the people of Israel.

Two of Aaron's sons, Nadab and Abihu, make a "strange fire" (a fire not made by following God's instructions for making holy fires) and the fire "devours them" (Lev. 10:1–2). Moses explains to Aaron that those who are in positions of power and greater holiness are held to exacting standards. The Soncino commentary explains that Nadab and Abihu were killed by the fire because they did not follow God's instructions. (The rabbis also theorize that these priests may have been drinking, for this scenario and the instructions to the other sons of Aaron not to mourn Nadab and Abihu are followed by strict instructions not to drink alcohol before performing rituals.)

Moses commands the priests to eat the sin offering, even though those in mourning do not eat. They do not want to eat and Moses becomes angry. Aaron explains to Moses that they do not feel worthy that day of eating a holy meal, and Moses is calmed.

From this we begin to learn some laws of kashrut, specifically, which animals are clean and which are not. For example, we can eat only animals that have split or cloven hooves and chew their cud (not one or the other, but both). Also, we can eat only fish that have both fins and scales. Among winged creatures, we cannot eat vultures, ospreys, kites, falcons, ostrich, hawks, owls, cormorants, pelicans, storks, herons, and bats. And among insects, we can eat locusts, crickets, and grasshoppers (which have jointed legs), but not flying bugs that have four legs that do not bend (like bees or flies). And finally, weasels, mice, lizards, chameleons, and crocodiles are not considered kosher (I know you're disappointed).

QUESTIONS FOR DISCUSSION

The sins of Nadab and Abihu were interpreted by the rabbis to include intoxication, unholy ambition, and arbitrary tampering with the service. In the Zohar (the original text of kabbalah, or Jewish mysticism), it is written "He who is moved to tears while reading this portion of the Torah [the story of Nadab and Abibu], taking its teachings to heart, will win forgiveness for his own sins and the blessing of old age for his children." Do you or don't you agree with that? Why?

The priests were punished with death. Should those in positions of authority be held to tougher standards? Why or why not?

This week we are introduced to the idea that what we eat or drink is connected to cleanliness and holiness. Why are the priests not allowed to drink hard alcohol?

Why do you think God cares what we eat? Why should we eat only what is deemed clean? Does what we eat make us more or less holy?

Do you keep kosher? How do you feel about keeping kosher? Are there times you are careful what you eat and times you are not?

Tazria

Tazria details rules for purification after childbirth, such as how long a mother is considered "unclean" and what type of animal she should give to the priest as a thanks sacrifice. We also read how a priest can identify leprosy and how long an infected person, leprous or not, is considered unclean and needs to be separated from the community.

Please remember, the notion of being unclean is not a pronouncement of sin. Rather, this was the way the Israelites tried to stop the spread of infection. As far as childbirth is concerned, it is a very holy act—"be fruitful and multiply" is one of the main mitzvot, or righteous acts, a person can do; however, the reality is that a lot of bodily fluid is discharged during and after childbirth. There were no hospitals or antibiotics in the desert, so this period of being "unclean" was a way to prevent a possible spread of illness or infection among the community.

QUESTIONS FOR DISCUSSION

Rabbis interpret these laws of purification for both hygienic and levitical (purely religious) reasons. Which do you think they were for?

Why did the priests make the diagnosis of leprosy? Do you think there were doctors back then? Why was the priest the doctor?

Why do you think a woman had to offer a sacrifice after she gave birth? Why is "be fruitful and multiply" such an important commandment?

Metzora

Metzora continues with more purification laws, including what ceremonies a person who is healed from leprosy must do when he or she returns to the society at large. This involves dipping a live pigeon into the blood of a dead pigeon and sprinkling the blood off the live pigeon onto the healed leper and finally releasing the bird into the wilderness. Afterward, the person bathes and shaves off all of his hair. (*Ewww* all around.)

God also instructs Moses what to do when the Israelites are living in the Promised Land and there is a house on which "I put the plague of leprosy" (Lev. 14:34). God says it this way to emphasize that everything that happens (both good and bad) is done by His will. The instructions are quite clear and involve removing the moldy stones and disposing of them outside the village in a place designated for other tainted things (similar to our hazardous or toxic waste dumps) and rebuilding the contaminated walls.

Finally, instructions are given for what to do with other infections (aside from leprosy) that cause "infectious secretions" (again . . . *ewww*).

QUESTIONS FOR DISCUSSION

Why is it important that these purification laws be established?

Discuss the phrase "I put the plague of leprosy in a house of the land of your possession." Do you think everything that happens, good and bad, happens by God's will? What does "by God's will" mean to you?

Acharei Mot

Acharei Mot begins with God's instructions to Aaron, the high priest, for performing the ritual of atonement for the people. Part of this ritual involves the priest placing his hands on a goat's head and confessing the sins of the people over the goat and then sending the goat off into the wilderness, bearing the full weight of the iniquities so that the goat essentially takes all the people's sins away. (This is the inspiration for the word *scapegoat*.)

The chapter continues with a law that forbids individuals to perform the actual ritual of making a burnt offering, but allows them to bring an animal to a priest, who will then make the offering. The chapter concludes with rules forbidding marriage between blood relatives and close relatives (your stepmother or an aunt by marriage, for example). Before this law was in place, Abraham was able to marry his half-sister and Jacob to marry two sisters.

QUESTIONS FOR DISCUSSION

Discuss the idea of a scapegoat. How have the Jewish people been scapegoats?

How is the idea of the scapegoat similar to what we do on Rosh Hashanah—throwing bread into a running stream, in the tashlich ritual?

Have you ever felt like a scapegoat? Have you ever used anyone as a scapegoat?

Kedoshim

In Kedoshim the Israelites are given the moral laws—laws that essentially make the Israelites more holy than other nations; *kedoshim* means "holies." God reiterates the Ten Commandments and then instructs the people in everything from not placing stumbling blocks in front of the blind to not eating the fruit of a tree within the first three years of its being planted.

The statement is made that we are all holy (or have the potential to be holy) because God is holy. The actual line is "Ye shall be holy; for I the Lord your God am holy" (Lev. 19:2). By following the everyday moral code established in Kedoshim, we may live holy lives.

QUESTIONS FOR DISCUSSION

What does it mean to be holy?

In Kedoshim we are told in the same sentence not to gossip and also not to stand idly by while a neighbor is being harmed. Here we are being told when to be silent and when to speak. By telling tales or spreading gossip, we destroy a person's reputation. By keeping silent and not seeking help when a neighbor is in need, we aid in the destruction of his or her life. Why are these two commandments linked in the same sentence?

Why does it make us holy to wait years before eating fruit from a newly planted tree?

Why are we commanded to "fear" our father and our mother? In this case, what does the word "fear" really mean?

We are commanded not to reap the corners of our fields, but leave them for the poor. Why does God not command us to give food to the poor? What does it say about Judaism that we leave the corners of our fields for the poor to glean on their own?

Emor

In Emor we are instructed to respect our bodies. We are not allowed to cut or maim ourselves, nor are we to marry anyone who has defiled themselves physically or "through harlotry." By respecting our bodies we show respect to God.

We are also instructed to respect certain sacred occasions: Shabbat, Passover, Lag b'Omer, Shavuot, Yom Kippur, and Sukkot. Again, by showing respect for these occasions, we show respect to God.

Emor ends with instructions to respect one another. If we harm or kill another, we are to be punished by the same rule: ". . . eye for eye, tooth for tooth."

QUESTIONS FOR DISCUSSION

Emor seems to be about the different ways of showing respect to God by respecting our bodies, sacred holy days, and one another. How else can we show respect?

Based on what we read in Emor, do you think tattoos and piercings are OK or not OK?

We have learned that only animals *without blemish* can be offered as a sacrifice to God. Do you think there is a link between this rule and that of not cutting or maiming ourselves (intentionally placing blemishes on our bodies)?

Why is it disrespectful to God to disrespect ourselves or others?

Where else in the Torah are we commanded to show respect? To whom are we to give that respect?

B'har

In this parashah God instructs the Hebrews to observe more than one Sabbath. We must observe a Sabbath day every seventh day, and a sabbatical year every seventh year. At the seventh occurrence of the seventh year (every forty-nine years), God declares to Moses "on the mountain" (*b'har*) that the shofar is to be blown to "proclaim liberty throughout the land unto all the inhabitants thereof." (This phrase is also inscribed on the Liberty Bell.) The fiftieth year of this cycle becomes a jubilee, when all slaves are emancipated and all mortgaged property reverts to its original owner.

B'har instructs on responsibilities of ownership. The chapter begins with instructions to let the land rest in the seventh (or Sabbath) year. This year of rest prevents the land from being overused and promotes its fertility. During this year, we are to eat what spontaneously grows from the fields and trees, but to not intentionally "sow thy field, nor pick thy vineyard" (Lev. 25:4). We are told that people do not own the land, but that the land belongs to God and we are merely using it. Therefore, we must care for the land under His instructions.

In the same way, we are told that we do not own our slaves. If our fellow man becomes so destitute that he must sell himself to another, the slave owner is to treat him humanely and must even take responsibility for caring for the slave's family. Again, we may assume that we "belong" to God; in other words, we are God's children and therefore are responsible for one another's well-being.

QUESTIONS FOR DISCUSSION

Why are the rules of caring for our land and caring for one another discussed in the same chapter? How are they linked?

Why is it important to take care of the land?

Why is care for the land discussed first and care for one another second? Does this mean the land is more important?

Are these rules for caring for the land merely because the Israelites were an agrarian society when these laws were made, or is there a larger reason?

Leviticus follows Exodus. In all the rules the Israelites received they are told to treat slaves humanely. Is this because of their own experience as slaves? If the Jews had never been slaves, do you think instructions about how to treat a slave would have been given? How did the experience in Egypt shape the development of Jewish society and culture?

Bechukotai

Bechukotai completes the book of Leviticus. Just as in Exodus we received our laws, in Leviticus we receive our code of ethics. In Bechukotai, God tells Moses to reiterate the rules to the people of Israel and (as added incentive) says that if they follow the rules, He will cause the Promised Land to be fertile, their enemies to fail, and their people to multiply. However, if they ignore these rules, they will be in big trouble: the land will not produce, their enemies will succeed, and they will be punished "seven times for [their] sins" (Lev. 26:24).

Bechukotai concludes with a monetary valuation of every man, woman, and child that is to be paid to God (through the priests at the Tabernacle). It is noted that the Israelites are not allowed to make an offering to God of the firstborn beast (ox, sheep, cattle, etc.) because the firstborn already belongs to God and is therefore not theirs to give.

QUESTIONS FOR DISCUSSION

What do you think the reaction of the people was when Moses gave them this message from God? Why was it necessary for God to basically say, "Do this and I'll reward you—if not, I'll punish you"?

What does it say about Judaism that we have an entire book of the Torah dedicated to laws of ethics and morality? Does this differ from other religions that existed in the time of Moses? How did this set the children of Israel apart?

Why do you think firstborns belong to God?

NUMBERS
Bamidbar

Bamidbar opens the book of Numbers. In Exodus, the Israelites receive the laws, in Leviticus they learn the code of ethics, and in Numbers Moses takes the census (hence the name, Numbers, in English).

God tells Moses to count the Israelites by tribe. He is to include only males over the age of twenty as only they are able to bear arms. God appoints one man from each tribe to assist Moses. The results of the census are:

Reuben: 46,500

Simeon: 59,300

Gad: 45,650

Judah: 74,600

Issachar: 54,400

Zebulun: 57,400

Ephraim: 40,500

Manasseh: 32,200

Benjamin: 35,400

Dan: 62,700

Asher: 41,500

Naphtali: 53,400

Total: 603,550

Each tribe was told to camp together under its own banner and were instructed where to camp in relation to the tent of meeting.

The Levites were not counted as they would not go to war. (The great rabbi Rashi explained that since the Levites formed the "Divine King's Legion" they were to be honored with a separate census.) Instead, they were appointed to serve God by assisting the priests and were put in charge of the Tabernacle—setting it up, disassembling, carrying, and protecting it.

God instructed Moses to count the firstborn sons of every woman (firstborn sons of the men had inheritance rights; in the days of the Bible, the men had many wives, so the firstborn son of a man's first wife was the rightful heir, but the firstborn sons of *each* wife were to enter the Lord's service. These firstborn were special because God consecrated every firstborn in Israel (Num. 3:13). However, God said that He would take the Levites *instead of* these firstborn, even though the firstborn were consecrated to Him. The Levites, therefore, symbolized the firstborn males of all the tribes. God then instructed the Levites (through Moses) how they were to take care of the Tabernacle.

God charged all sons of Kohath who were over the age of thirty with the special service of handling the most sacred and holy objects after Aaron and his sons covered the objects. (These men would be called kohanim.) God then told Moses that the people of Israel were to take care of the Kohath tribe.

QUESTIONS FOR DISCUSSION

By counting only the men who were old enough to carry arms and by instructing them to camp in tribes, was God preparing the Israelites for war, or was the ability to carry arms merely the determination of adulthood?

Why weren't the women counted?

Is your family a Kohen or Levite? Ask your grandparents or parents if they know.

Naso

Naso continues to instruct the priests in their duties—caring for the Tabernacle, dealing with those accused of sin, and collecting offerings from the heads of each of the twelve tribes.

Perhaps the most beautiful segment of Naso is the instructions God gives to Aaron for the Priestly Blessing. The priests, and only the priests, are allowed to give the blessing. Then, as today, the priest is to stand with outspread hands with the pointer and third finger split from the ring and pinky finger so the space between each pair of fingers makes a V. The blessing is (Num. 6:24–26):

> *The Lord bless thee and keep thee;*
> *The Lord make His face to shine upon thee, and be gracious unto thee;*
> *The Lord lift up His countenance upon thee, and give thee peace.*

God explains that through this blessing, the priests shall "put My name upon the children of Israel, and I will bless them" (Num. 6: 27). And with that, we again hear how the priests are the vehicle by which the Israelites will speak with God.

QUESTIONS FOR DISCUSSION

Can you think of times you've heard a rabbi give the Priestly Blessing? How did you feel?

Some prayers in the siddur (prayer book) were written by rabbis over the ages. How does knowing that the words of this blessing were actually given by God change the meaning of this prayer?

In your opinion, how does the language (Hebrew or English) affect the feeling imparted by the blessing?

Beha'alot'cha

Beha'alot'cha touches on a number of topics. The parashah describes a menorah and the commandment to light the lamp in the Tabernacle. We also read of two silver trumpets used to call the community to prayer as well as war. (These were not shofars. The shofar was used in times of jubilee.)

We also learn that a cloud would, at times, cover the Tabernacle. The cloud was thought to be the spirit of God, and when it was upon the Tabernacle, the people would make camp. Once the cloud lifted, the people would begin to journey again. The cloud (Divine Spirit) essentially guided the Israelites through the wilderness.

In Beha'alot'cha, the people begin to rebel again; they are hungry for meat (having only manna to sustain them) and are beginning to think life was better in Egypt. Moses begs God to kill him and put him out of the misery of dealing with the unhappy people. God tells Moses to gather the leaders of the rebellion so He can give them a vision. The vision does not allow them to see the future, but rather, they are allowed to feel God and be admonished directly by God. God then sends meat for the rebellious people to eat, but those who eat become ill and die. The land where this happened is then renamed Kivrot Hata'avah "because there they buried the people that lusted" (Num. 11:34).

Moses' authority is once again tested and defended by God when his sister, Miriam, and brother, Aaron, protest Moses' taking a Cushite woman as his wife. God appears to Miriam and Aaron and admonishes them for questioning Moses, who "is trusted in all My house; with him do I speak mouth to mouth . . ." (Num. 12:7–8). God then strikes Miriam with leprosy (the biblical punishment for slander) and sends her away for seven days before healing her.

QUESTIONS FOR DISCUSSION

Why is it important that we read about Moses becoming frustrated with being a leader? What does this say about his leadership? Does this make him weak or strong?

Why is it necessary for God to be so severe in His punishments? What may have happened if God had just said, "OK, here's some meat, now stop complaining?"

Miriam is such a tragic figure. It was she who watched over her brother Moses during his journey down the river as a baby, and it was Miriam who led the women in song after the Israelites crossed the Red Sea. How does it make you feel that, in the end, she incited people against Moses?

What do you think the cloud symbolizes? Why is it a cloud that guides the people (and fire by night) in their journey to the Promised Land?

Shlach Lecha

Commentary from the Soncino Pentateuch on this parashah explains that the Israelites had just had a tremendous victory over the king of Arad. Because of this victory, Moses believes the people were poised to take over the Holy Land. He sends out a group of men to survey the land and its inhabitants. The spies come back with a large vine of fruit balanced on a rod by two men and declare that the land "flows with milk and honey" (Num. 13:27) and show the abundance of fruit they found. However, the spies (with the exception of Joshua, the son of Nun, and Caleb, the son of Jephunneh) are afraid to enter Canaan and spread rumors among the Israelites that the inhabitants of the land are so large they make the Israelites look like grasshoppers (Num. 13:33).

The Israelites are afraid. And even though Caleb and Joshua try to convince them that the land is wonderful and worth the fight, the people complain to Moses that they are afraid they will be killed in battle and wish to return to Egypt.

God is angered that the Israelites do not trust Him. He understands that those who are born into slavery will never have the strength of spirit to fight for freedom, yet those who are born in the desert will fight. He pronounces that the Israelites will wander for forty years. Within that time, those who were slaves will die and not live in the land God promised (and which they rejected). Their children, however, will live there. God makes an exception with Caleb and Joshua, because they believe and trust in God and tried to convince the Israelites to fight; they will be allowed to enter the land of Israel.

Also, in Shlach Lecha, the people of Israel find a man gathering sticks on the Sabbath. They are commanded by God to stone the man to death because he broke the Sabbath. God commands Moses to tell the people to make tzitzit, fringes, on the corners of their garments with a special blue thread tied into each of the four corners. These fringes will remind the people of the commandments.

Do you agree with God's decision to make the people wander for forty years? What is the significance of the number forty?

Why would a slave not want to fight for freedom? Doesn't it make more sense to think that experiencing slavery would make one want to fight harder for freedom?

How does fear stop us from doing things we want to do? Have you ever let fear stop you from doing something you wanted to do? Have you ever lost anything because of fear?

Korach

In Korach the seeds of mutiny grow. Korach, a Levite, along with Datan and Abiram, from the tribe Reuben, try to rally the people against Moses and Aaron. They confront Moses and basically say that all people are holy, so who is Moses to appoint himself a leader over the rest of the people?

Moses talks to God, and God tells Moses to stand back because He is going to kill them all in one swoop. Moses asks God's forgiveness for those who are innocent and not part of the rebellion. God gives Moses the chance to speak to the people.

Moses gathers the congregation and tells them that if they are not part of the rebellion with Korach, Datan, and Abiram, they should move as far away from those tents as possible, for those men, their families, and supporters will die. Moses notes that if these men die in a normal manner then it is not God Who has killed them; however, if they die in a spectacular way, the congregation will know these deaths are God's will.

Sure enough, the ground opens up and swallows the rebels and their homes and then closes over them—thus proving God's power as well as His support of Moses and Aaron.

QUESTIONS FOR DISCUSSION

Was it right for Korach to rebel?

Do you think there was any other way for God or Moses to handle the rebellion?

Have you ever wanted to rebel against authority? What did you do and why?

How did God's action ensure the unity of the people of Israel?

Chukat

Chukat begins with an unusual and controversial commandment in which God instructs Moses and Aaron how Eleazar, the priest, should sacrifice a red heifer (a special red cow that no longer exists today) and from the ashes of the heifer make a mixture with water that an unclean person would sprinkle on him- or herself to become clean. (By "unclean," I do not mean having some dirt on you and needing to wash it off; rather, the ritually "unclean" of doing something, like touching a dead body, that would make one unclean or impure in the eyes of God.) The interesting thing about this commandment is that by performing it, the priest himself becomes unclean and needs to exile himself from the others until the evening.

In this chapter, the Israelites also journey to the wilderness of Zin, where Miriam, Moses' sister, dies. There is no water in the place, and the people complain to Moses and Aaron, who then beseech God on behalf of the people. God tells Moses to take his rod and in front of the congregation speak to the rock, and water will spring from the rock. However, Moses hits the rock *twice*. As a result, God says, "Because you believed not in Me, to sanctify Me in the eyes of the children of Israel, therefore you shall not bring this assembly into the land which I have given them" (Numbers 20:12). Moses and Aaron will never enter the Promised Land.

(What exactly did Moses and Aaron do to make God refuse them entry into the Promised Land? Yes, they were angry. Yes, they complained on behalf of the people. What was it about this time that caused God to punish them? Some rabbis claim that we will never

205

know—that we aren't supposed to know or to understand. Some commentators believe that it is explained by God's statement that because Moses hit the rock twice, he no longer had faith in God. And the rabbis of the Midrash think that Moses did not even want to be associated with the generation of Israelites in the desert or be punished along with them for their sins, so he asked that if he were not to be allowed into the Promised Land that it be written in the Torah that God punished him for another reason. What do you think?)

Then the Israelites journey to Mount Hor. Here God tells Moses to take Aaron to the top of the mount and remove Aaron's garments and place them on Aaron's son Eleazar (thus making Eleazar successor to Aaron). Aaron dies on top of the mountain. The people mourn for thirty days.

The journey continues through other lands and other battles. When they are circling around Edom, the people complain they have no bread. God is very angry and sends serpents to bite and kill the people who complained. The people tell Moses they are sorry they didn't trust God and ask Moses to pray for relief from the snakes. Moses does so, and God tells Moses to make a brass serpent and put it on a pole. From then on, anyone bitten by a snake could look at the brass serpent and be healed.

Chukat ends with the people resting in the plains of Moab, beyond the Jordan River at Jericho.

QUESTIONS FOR DISCUSSION

Do you think it's fair for God to have punished Moses and Aaron?

Do you think it would have been fair if Moses and Aaron had been allowed to go into the Promised Land, but the rest of the "generation of the desert" were not allowed?

The people were punished and not allowed into the Promised Land because they did not have enough faith in God. Was it Moses' responsibility that the people had enough faith?

If you were leading a group and the group did something wrong, should you also be held responsible?

Balak

I find Balak to be a very intriguing parashah. In it, Balak, the king of Moab, learns that the Israelites are approaching. The Israelites have successfully defeated many nations on their way to the Promised Land, and Balak and the Moabites are afraid. So Balak sends messengers to Balaam, a heathen prophet, to ask Balaam to curse the Israelites on behalf of the Moabites. However, God speaks with Balaam in a vision and tells him not to curse the Israelites because He has blessed them. God instructs Balaam not to go with the messengers of Balak.

Balak's messengers go to Balaam and ask him to return with them to Balak, promising much honor if he comes. Balaam tells the messengers that he cannot, that he was instructed by God that the Israelites are blessed, and he is unable to remove that blessing. Desperate, Balak sends Moabite princes to Balaam with promises of riches and honor if he comes. This time, God tells Balaam to go to Balak, but on the condition that Balaam speaks only what God tells him to speak. Balaam goes, but God becomes angry and sends an angel to stop him. (Now, why is God angry if He had allowed Balaam to go? Good question. Ibn Ezra's commentary explains that God can read Balaam's heart so He knows that Balaam is hoping to go to Balak and find a way to curse the Israelites so he can get his monetary reward.) On the way, Balaam's donkey sees the angel of the Lord and stops. After Balaam finally coaxed his donkey to continue, the angel appears again, and the donkey responds by throwing itself against a wall. Balaam gets mad and beats the donkey. After the donkey stops a third time, Balaam beats the animal a third time. Finally, God causes the donkey to be able to speak, and she says, "Why have you beaten me these three times?" Then God lets Balaam see the angel, who says to him, "Behold, I am come forth for an adversary because thy way is contrary unto me" (Num. 22:32). Balaam admits to the angel that he has sinned and promises to speak only God's words.

Balaam meets with Balak and refuses to curse the Israelites and predicts great victories for the Israelites.

Here's where it gets intriguing: The Israelites are invited by the Moabite women to take part in the Ba'al Pe'or ceremony. This is a *very* hedonistic pagan ceremony. There is much harlotry (as the Torah says, or "whoring" in some editions) committed. God is not happy with the Israelites for acting in such a way. Moses tells the judges to gather all the men who participated in the Ba'al Pe'or activities and stone them, because he fears that

God will turn away from the Israelites because of these sins. By killing these men, God's anger will be assuaged.

Now, why did the Moabite women invite (perhaps "seduce" is a more appropriate word here) the Israelites to the Ba'al Pe'or? The Soncino commentary suggests that Balaam reverted to his sneaky, pagan self after giving his prophecy to Balak, and suggests this idea to Balak as a way of getting the Israelites to bring a curse upon themselves.

QUESTIONS FOR DISCUSSION

What do you think of this story?

What does this story prove about God's intentions for the people of Israel, that He talks to Balaam?

Do you think Moses acted correctly in his treatment of those who sinned at the Ba'al Pe'or festivities? Did he have any other choice?

What would you have done if you were Moses?

Has anyone ever betrayed you?

Have you ever pretended to help someone but then betrayed them?

Pinchas

Four key elements emerge in Pinchas that are significant in moving forward with the story of Moses:

1. Pinchas, son of Eleazar, son of Aaron (in other words, Aaron's grandson), is granted the covenant of an everlasting priesthood.
2. Daughters are given inheritance rights in families without sons. (The first to inherit is the son; when no son, the daughter; when no son or daughter, the man's brothers.)

3. Moses and Eleazar count the Israelites, and there is no one left from the generation who originally came out of Egypt, with the exception of Caleb and Joshua (who, if you remember, were both given the right to enter the Promised Land because of their faith in God).

4. Moses asks God to pick his successor. God tells Moses to get Joshua and bless him in front of the people Israel, thus naming Joshua Moses' successor.

QUESTIONS FOR DISCUSSION

What does it say about Moses that he asks God to appoint his successor? Why is it important to have a successor in place while you are still the leader? Why not leave it up to the people to decide once you are no longer able to lead?

If you were in charge of something, is it enough to be a good leader during your term? What if you didn't care what happened after you were finished? Should you still be considered a good leader?

Why does Moses ask for a successor at this moment?

Why is Joshua chosen? What do we know about him that makes him the right choice? (Remember, in Shlach Lecha he was one of the spies Moses sent to scout the Promised Land, and along with Caleb, he encouraged the frightened Israelites to push forward and fight and have faith in God that they would succeed.)

In addition to Joshua's appointment, how do the other elements discussed in the parashah ensure the future success of the Jewish people?

Mattot

Mattot begins with Moses explaining to the children of Israel what God has decreed about vows. Basically, if a man makes a promise or vow, he must keep his word. If an unmarried woman, who lives in her father's house, makes a vow, and her father agrees with the vow, she must keep the vow. If, however, her father disagrees with her vow, the vow is null and void. The same goes for a married woman: her husband must agree with the vow in order for the woman to be able to keep her vow. (Remember, at the time the Torah was written, women were wholly submissive to their husbands. I believe we can now read these lines to mean that all men and women are required to keep their word.)

The parashah continues with Israel defeating the Midianites (even killing Balaam, who betrayed them in the previous chapter). The tribes of Reuben and Gad find land perfect in Jazer and Gilead for their great numbers of cattle and ask Moses if they can stay there, rather than cross the Jordan River with the rest of the children of Israel. Moses explains that he is concerned that God will be angered and believe that their not wanting to enter the Promised Land is a sign of their lack of faith and will forbid this generation to enter the land as He had done with their parents' generation. Reuben and Gad want the land in Jazer and Gilead, but promise to fight for the Promised Land alongside the other tribes until everyone is settled peacefully in Israel. This satisfies Moses.

QUESTIONS FOR DISCUSSION

Talk about the importance of one's promise, vow, or giving your word—what does it mean to give your word?

What does it mean that Moses wasn't satisfied until the tribes of Reuben and Gad promised to fight for the Promised Land together with the rest of the Israelites and go on their way only when everyone is settled? What does this show about the tribes truly becoming one people? Have you ever stayed with something just because you were part of the team?

Massei

Massei begins by recounting the entire journey of the children of Israel from Egypt to the land of Canaan. The Midrash suggests that this rehashing of all their travails "may be likened unto a king who had taken his ailing son to a distant place to be cured. On the return journey, the king would lovingly recount to the lad all the experiences they went through at each of their halting-places." Essentially, the journey was a significant experience, so telling it again, even in a shorter way, emphasizes its importance.

After this summary, God tells Moses how Canaan will be divided among the tribes. These boundaries set up the social order of the people. In addition, God sets up procedures for how murderers will be punished. In other societies at this time, murder was avenged on any person in the murderer's family. Here, God says that the Israelites will not do it this way. Instead, should a murder occur, only the one who commits the murder is to be killed in vengeance and even then, only if the murder was seen by at least two witnesses (so that the murder could be proved). This rule marks a significant step forward in the evolution of society. (Here, God has set the limits—or boundaries—to which a person can go, in avenging a heinous crime.)

Finally, the parashah ends with another set of boundaries, this time for women. A story is told that Zelophehad died leaving only daughters. In Pinchas, God decreed that daughters could inherit their father's land if there were no sons. However, it was now time for Zelophehad's daughters to marry. God declared that they could marry whoever they liked; however, they must choose husbands only from within their own tribe. The daughters, therefore, married their cousins. The Torah uses the phrase "Even as the Lord commanded Moses, so did the daughters of Zelophehad" (Num. 36:10). The wording "so did the daughters" implies that they did what they were commanded, but it was against their better judgment to marry their cousins. By requiring women to marry within their father's tribe, the boundaries were set so that the ownership of their land remained in their ancestral tribe.

Questions for Discussion

Talk about boundaries—why are they important in a society? What about within your household? What kind of boundaries are set and why?

Why was the new rule about murderers significant? How does this advance society? How does our modern judicial system reflect this?

Do you think it was right for the daughters to be commanded to marry within the tribe? Did it restrict them, or was it a way of keeping the tribe's land rather than transferring it through marriage to another tribe? What could have happened if the five daughters had married into five different tribes—would the divided land have caused more problems? Was the rule actually a way of looking out for the greater good?

DEUTERONOMY
D'varim

The fifth, and final, book of Moses starts with the words *Eileh had'varim*, meaning "these are the words." *D'varim* means "words."

"Words" has many meanings in this book. In D'varim, Moses again recounts the journey of the children of Israel from Egypt to the Holy Land. Here, the "words" of the journey are spoken (in parashah Massei they were written). Moses also summarizes God's laws, rules, and even His promises, thereby giving the "word" of God in this book. And finally, as he is dying, Moses gives his blessing to the people he has led and makes clear that Joshua is his successor, thus giving his "word," or vow.

In the first chapter, Moses not only recounts the beginning of the journey, but also reminds the people that the generation of Israelites who left Egypt (all of whom are dead, except for Caleb and Joshua) did not have strong faith in God. Rather than trusting that God was with them, leading and protecting them, they constantly feared for their lives. This fear, distrust, and lack of faith angered God and caused Him to declare that the Israelites would wander in the desert until all who had initially left Egypt had died. Only Caleb and Joshua (who trusted God) and the children who were born in the desert would venture into the Promised Land. Moses continues to explain that the people's lack of faith was viewed by God as Moses' own failure, giving this as the reason why Moses will die before entering the Promised Land.

But in spite of all this, Moses emphasizes that God has been with the Israelites throughout the entire journey, that He has fought with them and for them, because the Israelites are truly God's children.

QUESTIONS FOR DISCUSSION

Are Moses' words also a cautionary tale? He is talking to the children of those who left Egypt. Is he reiterating the punishment given to their parents to warn them what might happen if they lose faith? Or explaining the caveat to God's vow?

Even though God was often angry with the Israelites, He never abandoned them. Is this the truest example of God as parent?

Talk about "words." The Jewish people are known as the "people of the book," and the first chapter of the final book of the Torah is titled "Words." Why are words so important?

Talk about the power of words. In the Torah, the people *did* what God commanded; however, they *spoke* their fears and distrust. Their words were more powerful than their actions and revealed their true feelings. Which is more important—what you say or what you do?

Va'etchanan

Va'etchanan continues Moses' discussion with the children of Israel. In this chapter, he again painfully states that as much as he wants to go to the Promised Land, he is not allowed to go and that this is for the sake of the people. He reiterates the Ten Commandments and explains the Israelites are unique as an ethical society. "Observe therefore and do them; for this is your wisdom and your understanding in the sight of the peoples, who, when they hear all these statutes, shall say: 'Surely this great nation is a wise and understanding people'" (Deut. 4:6). He recites the *Sh'ma*, the cornerstone of Judaism.

The most important rule, and the one that preserved Judaism from being incorporated into other religions throughout the thousands of years since Moses, is contained in the Sh'ma:

Hear, O Israel, the Lord, Our God, the Lord is One.

The concept of one God, this jealous God, Who denies the existence of other gods and forces His people to refuse the idea of other gods, is what kept Judaism alive when the Greeks (who were great admirers of the Jews) wanted to incorporate the Jewish God into their pantheon of gods. The commentary in the Soncino Pentateuch explains that "the same reasons that would not permit the Jews to bend the knee to the gods of pagan Rome, prevented them in later generations from allowing themselves to be absorbed by the two great religions that issued from Israel's bosom. Here too they found, both in dogma and morality, novelties and concessions that were repugnant to the austere simplicity of their absolute monotheism" (Hertz, 761).

Finally, Moses cautions the people not to doubt God or turn from Him for fear of grave and terrible punishment.

In the Midrash, Rashi uses this parashah to suggest a reason for why Moses is not allowed into the Promised Land. Rashi explains that Moses begs God to at least let him be buried in Israel, as he says that the bones of Joseph will one day be taken from Egypt and laid to rest in the Holy Land. Rashi suggests that God explains to Moses that even at the height of Joseph's power in Egypt, he always considered himself a Hebrew, not an Egyptian, and felt he was taken from the land of the Hebrews. Moses, however, was silent when the daughters of Jethro identified Moses as an Egyptian; Moses did not correct them or identify himself as a Hebrew.

When Moses met the daughters of Jethro, he had only recently learned that he was not an Egyptian. He had spent his entire life (except for the trip down the Nile when he was an infant) raised as an Egyptian prince. He had not, at that point, spoken to God through the burning bush or truly had time to understand his heritage—couldn't God ultimately forgive Moses' silence and not hold it over everything else that Moses had accomplished in his life and allow him to complete his journey? But perhaps *this* is how Moses is to complete his journey, by setting another example for the Jewish people. As a great leader, he must replace himself—he must allow another leader (Joshua) to take up the mantle and be the one to lead the people into the Promised Land. If the people see Moses hand over the reins, this gives rise to a stronger transition of allegiance to the leader. God's refusal makes Moses the ultimate example of why the Israelites must trust and follow God; God does not bend or fluctuate or accept excuses or transgressions even for great men like Moses.

In this chapter, Moses says, "Behold, I have taught you statutes and ordinances, even as the Lord my God commanded me, that ye should do so in the midst of the land whither ye go in to possess it" (Deut. 4:5). It is these rules and statutes that took the Israelites from a people enslaved to enlightenment. These rules make the Jews a nation admired for their principles and advances in ethics and philosophy, and the only way for the nation to survive is to adhere to these laws that even Moses is not above.

QUESTIONS FOR DISCUSSION

Talk about some of God's laws and how they apply today. For example, is it still important to keep kosher and why?

How would things have been different if Moses had been allowed into the Promised Land?

How did God's strictness with the laws and harsh punishment for those who broke the laws ensure that the Jewish people would survive as a nation?

Ekev

In Ekev, we learn that God is allowing the Israelites to enter to the Promised Land not because they were righteous in the desert, but because He promised their forefathers Abraham, Isaac, and Jacob. He also promised that the Jews would be as numerous as the stars in the heavens, and in Ekev, Moses points out that the forefathers first came to Egypt with threescore and ten persons (seventy) and are now numerous. Moses tells the children of Israel that the people who currently inhabit the land of Canaan are large and fierce and have grown wicked in their rituals. God will travel ahead of the Israelites as a cloud of fire and destroy them because He wants to replace them with a people loyal to Him. That said, *the* reason the Jews are given the land is because of His promise.

It is in Ekev that we read the words "man does not live by bread alone" (Deut. 8:3). This means when the Israelites were in the desert, God purposefully allowed the people to be hungry so that they would learn that they were sustained not by manna but by faith. Although the Israelites complained, they held fast to their faith. Now the reward is a land flowing with milk and honey.

QUESTIONS FOR DISCUSSION

Talk about the phrase "man does not live by bread alone." What does this mean to you? What do you need to survive? Is food enough?

How were the Hebrews starved in the desert? Was it just for food? How did God fill their hunger?

Is the story Moses tells the Israelites about God destroying the current inhabitants of Canaan a warning? Could we be replaced if we lose our faith?

Re'eh

Re'eh continues Moses' discourse with the people of Israel. Here he reiterates the rules of kashrut (the dietary laws), methods for sacrifices to God, the observance of Passover, and warns against false prophets. Rules about mourning, debt forgiveness, and tzedakah (charity) are reiterated.

Regarding the rules of kashrut, Moses explains that Jews may eat only animals that both chew their cud and have split hooves. (Pigs have split hooves but do not chew their cud and are therefore unclean.) There is a strict order not to eat blood (this is the reason Jews salt meat after killing the animal—to draw the blood from it). This is because blood is life and no one shall eat life.

The rules discussed in Re'eh are connected through the basic law that Jewish people are to respect life. God did not allow His people to offer human sacrifices as was the custom of many other religions at the time; this would be a great offense to God. Jews are not supposed to eat blood or flesh that contains blood because of respect for life. For this same reason Jews are commanded not to cut or disfigure their own bodies in any way during mourning (also popular custom) because as God's children we are precious and must respect life.

In this chapter God commands that no one is to follow anyone (including a family member) who claims to have a dream or prophecy that we should follow another god or gods (this is the law of false prophets). The law goes as far as instructing to stone anyone who tries to turn us away from God. To disobey God would bring His wrath upon the people as occurred several times during the forty-year journey through the desert. In essence, this law preserves the Jewish way of life.

And finally, God commands the Israelites to forgive debt every seven years. And He also tells them to give to those in need, even strangers. In other words, respect the lives of others and help to ease their pain and strengthen their lives when they are in need.

Again, all of this truly sets apart the Jewish people from the other religions of the day and emphasizes the deep ethical grounding of Judaism.

QUESTIONS FOR DISCUSSION

Even though the gazelle is considered clean and permitted to be eaten, the Jews were not allowed to sacrifice it because it was not a domestic animal. Only domestic animals were acceptable sacrifices. Is this because they were owned and something can be considered a sacrifice only if it is personally owned?

Jews no longer sacrifice animals. What is something we sacrifice today to God, and how does it relate to the idea of domestic vs. wild animals?

Discuss the idea of tzedakah. Why is it important to give to those in need? How can you incorporate tzedakah in your life?

Shoftim

Shoftim focuses on laws relating to criminals and warfare. Basically, if someone commits manslaughter (killing another unintentionally), he must separate from his family (this is his punishment) and go to one of three cities designated as a sanctuary, where he may live safely from revenge from the victim's family. Again, this is available only in cases of manslaughter but not murder (where the individual intended to kill).

In warfare, God's rules for the Israelites were once again ahead of their time in their respect for humanity. Certain men were exempt from warfare (for example, newly betrothed men). War must also be the last resort. God declared that upon approaching a city, the Israelites were to first offer peace. If the offer of peace was declined, then war could ensue. After the Israelites take possession of the city, they were not to harm the women and children (as was done by other peoples of that time), and they were not to cut down any fruit trees (because trees are not man's and should not be harmed). Fruit trees were also kept from destruction because they provide food.

Finally, Shoftim ends with the ritual for what happens if a slain body is found in a field: the elders of the town closest to the body are to kill a heifer in an uncultivated field near a stream and pray for forgiveness. This is because murder is not only a sin against man but a sin against God. When the murderer is not known, the entire community is held responsible.

QUESTIONS FOR DISCUSSION

Does modern-day Israel follow the rules in Shoftim?

Talk about who is exempted from going to war. Debate whether or not this is a good idea. For example, could one argue that a man should be exempted if he has been married a long time and has a family to care for, whereas the newly married man does not have children yet? What other individuals should be exempted?

Talk about God's rule that an entire community will be held responsible for an unsolved murder. What does this mean for a society? What other examples of communal responsibility have we read about in other parashahs? How does this relate to modern-day disasters?

Ki Tetze

Ki Tetze discusses a variety of laws, including one for constructing a parapet around the roof of a house (to prevent people from falling off), a law against mixing seeds in a field as well as mixing wool and linen, and one against plowing a field with an ox and an ass paired together. This parashah also reviews the laws of decency toward wards, sons, wives, strangers, orphans, and widows. Various rules and punishments are established for respecting women and protecting them from being violated. This runs the gamut from women of conquered cities (they should be married and not taken as slaves), to maidens in a field, to a wife a husband may hate (especially if he has more than one, as was the custom). Concerning this last group, the Torah states that if a man has two wives and he hates one, but that one gave birth to his firstborn son, that son still inherits his due as firstborn; the fact that his father hates his mother cannot interfere with his inheritance rights.

The Torah also states that if a son is very disobedient and does not listen to his mother or father, the parents may take him to the elders of the town and have him stoned to death, for he is a bad mark on the community.

As harsh as that is, at the same time the Israelites are told to be very kind and sympathetic with those in need. For example, if a poor man is in debt to you and gives you his coat to secure the debt, you must return his coat to him at night so that he can be warm (it gets very cold at night in the desert). This law led the Torah commentator J. H. Hertz to remark: "No other system of jurisprudence in any country at any period is marked by such humanity in respect to the unfortunate."

QUESTIONS FOR DISCUSSION

What do you think of all the rules for not mixing things? Why do you think they exist? The commentary in the Soncino Pentateuch suggests that this may come from the concern over obliterating things in the natural world by intermixing them. Can you relate this to anything now? Do the rules also relate to who we can marry?

What do you think of the rule for stoning wicked sons? Why could this have been necessary (given the time period)? If your child was guilty of a heinous crime against society, do you protect and harbor him or turn him in?

Many of the rules in Ki Tetze about sympathizing with those in need heed us to remember the Israelites were once slaves in Egypt. How did the experience of being slaves shape Jewish society?

219

Ki Tavo

Ki Tavo begins with outlining the structure of the tithes (taxes).

After this, Moses instructs the Israelites that once they cross the Jordan River, they must erect large stones, plaster them, and write all the laws on them. Interestingly, Moses tells them to write simply—so that everyone can read and understand the laws. The Israelites are then to build an altar. (It is noted in the Soncino commentary that the first duty of the Israelites upon entering the new land is to create a space for public worship.)

Ki Tavo concludes with the blessings and the curses or dooms, which reinforce the blessings that will be given those who follow God's law and the punishments for those who disobey. Again, it is also repeated that the Israelites came to Egypt small in number and multiplied there. The children of Israel were treated harshly by the Egyptians but God led His people from Egypt and slavery across the desert, providing for and protecting them, and brought them to the Promised Land.

QUESTIONS FOR DISCUSSION

Moses instructs the people of Israel to write the laws "simply" so that everyone can read and understand them. Why is this important? Why wasn't it enough that the priests or judges understood the laws?

Perhaps the need for everyone to understand the laws establishes the religion as one that allows and encourages individuals to have a personal relationship with God—that the priest should not be the go-between. Do you agree or disagree? Do you feel like you can pray directly with God, or does your rabbi have a different relationship with God?

Moses was not a king. His successor, Joshua, is not made a king either. Why? Is this because they are the representatives of God, and God is the king and not Moses or Joshua? What does this say about equality of souls?

The Israelites were told to build a space for public worship. Does this remain an important responsibility for modern Jews? When Jews move to a new area, how important is it to build a synagogue and religious school? How important is it to affiliate with and support a local synagogue?

Nitzavim

Nitzavim is a relatively short parashah as the life of Moses and the book of Deuteronomy come to a close. The promise that God made to Abraham has been kept. It is now up to the people to accept their side of the covenant.

In Nitzavim, Moses basically tells all assembled that they have walked through many other nations, they have seen idolatry, they have witnessed the blessings God has given to those who follow Him and the curses on those who forsake Him. Moses states that the laws are not difficult to understand (but note that he does not say that they are not difficult to follow). Every person is able to walk the ways of God—the laws are not set up for only the priests to interpret. Moses recognizes that with all the people have seen and heard and learned, it is still up to each individual to choose for him- or herself whether to follow God, and he describes the choice to follow God as choosing life and the choice to forsake God as choosing death. He says, "I call heaven and earth to witness against you this day, that I have before thee life and death, the blessing and the curse; therefore choose life, that thou mayest live . . ." (Deut. 30:19).

Questions for Discussion

What does it mean to "choose life"?

What does it mean to live a Jewish life?

If you were Moses, what would your final words have been? What message would you leave with those who had followed you for forty years through the desert? What would you say to convince them to continue following Judaism even after you were no longer leading them?

Imagine being with Moses at this moment—how would you feel? What would you choose to do? Do you feel you have a choice in what and how you believe? How do you choose what to believe? Does it change? What do you believe now?

Vayelech

Vayelech begins with Moses announcing that he is 120 years old and can no longer "go out and come in" (Deut. 31:2), which refers to his not being able to serve as a military leader, and that he is going to die. He therefore summons Joshua to him and officially anoints him his successor. God then appears to Moses and Joshua as a cloud and appoints Joshua as Moses' successor.

Moses then writes the Torah and gives it to the priests with the instruction to teach it to the people.

After this, God instructs Moses to write a song that will be sung to the people and specifically notes that this song should be heard by the children who did not live in the desert and therefore "who have not known" (Deut. 31:13). The song will speak about God and teach the listener to "fear the Lord your God, and observe to do the words of this law" (Deut. 31:12). After writing the song, Moses teaches it to the people.

Moses then charges Joshua saying, "Be strong and of good courage for thou shalt bring the children of Israel into the land which I swore unto them; and I will be with thee" (Deut. 31:23). He then tells the Levites to place the Torah by the side of the ark, and there it will serve as a witness. He then asks to speak with the elders of the tribes and predicts that after his death they will turn away from God and "deal corruptly" (Deut. 31:28). (According to the commentary, this prediction comes true for many of the priests in the days of Judges.)

QUESTIONS FOR DISCUSSION

Why does Moses give his final message in the form of a song? Think about oral history—how many people could read at the time? Why is a song preferred over a traditional speech?

Why does Moses write the Torah?

Think about Moses calling the Torah a "witness." What do you think it was a witness of? How does this image change the way you think about the Torah when you are at synagogue services?

Why was it important for both God and Moses to declare Joshua the leader?

What do you think Joshua is feeling now? How would you feel?

Why does God emphasize that the song be taught to the children? How does that relate to the discussion you are having with your children at your Shabbat table?

Ha'azinu

Just as Moses sang a song of praise and triumph at the Red Sea, he sings to the children of Israel as his last message.

In Ha'azinu, Moses sings the history of the people and their disappointment in their relationship with God. He recounts the days when the people turned from God and worshipped idols. He tells how then God turned away from the children of Israel to see what would happen to His children. He even sent "no-people" (Deut. 32:21), or barbarians, against them.

In the end, God turned back to His people and led them to the land He promised Abraham; however, Moses acknowledges that the nation Israel still does not give God His due. Moses sings (Deut. 32:28–30):

> For they are a nation void of counsel,
> And there is no understanding in them.
> If they were wise, they would understand this,
> They would discern their latter end.
> How should one chase a thousand,
> And two put ten thousand to flight,
> Except their Rock had given them over,
> And the Lord had delivered them up?

This is a powerful statement: how indeed did the nation of Israel accomplish so much when they were so greatly outnumbered and outarmed? Surely, the people should have died in the desert. Why didn't the nation give God His due?

This is the reason Moses cannot cross the Jordan and enter the Promised Land. God tells Moses that although Moses convinced Pharaoh of God's might and caused Edom and Moab to tremble before God, he failed to inspire the same fear and faith in the people of Israel.

And this is the point on which the chapter ends . . . this is Moses' failure.

QUESTIONS FOR DISCUSSION

Do *you* think Moses failed?

Is not being allowed into the Promised Land too severe a punishment? On Yom Kippur Jews pray for forgiveness—why wasn't Moses forgiven? Or was he?

Moses' song is difficult to hear/read because it seems to be full of anger and disdain.

Do you think Moses was angry for not being allowed into the Promised Land? If you read it like this, is he angry at Israel or at God?

Does God repeat that Moses is not allowed to cross the Jordan River into the Holy Land to emphasize that Moses is human and as such is imperfect? Why is Moses' imperfection one of our final images of him?

If you were Joshua, what would you plan to do differently? How would you inspire faith?

Make up your own song—what would you sing if you were Moses?

Vezot Habrachah

This is the final chapter.

In this beautiful parashah, Moses walks through the tribes and blesses them individually with strength and prosperity. He has completed his teachings. He is done with admonitions. He is bereft of warnings. He is at the end of his journey and ready to bless the people of Israel, as a dying father blesses his children.

Moses then walks to the top of Mount Nebo, and there God shows him all the land that He promised Abraham, Isaac, and Jacob. By doing so, God allows Moses to die peacefully, knowing that his life's struggle and sacrifice allowed the people to reach the point where God could finally complete the promise. The Israelites could not get to the Promised Land—not only physically reach the land, but more so spiritually be ready to enter the land—without Moses. No other human had this kind of relationship with God. Abraham may have fathered the Jewish nation, but it is Moses who raised it.

After seeing the land, Moses dies. Although he was 120, Moses' "eye was not dim, nor his natural force abated" (Deut. 34:7). This is the reward of the righteous; the rabbis explain that the phrase "So Moses the servant of the Lord died there . . . according to the word of the Lord" (Deut. 34:5), which in Hebrew is literally "at the mouth of the Lord," means that God gently takes the soul of the righteous with a kiss. Significantly, Moses dies alone, just as he truly lived alone (after all, we do not really learn about his relationships with his wife or children, and no one can really understand what he endured as a leader).

And since no other person witnesses his death, the rabbis tells us that God buried Moses, keeping his grave hidden from humankind and preventing it from becoming a pilgrimage site. This peace and anonymity is a gift.

At this moment, Joshua is empowered with "the spirit of wisdom" (Deut. 34:9), or the spirit of God. As the Talmud says, "No sooner did the sun of Moses set, than the sun of Joshua rose."

Thus ends the book of Deuteronomy and the Five Books of Moses. And we say:

Chazak, chazak, v'nit' chazek
Be strong, be strong, and let us strengthen one another.

Questions for Discussion

Moses died alone with no witnesses on the mountain. But do you think he was truly alone if God was with him?

Moses wrote the Torah before he died. How do you think he felt writing of his own death? Do you think it was how he wished it would be?

Have a general conversation about everything you have learned this year about the Torah. What did you learn that you did not know before? What was the most interesting parashah or story you discussed?

Talk about what it must have been like to journey with Moses.

What's with All the Yiddish? Glossary of Yiddish and Hebrew Words Used

A NOTE ON SPELLING: I used the letter *k* to represent the letter *koof* (*kabbalah*, *kiddush*), and *ch* for the Hebrew *chaf* (Shechinah) and *chet* (*orchim*). Pronounce *ch* as you would the *ch* in *blech*! *Sch* is read like shhh! (be quiet), and *eit* (as in *beit*) is read like "ate." The *i* in *mi* and *bi* is long and read like *ee* (*mikdash* and *bimah*). And to read *ts*, you have to run the two sounds together (ask your mother how to say *tsuris*).

Also, some of the words are masculine (m.) or feminine (f.) and I have marked them as such.

ach! How do I define this? It's not "ah"—it's more of a guttural, phlegmy *ecch*, as if you have something in your throat similar to "ah" but used in a sense like *oy*.

Ashkenazi. n. If your family lived in Germany, Poland, Austria, or Eastern Europe between the tenth and twentieth centuries, you are Ashkenazi. This is where the Yiddish language comes from.

ba'al t'shuvah. *n.m.* (feminine version is *ba'alat t'shuvah*) Literally, an owner of righteousness. The term now refers to a person who has become very (and I mean *very*) observant—think "born again" but Jewish.

Beit Mikdash. n. Literally, "house of holiness," it refers to the two Temples.

bentscher. n. Small prayer book containing the grace after meals (**birkat hamazon**), blessings, and songs (**zmirot**) traditionally sung after eating. To **bentsch** is to recite a blessing or grace.

besamim. n. Spices.

bikur cholim. Visiting the sick (a mitzvah).

bimah. n. The raised platform in the sanctuary of a synagogue where the Torah is read. When you read from the Torah, you are "called up" to the bimah. This is known as an **aliyah,** which means "ascent"—not only because you physically walk up steps to the bimah but because you are elevated by the honor of reading the Torah.

brachah. n. Blessing (plural is **brachot**).

challah. n. Braided loaf of white bread. (Plural in Hebrew is **challot,** but as *challah* is used commonly today, I refer to more than one challah as challahs.)

chazzan. n. Cantor.

chazzerai. n. Junk. This is from the Yiddish word **chazzer,** which means "pig."

chuppah. n. Wedding canopy—four poles with a cloth draped over the top.

d'var torah. n. Discussion of weekly Torah portion.

farkakta. adj. Lousy, as in "my *farkakta* dog" or "that is a *farkakta* idea" or "the *farkakta* phone won't stop ringing"—you get the idea! My very favorite word!

fleishchig. n. Meat (flesh).

frum. adj. Pious, religious.

hachnasat orchim. n. Inviting guests to your house (a mitzvah).

hak. v. Pronounced "hock," rhymes with "clock"—to nag (literally, "to bang"). May be short for the phrase **hak meer nit kayn tshaynik,** meaning "stop talking so much"—it literally refers to the rattling of a teakettle. So, in true Yiddish fashion, an annoying talker is colorfully compared to a rattling teakettle!

halachah. n. Law (plural is **halachot;** adjective is **halachic,** or according to the law.)

kabbalah. n. A strain of Judaism that focuses on the mystical and spiritual.

kaddish. n. The mourner's prayer.

kashrut. n. Jewish dietary laws (pronounced kash-ROOT).

kiddush n. Blessing over the wine. (The word comes from the Hebrew word *kadosh,* meaning "holy.")

kippah. n. Skullcap (plural is **kippot**). See also **yarmulke**.

kohanim n. Priests (descendants of Aaron, the first high priest, who was the brother of Moses).

kosher. adj. According to Jewish dietary law (*kashrut*).

kvell. v. To gush with pride (usually over something your children have done).

kvetch. v. To whine or (n.) one who whines and complains.

lashon hara. n. Evil language or malicious gossip.

macher. n. Big shot (literally, a "maker").

mensch. n. Literally, "man," but the word connotes good, thoughtful, or upstanding and respectable behavior. (What every nice Jewish boy should grow up to be!)

meshugge. adj. Crazy, nuts. The **meshugganeh** (n.) is acting **meshugge**.

mezuzah. n. Literally "doorpost," it is also a small case that contains a parchment which on one side has written the Shema and the passage from Deuteronomy 11:13–21 and the other side has written the name of God. Jews are commanded to affix a mezuzah to their doorposts as a constant reminder of God and the commandments.

Midrash. n. Rabbinical and scholarly Torah commentary.

mikdash me'at. n. Little sanctuary—refers to the home during Shabbat

milchig. adj. Dairy.

mitzvah. n. Righteous or good deed (plural is **mitzvot**).

muktzeh. n. An instrument of work that we are forbidden to use on the Sabbath.

naches. n. Pleasure, joy, or pride (usually because of something your child has done).

niggun. n. Wordless song.

oy vey iz mir! Oh, woe is me! Same as **oy!** or **oy vey!** Just longer and more dramatic.

parashah. n. Weekly portion of the Torah.

pareve. n. Neither meat nor dairy (i.e., fish and margarine are both considered pareve)

patshkeh. n. A fuss. (Can also be used as a verb—stop **patshkeing**.)

schlep. v. To drag (and object); to lag, to act slooooowly.

schmaltz. n. Chicken fat; as an adjective—**schmaltzy** for overdone, corny, dramatic.

schmatte. n. A rag; a cheap, worn-out piece of clothing that your mother would be embarrassed to see you wearing, so go change immediately!

schmear. v. To spread. (n.) A small amount of cream cheese for a bagel as opposed to the huge glunk they usually put on.

schtunk. n. A stinker.

seder. n. Literally means "order"—but refers to a religious service or ceremony that is conducted during a meal. Usually refers to the first two dinners during Passover (in the Diaspora), but it is also appropriate to call the Friday night meal a seder.

Sephardic. adj. Refers to Jews of Spanish, Portugese, African, or Asian descent. Ladino (as opposed to Yiddish) is the traditional language of the Sephardim.

Shabbes. n. Yiddish for the Sabbath (Shabbat in Hebrew).

shabbesdik. adj. Befitting the Sabbath spirit.

shalom bayit. n. Peaceful home.

Shamor. v. To guard.

Shechinah. n. The Divine Presence of God.

shmush. v. To mash together.

shomer shabbes adj. Observing (or guarding) Shabbat piously, according to all the laws.

shul. n. Synagogue (from the Yiddish for *school*).

Talmud. n. Commentary and teachings of the oral law, written in the second and third centuries, which include the **Mishnah** (oral law) and the **Gemara** (discussion on the Mishnah). Talmud stipulates how the teachings of the Torah (halachot) may be applied to problems of law, ethics, ceremony, and traditions.

Torah. n. The Five Books of Moses; Genesis, Exodus, Leviticus, Numbers, and Deuteronomy. Do not refer to the Torah as the Old Testament unless you believe in the New Testament!

t'shuvah. n. Repentance; literally, "return."

tuches. n. Also **tushy**; your rear end.

tzedekah. n. Charity.

yarmulke. n. Skullcap (in Hebrew, **kippah**).

yontif. n. Holiday; from the Hebrew *yom tov*, meaning "good day."

zachor. v. To remember.

zmirot. n.pl. Songs (**zmirah** is singular).

Resources

THE FOLLOWING IS A LIST of books, magazines, and Web sites that have been tremendously helpful to me. Like any good Jewish mother, I want to make sure you are well fed. In this case, I list these for you in hopes that you are hungry to learn more.

JEWISH HOME

Abramowitz, Yosef I., and Susan Silverman. *Jewish Family & Life: Traditions, Holidays, and Values for Today's Parents and Children.* New York: Golden Books, 1997.

Diamant, Anita, with Howard Cooper. *Living a Jewish Life: Jewish Traditions, Customs and Values for Today's Families.* New York: HarperResource, 1991.

Ehrlich, Elizabeth. *Miriam's Kitchen.* New York: Penguin, 1997.

Greenberg, Blu. *How to Run a Traditional Jewish Household.* New York: Fireside, 1983.

JEWISH LIFE

Drucker, Malka. *The Family Treasury of Jewish Holidays.* Toronto: Little, Brown, 1994.

Eisenberg, Ronald L. *The JPS Guide to Jewish Traditions.* Philadelphia: Jewish Publication Society, 2004.

Kolatch, Alfred J. *The Jewish Book of Why*. Middle Village, NY: Jonathan David Publishers, 1985.

————. *The Second Jewish Book of Why*. Middle Village, NY: Jonathan David Publishers, 2000.

Kushner, Harold S. *Living a Life That Matters: Resolving the Conflict Between Conscience and Success*. NewYork: Knopf, 2001.

Olitzky, Kerry M., and Daniel Judson. *Jewish Ritual: A Brief Introduction for Christians*. Woodstock, VT: Jewish Lights Publishing, 2005.

Remen, Rachel Naomi. *My Grandfather's Blessings: Stories of Strength, Refuge, and Belonging*. New York: Riverhead, 2000.

JEWISH PARENTING

Diamant, Anita, with Karen Kushner. *How to Be a Jewish Parent: A Practical Handbook for Family Life*. New York: Schocken, 2000.

Mogel, Wendy. *The Blessing of a Skinned Knee: Using Jewish Teachings to Raise Self-Reliant Children*. New York: Penguin, 2001.

Olitzky, Kerry M., Steven M. Rosman, and David P. Kasakove. *When Your Jewish Child Asks Why: Answers for Tough Questions*. Hoboken, NJ: Ktav Publishing House, 1993.

Wolpe, David J. *Teaching Your Children About God: A Modern Jewish Approach*. New York: Henry Holt, 1993.

JUST FOR FUN

Diamant, Anita. *The Red Tent*. New York: Picador USA, 1997.

Ellenson, Ruth Andrew, ed. *The Modern Jewish Girl's Guide to Guilt*. New York: Dutton, 2005.

Glasser, Natasha. *The Bubbelah Factor*. London: MQ Publications, 2005.

Traig, Jennifer, and Victoria Traig. *Judaikitsch*. San Francisco: Chronicle Books, 2002.

Wolfson, Paula. *Jewish Mothers: Strength, Wisdom, Compassion*. San Francisco: Chronicle Books, 2000.

MULTIMEDIA

Jewish Lullabies (CD), Sony BMG Music, 1993.

Oy Baby 2 (DVD and CD), OyBaby LLC, Mercer Island, Washington, 2005.

Paul Zim. *The Friday Night Sing-a-Long* (CD). Paul Zim Productions, 2001.

Shabbat at Home (CD). Paul Zim Productions.

Rick Recht. *Shabbat Alive!* (DVD and CD), 2005.

RECIPES

I love both *Bon Appétit* and *Gourmet* magazines, especially for their delicious and elegant holiday recipes.

These cookbooks are quite wonderful for all occasions:

Brooks, Karen, Diane Morgan, and Reed Darmon. *Dressed to Grill: Savvy Recipes for Girls Who Play with Fire.* San Francisco: Chronicle Books, 2002. (This isn't a Jewish cookbook, but I love her recipes and have used them for many a Shabbat dinner—I especially recommend her "Mod bods" mustard marinade.)

Brownstein, Rita Milos. *Jewish Holiday Style: A Beautiful Guide to Celebrating the Jewish Rituals in Style.* New York: Simon & Schuster, 1999.

Cohen, Jayne. *The Gefilte Variations: 200 Inspired Re-Creations of Classics from the Jewish Kitchen, with Menus, Stories and Traditions for the Holidays and Year-Round.* New York: Scribner, 2000. (These recipes are challenging, but the book is beautifully written and the hamantaschen recipe is so good!)

Fishbein, Susie. *Kosher by Design Entertains.* New York: ArtScroll, 2005. (Actually, any cookbook by Susie Fishbein is wonderful!)

Goltz, Eileen. *Perfectly Pareve Cookbook.* Jerusalem: Feldheim Publishers, 2001. (Helps solve the dilemma of good pareve desserts—a must if you keep kosher.)

Granger, Bill. *Bill's Open Kitchen.* New York: Morrow, 2004. (Again, not a Jewish cookbook, but so yummy!)

Zeidler, Judy. *The Gourmet Jewish Cook.* New York: Morrow, 1988. (I think I got this at my bridal shower. It's a classic.)

———. *Master Chefs Cook Kosher.* San Francisco: Chronicle Books, 1998. (For when you're feeling fancy-schmancy.)

SHABBAT

Ben David, Aryeh. *Around the Shabbat Table.* Jerusalem: Jason Aronson Publishers, 2000.

Weisblum, Moshe Pinchas. *Table Talk: Biblical Questions and Answers.* Middle Village, NY: Jonathan David Publishers, 2005.

Wolfson, Ron. *Shabbat: The Family Guide to Preparing for and Celebrating the Sabbath.* 2nd ed. Woodstock, VT: Jewish Lights Publishing, 2003.

Zion, Noam Sachs, and Shawn Fields-Meyer. *A Day Apart: Shabbat at Home.* Jerusalem: Shalom Hartman Institute, 2004.

TORAH

Berlin, Adele, and Marc Zvi Brettler, eds. *The Jewish Study Bible.* New York: Oxford University Press, 2004.

Feiler, Bruce. *Abraham: A Journey to the Heart of Three Faiths.* New York: Harper Perennial, 2005.

Friedman, Richard Elliott. *The Bible with Sources Revealed: A New View into the Five Books of Moses.* San Francisco: HarperSanFrancisco, 2003.

Goldstein, Elyse, ed. *The Women's Torah Commentary: New Insights from Women Rabbis on the 54 Weekly Torah Portions.* Woodstock, VT: Jewish Lights Publishing. 2003.

Hastings, Selena. *The Illustrated Jewish Bible for Children.* New York: DK Publishing, 1994.

Hertz, J. H., ed. *The Soncino Press Pentateuch and Haftorahs.* 2nd ed. London: Soncino Press, 1960.

Lieber, David L., and Jules Harlow, eds. *Etz Hayim: Torah and Commentary.* New York: United Synagogue of Conservative Judaism, 2003.

Plaut, W. Gunther, ed. *The Torah: A Modern Commentary.* New York: Union for Reform Judaism, 2004.

Rosenblatt, Naomi Harris. *After the Apple: Women in the Bible—Timeless Stories of Love, Lust, and Longing.* New York: Miramax Books, 2005.

YIDDISH

Kogos, Fred. *A Dictionary of Yiddish Slang and Idioms.* New York: Citadel Press, 1989.

Rosten, Leo. *The New Joys of Yiddish.* Revised by Lawrence Bush. New York: Three Rivers Press, 2001.

Weiner, Ellis, and Barbara Davilman. *Yiddish with Dick and Jane.* New York: Little, Brown, 2004.

Wex, Michael. *Born to Kvetch: Yiddish Language and Culture in All of Its Moods.* New York: St. Martin's Press, 2005.

WEB SITES

www.modernjewishmom.com. OK, this is my own Web site . . . so what can I say? It's full of advice, projects, recipes, and information about holidays, b'nai mitzvot, tzedekah, and more. I cannot recommend this site highly enough!

www.aish.com. This is an Orthodox site and the one I went to for preparing my family's divrei torah before I started writing my own. They try to put a "cool" spin on their divrei torah, but they end up being a little convoluted. Still it's a strong source for information, just not the easiest to read and translate for less observant families.

www.anshe.org. Nice parashah summaries that include questions and answers about the text—you can even download them to your handheld.

www.askmoses.com. Interactive site—type in a question and they claim a rabbi will answer it within minutes. Worth a try if you don't have access to a rabbi at the moment you have a question.

www.chabad.org. OK, if you're interested in hearing a gefilte fish (yes, a gefilte fish) give a news report as a way to explain the parashah, this site is for you. This is the Chabad-Lubavitch Web site.

www.eparsha.com. A warehouse of divrei torah from a variety of sources (from Orthodox to feminist).

www.everythingjewish.com. Good, basic information, plus links to major news sources and Jewish organizations.

www.hebcal.com. The Hebrew calendar site. It allows you to download calendars to your handheld—you'll never have to wonder again when Rosh Hashanah falls ten years from now!

www.hebrewsongs.com. Fun site that gives you the words (transliterated) to a library of Hebrew songs. Some songs are even available to download and listen.

www.hillel.org. Official site for the Foundation for Jewish Campus Life. Over the years, Hillel has been very successful in their outreach on American college campuses and is popular with Jewish college students. Definitely check this site out if you have children in high school or college.

www.interfaithfamily.com. Really nice site with information and advice for interfaith families.

www.jewfaq.com. Also known as Judaism 101. This wonderful site is written by Tracey

R. Rich, an Orthodox woman. Jewfaq.com has everything you need to know about Judaism presented in a straightforward, easy-to-read manner.

www.judaism.about.com. Written by a modern Jewish mom in Israel, this site is chock-full of information. You can even sign up for free newsletters to update you on various topics of Jewish interest.

www.masorti.org. Masorti is the Conservative Jewish movement in Israel. I highly recommend their weekly parashah summaries.

www.oukosher.org. Official site of the Orthodox Union answers all your questions about keeping kosher. It also has updates on newly certified kosher products.

www.perpetualpreschool.com. This site seems to be a blog for preschool teachers. It's not a Jewish site, but you can find great ideas for projects and songs for the Jewish holidays that are suggested by the bloggers.

www.torahtots.com. This is a wonderful kid-friendly site with information about holidays and parashah summaries.

www.ujc.org. The official site of the United Jewish Communities, the Federations of North America.

www.urj.org. This is the official site for the Union for Reform Judaism. It includes a wonderful family Shabbat table talk page.

www.uscj.org. The official site of the United Synagogue of Conservative Judaism.

www.yoyenta.com. I love this blog. Head Yenta rants about everything Jewish—from the latest Jewish celebrity couple to cleaning her house—oy, such fun!

Ach-knowledgments

TO MY BEST FRIEND, my business partner, my sister, Jennifer, without whom this book would not have happened. From your early edits of the query letter to the late nights "putting the funny in," you are an indelible part of this book. Just knowing you were willing to take time out from being the busy Modern Jewish Mom of Jake and Drew to help me, let me know that I was on the right track and I wasn't doing this alone. And to her husband, Michael, who is more like my brother than brother-in-law, for being the first person in the world to pre-order the book.

To Allison Fine, who first said, "You should write a book." I don't think I would have considered it otherwise.

To my talented illustrator, Jackie Ross, for brilliantly taking my musing "I don't know, maybe she should have her face in her hands . . . and make her look nice" and somehow creating a face for Modern Jewish Mom (even though you were exhausted from sleepless nights of being a new Modern Jewish Mom).

To my Web designer, Amy Kramer, for building such a warm and welcoming public home for Modern Jewish Mom, and who became a Modern Jewish Mom when baby Jory was born nine months after our launch. (I knew it was *beshert* that we work together!)

To all my wonderful "Yentas" for being with me from the beginning and for reminding me that this is a message that moms want to hear.

To Rabbi Stuart Weinblatt, who taught me so much by simply suggesting I "do one thing more each year." To Cantor Marshall Kapell for clueing me in to the power of the niggun. To Jodi Kern, Susan Kressler, and everyone at Congregation B'nai Tzedek, I would not be who I am today were it not for all of you. You have encouraged, supported, and inspired me. I never thought I would consider any other synagogue besides the one I grew up in, "my shul"—but you have done just that—you are my shul and my *mishpocheh*. And to Temple Sinai, back in Philly, for teaching me that a synagogue can be as comfortable as a home.

To Rabbi Susan Shankman of Washington Hebrew Congregation, for giving the book the "Rabbinic Seal of Approval" from a Modern Jewish Mom rabbi!

To Jill Cohen, for giving so much of your time to reading my first draft—I look forward to doing the same for you.

To Rabbi Yaakov Lipsky for teaching me what little I know of kabbalah and inspiring me to study Torah.

To Carol Berman and her son Casey, for your incredible inspiration.

To Evie Stoller and Michelle Bennaim for teaching me about the beautiful Sephardic culture.

To all my "genius mom" friends for so generously sharing your ideas, stories, and lives with me: Lianne Aaron, Robin Brown, Sherri Farrell, Shari Friedman, Gail Gaspar, Holly Gelfond, Laura Goldschein, Suzi Guardia, Elinor Jacobs, Debbie Katz, Paula Lowe, Jennifer Millstone, Lisa Rudden, and Lisa Schneider.

To Jane Greenblatt, Adrienne Maman, Patrick Moulet, Dori Oshinsky, Karen Shapiro, and Emily Stashower for sharing your top-secret family recipes.

To Sheri Freedman for your advice column but, more importantly, for your advice.

To Andrew Buerger and Neil Rubin of the *Baltimore Jewish Times* for your generosity.

To Sandy Abrams, Michelle Cohen, Lee Gorsky, Sandy Liss, and Rikki Postal for your friendship.

To Laurie Sheer for encouraging me "onward."

To Toni Levin for being the "Queen of Everything."

To the Jacobs family for all your support and love.

To my amazing aunts and uncles: Beverly and my late uncle Jerome Levinson, Cantor Saul Z. and Aileen Hammerman, and Dr. William and Natalie Feinblum. Thank you for always loving me like a daughter. You mean so much to me.

To my brilliant editor, Joelle Yudin. Because of you this book is so much better than I ever could have made it on my own. Thank you for believing in and championing this project. I had once heard about a book finding a "home"—I now know what that means. And thank you to Dr. and Mrs. Yudin for raising your children with Shabbat! Thank you to everyone at HarperPaperbacks—Jen Hart, Leslie Cohen, Gregg Kulick, Lauretta Charlton, Nicole Reardon, Sarah Maya Gubkin, and May Vlachos—for your amazing enthusiasm. It means so much to me.

To Anne Greenberg for your careful and thoughtful copyediting (and Torah study).

To my unbelievable agent and friend, Joanne Brownstein. Thank you for opening my envelope. Thank you for taking the chance on me. Thank you for believing that this would happen because "we are good Jewish girls doing a good thing." Thank you for setting my life on a path I never allowed myself to dream I would take. And, most importantly, thank you for sprinting with me!

To my children, Sofie and Jules. I am "blessed to be your Mommy" every day of my life, not just Shabbat. Thank you for inspiring me. Thank you for sharing me with this book and for being proud of me. You are my treasures and my blessings, and I thank God every day for you.

To my husband, Jonathan. You know me better than anyone in the world. You are my support and strength. I have grown tremendously because of your love and your belief in me. I can never thank you enough. And yes, you may now read the book.

And finally to my parents, Ellen and Ralph Levin. This book is a tribute to you. You are my role models—as parents, as partners . . . as people. Thank you for raising me in a home that I want to recreate for my children. I am forever grateful for the foundation you have given me—it is deep and it is secure. The only way I can possibly thank you is to try to give to Sofie and Jules what you have given to me and Jennifer.

Bread Machine Challah recipe used with permission of Dori Oshinsky.

Apple and Raisin Kugel recipe used with permission of Karen Shapiro.

Emily's Chicken Soup recipe used with permission of Emily Stashower.

Shabbat Box project (including Shabbat Box, Shabbat Candlesticks, Kiddush Cup, and Challah Cover) used with permission of Phillip Ratner.

Shabbat tablecloth project used with permission of Judy Tepper.